Becoming Human Together

Becoming Human Together

The Pastoral Anthropology of St. Paul

Third Edition

by

Jerome Murphy-O'Connor, O.P.

Society of Biblical Literature
Atlanta

BECOMING HUMAN TOGETHER
The Pastoral Anthropology of St. Paul

ISBN: 978-1-58983-361-6

Library of Congress Control Number: 2009932173

17 16 15 14 13 12 11 10 09   5 4 3 2 1
Printed in the United States of America on acid-free, recycled paper conforming to ANSI/NISO Z39.48-1992 (R1997) and ISO 9706:1994 standards for paper permanence.

CONTENTS

For
K. ASHE
in gratitude

FOREWORD

The story is told of a wise old Jewish rabbi who was informed that some say that the Messiah had already come. He made no answer but went to the window, opened it, and looked out into the world. After a moment he turned and sadly shook his head. If the Messiah had in fact come, things would have been different, but nothing had changed.

When we Christians look out at our world we experience moments of joy and wonder, but their duration is short-lived and their poignancy is intensified by their unexpectedness. They are an irruption into an existence of meaningless boredom. Yet such moments ensure the vitality of hope. Despite the prevailing mood of pessimism, people always crowd to the window of promise. They continue to dream of better things, because only such a withdrawal from reality makes life bearable.

For nearly two thousand years the church has been preaching the good news of a new creation, of a radical change in the structures of human existence. Countless numbers of men and women endowed with good-will, talent and energy have spent themselves without reserve in this service. Yet what is there to show for it? So little, unfortunately, that many generations ago Christians began to develop a theology which shifted the emphasis from achievement to mere effort. It was thought wrong to judge others in terms of their success in bringing about change. The fact that they had failed to bring others to a real encounter with Christ was passed over in silence in favour of praise for the efforts they had made.

The late, but logical, outcome of this tendency was the development of a concept of anonymous Christianity in which all were considered to be Christians whether they knew it or not, whether they denied it or not. The motives which led to the elaboration of this theology were not all bad. This, however, should not be permitted to obscure the fact that it is rooted in pessimism. Its proponents see no real possibility of creating a better world. Inevitably, therefore, their reflection gravitates to the justification of the status quo. It is hardly surprising that the world remains unchanged.

Fortunately, there are Christians who reject this approach. Misery and unhappiness batter their conscience to the point that complacency becomes the ultimate sin. Their concern for the oppressed surfaces in a commitment to changing the structures of society which are the instruments of oppression. No Christian could desire to do less. A fully authentic Christian, however, must desire to do more. Oppressive structures will not be successfully modified until hearts are changed. It is true that human beings change as new structures emerge, but the consistent lesson of history is that without genuine conversion the new structures will prove to be no less oppressive.

Failure to recognise this truth has meant that many Christians committed to freeing the oppressed through the modification of social structures have become discouraged, but because of their dedication their disillusionment with the pace of change tends to display itself in anger which finds an outlet in a theology of revolution. It is presumed that by removing the obstacle occasioned by the complacency of the rich the problem will be solved.

The simplicity of this solution is attractive. But when it is a question of human nature simplicity is suspect. Once again, the lesson of history is that violent disruption of the status quo has never in fact been the prelude to a better society. The poor are just as much in need of redemption as the rich. Unless the hearts of the have-nots are changed they will inevitably produce structures which inhibit the human development of others.

All, therefore, need liberation. Where do we begin? And if we begin, are there any grounds for optimism? To reflect on these questions purely on the basis of the reality in which we are immersed can only lead to pessimism and despair, as is evident in the works of the majority of the existentialist philosophers. If we are to continue to hope, and without hope there is no striving, we must find another perspective.

Just this alternative is provided by the New Testament. The situation that we face is not new. The first generation of Christians was faced with the same problem. They were a small minority and they were confronted with the gigantic task of changing the world. The fact that they did eventually bring about radical modifications in social structures gives them a claim on our attention which supercedes that of any other reformer. Of all the first-century theologians who articulated the dimensions of the problem, the apostle Paul stands preeminent. His analysis of the contemporary situation that he had to deal with could be an analysis of our society. This at once gives him an extraordinary credibility. He knows the difficulties. His answers, therefore, are not coloured by the utopianism which stirs intellectual excitement but fails to move to action. Realism and responsibility are so characteristic of his vision of what the human creature can become that we are forced to concede with Chesterton that Christianity has not failed; it simply has never been seriously tried.

Paul explicitly rejects any frontal attack on the structures of society. His eschatological vision was responsible for this, and we (however unrealistically) no longer share his belief that the end of the world is imminent. Nonetheless, a valid point can be extracted from his attitude. It is fundamentally unchristian to conceive one's mission as concerned with the rich, the workers, or the poor, because this approach effectively reduces persons to the status of units in a class. It fails to respect the dignity of their uniqueness. On a more practical level, to attempt to deal with the problem of oppression and freedom in terms of social classes places the problem in a perspective which makes it virtually insoluble, simply because the numbers involved are so vast.

If we perceive this, it was not any less evident to Paul. His realism comes to the fore in his recognition that the individual is powerless in the face of the forces at work in society. Those who belong to a society are deeply conditioned by its orientation. They may reject certain aspects, and this gives them the impression of freedom. Paul's radical vision had no place for such a naive illusion. He denied the reality of free will to those who belonged to an inauthentic society. It remained as a theoretical possibility, but his concern was with the reality of freedom. It is only the free who can liberate the slaves.

In order to be free, we must be detached from the grip of a society that moulds us despite ourselves to its own image. Fundamentally, it is a question of some form of protection which inhibits the influence of pressures that distort our self-understanding. Paul saw that such protection could be provided only by the setting up of an alternative environment in which we would be subject to inspiration supportive of our quest for authenticity. This environment is nothing other than the local Christian community which is not only the form of freedom and salvation, but is also the critical instrument for change in the world.

Though his vocation was to preach the Word, Paul saw clearly that words alone would never modify societal structures. It is too easy to talk and the world is tired of listening to barren proclamations. Neither is it sufficient to do things for people. What is crucial is that Christians *be* in a special way. The very style of their existence is the power which creates the possibility of change for others. Yet for Christians to exist in such a way, they too must be empowered. Hence, their mutual dependence on each other in the unity of the Body of Christ.

If the church is, once again, to release the power that is effective of lasting change it must recapture the basic concept of Christian community, and Paul, because of his success, has the first claim to be our guide. The purpose of this book is to show that community is the key element in his thought. Once this is grasped, all that he says in his epistles falls into proper place, and becomes a radical challenge that pierces to the heart of contemporary concern. It is only when we are convinced that community is the basic Christian reality that we can commit ourselves totally to bringing it into existence.

The book falls into three parts. The first part is devoted to Paul's anthropology, because the Apostle's insight into what the human creature can and should be is the basis of his whole approach. This will involve a discussion of his understanding of Jesus Christ because it was in him that Paul found a concrete historical model of authentic human existence. The second part examines the structures of inauthentic existence. It is here that we shall see that Paul's description of the society with which he had to deal can be applied with very little modification to our contemporary world. If he saw the problems we perceive, there seems to be no reason to deny that the solutions that worked for him should work for us. Hence, in the third part, I try to present his comprehension of the structures of authentic existence in the Body of Christ. It is here that we shall see the true nature of Christian community of which freedom is the primordial characteristic.

The understanding of Paul that I here put forward is the result of a long period of maturation to which many factors contributed. The original impetus to undertake this type of reflection was an invitation to deliver a series of talks on Pauline Moral Theology to the New England Summer Institute for Priests at Stonehill College, North Easton, Mass., in 1970. At this point I was concerned to determine exactly what weight Paul attached to the moral imperatives with which his epistles abound. The conclusions at which I had arrived were corrected and developed in dialogue with other audiences, and the preliminary publication in the form of three articles in *Doctrine and Life* (Jan., Feb., and March 1971) was eventually expanded into a book published in France under the title *L'existence chrétienne selon saint Paul* (Paris: Editions du Cerf, 1974) and in Brasil under the title *A Vida do Homem Novo* (Sao Paulo: Ediçoes Paulinas, 1975). Subsequent discussions with audiences in Ireland and the United States, in Peru and Brasil, and in Australia and New Zealand revealed, however, that the section of this book which dealt with anthropology and the structures of inauthentic and authentic existence was much more relevant to the contemporary situation of the church than the rather technical investigation of Paul's moral imperatives. Hence, I decided to develop this section and to publish it separately in the hope that it will be of some service to those who are trying to build the church in the modern world.

I have tried to be as brief as is consistent with clarity, and footnotes have been reduced to the bare minimum. I have adoped this alternative to a scientific treatise because of my conviction that the audience I want to reach would be more receptive to a study that respects its order of priorities. A dialogue between academics on minute points of interpretation has little value for those whose burden of work in parishes and on the missions allows them only minimal leisure. I also feel that in chosing this approach I am repaying a debt. My obligation to those who have written on Paul is immense, but I owe more to the selfless labourers in the vineyard whose urgent questions have directed my attention to aspects of Paul's though whose importance has not always been recognised. Their commitment to 'life' (in the Pauline sense) provided stimulus and criticism which I acknowledge with a gratitude that I can never adequately express.

Preface to the Second Edition

The understanding of Paul that I outlined in the first edition of this book rested on the study of only certain aspects and themes, but the vision I presented necessarily went beyond the evidence I could then control. Most of my research in the intervening five years has been devoted to detailed st idies of particular passages in the Pauline letters. The result has been a series of fully annotated articles published in *Revue Biblique, Journal of Biblical Literature,* and *Catholic Biblical Quarterly.* Nothing I found obliged me to alter my conception of the basic pattern of Paul's thought. On the contrary, the insight into his mind developed here enabled me to throw new light on texts which have long been bones of contention. My hypothesis, in other words, successfully passes the classical test; it clarifies points not considered in the formulation of the hypothesis. I have also been reassured by the convergent conclusions of other scholars, notably J. D. G. Dunn's firm rejection of any hint of the divinity of Christ in Paul, E. P. Sanders' refusal to see justification by faith as the key to the Apostle's theology, and F. Mussner's treatment of Sin and Liberty. All so many hints that this generation might see Paul freed at last from the alien categories which served only to obscure his relevance.

In addition to correcting minor errors, the generosity of my publisher and friend, Michael Glazier, has permitted me to add new material, the greater part of which appears in chs. 1 and 3. The former situates Paul historically by trying to specify how much he knew of the earthly ministry of Jesus. The latter deals, perhaps too briefly, with a number of concepts which, if misunderstood, necessarily involve a radical distortion of Paul's vision of Christ. I have also added a section on 'Women in Christ' in ch. 10, not simply because the problem is topical, but because misrepresentations of Paul's position on this issue have proved an obstacle to sympathetic appreciation of his contribution to our understanding of what genuine community should be.

In response to the suggestions of teachers who use my work as a basic introduction to Pauline thought I have added bibliographies at the end of each chapter. In no respect are they intended to be exhaustive. I include studies that have proved formative of my own thought, even when I am not always in complete agreement, and also books and articles that deal with the same topics from a different perspective. Any tensions between my conclusions and theirs should serve as a stimulus to personal thought. All the passages from 1 Cor to which I refer are treated in context in my commentary on *1 Corinthians* in the New Testament Message series (Glazier: Wilmington, 1979); it can also serve as a test of the extent to which the vision of Paul presented here illuminates the reading of one of his letters.

Jerome Murphy-O'Connor, O.P.
Ecole Biblique de Jérusalem
January 1982

Part 1
HUMAN BEING

I
PAUL AND JESUS

Paul's vision of humanity is rooted in his understanding of Jesus Christ. Much of what we find in his letters relative to Christ is the fruit of his own reflection, but he must have had something on which to meditate. Hence, we must begin by asking what Paul actually knew about the historical Jesus. This has the double advantage of underlining his relationship to the early church and of emphasizing how personal his Christology is.

From data supplied by his own letters we can be certain that Paul had three sources of information concerning the historical Jesus: the Pharisaic tradition, his conversion experience, and the tradition of the Christian communities in which he spent the first years after his conversion.

The Pharisaic Tradition

In 2 Cor 5:16 Paul says "even though we once knew Christ in a fleshy way, we know him so no longer". He is evidently referring to the knowledge that he had of Christ in his pre-conversion stage when he was a persecutor of the church (Gal 1:13; Phil 3:6; cf. Acts 9:1ff.). To discover where he got this information we have only to look at the Apostle's background.

He proudly claimed to be "of the race of Israel, of the tribe of Benjamin, a Hebrew of Hebrews and, as regards the Law, a Pharisee" (Phil 3:5). Many Jews of the tribe of Benjamin lived outside the borders of the Holy Land, and Paul was in fact from Tarsus on the south coast of Asia Minor (Acts 22:3), but his insistence that he was not only an Israelite but a Hebrew (cf. 2 Cor 11:22) emphasizes that he was of Palestinian stock. His parents, or at most his grandparents, were from Judea. It is very probable, therefore, that he had relatives living in Judea and, in consequence, there is nothing implausible in Luke's assertion that he was educated in Jerusalem (Acts 22:3). This text actually says that he was 'brought up' in Jerusalem which some have interpreted to mean that he did most of his schooling, and not merely his professional training (cf. Acts 26:4), in the Holy City.

Be that as it may, Paul was certainly a 'Pharisee'. The claim of Phil 3:6 is implicitly confirmed by Gal 1:14, "I was extremely zealous for the traditions of my fathers", because according to Josephus, "The Pharisees have imposed on the people many laws from the traditions of the fathers not written in the law of Moses" (*Antiquitates* 13:297); the importance given to traditional oral teaching was one of the distinguishing features of Pharisaism. This guarantees Luke's statement that Paul "lived as a Pharisee according to the strictest party of our religion" (Acts 26:5) and, this being the case, there is no good reason to doubt his assertion that Paul had studied under Gamaliel I (Acts 22:3).

This great teacher flourished in Jerusalem about A.D. 20-50. His reputation was so great that the Mishnah says, "From the time that Rabban Gamaliel the Elder died, respect for the Torah ceased; and purity and abstinence died at the same time" (Sotah 9:15). Were Paul a rabbinical student in Jerusalem he could not have escaped his influence. The dates fit perfectly, because Paul's conversion must be dated a year or so before A.D. 34.

We don't know his exact age, but at the time of his conversion Paul was certainly more than a mere student. Otherwise his commission to root out the Christians in Damascus (Acts 9:1) would be incomprehensible. It is even probable that he was already a member of the Sanhedrin. The key text is Acts 26:9-11, "I myself was convinced that I ought to do many things in opposing the name of Jesus of Nazareth, and I did so in Jerusalem. I not only shut up many of the saints in prison, by authority from the chief priests, but when they were put to death I cast my vote against them. And I punished them often in all the synagogues and tried to make them blaspheme, and in raging fury against them, I persecuted them even to outside cities." Here Paul is said to have voted in capital cases. Only the Greater (71 members) or Lesser (23 of the 71) Sanhedrin had competence in such cases, and only full members were entitled to vote. If we take the text at its face value, Paul was certainly a member of the Sanhedrin, but since all do not agree on this interpretation we must look a little more closely at the historical value of Luke's affirmation.

A number of scholars have tried to develop arguments against the historicity of Acts 26:9-11 but none carry conviction:

(1) Paul, it is said, was too young to be a member of the Sanhedrin in which the Pharisees occupied only about one-third of the seats. In fact, however, we know nothing definite regarding Paul's age - the term 'youth' (Acts 7:58) covers the 25-40 age group — and still less concerning the method of appointment to the Sanhedrin.

(2) Alternatively, it is claimed that 'to cast a vote' may be used very loosely and may mean nothing more than the vague 'to consent' used in Acts 8:1 and 22:20. However, a pure possibility is merely a warning not an argument. It is equally possible that Acts 8:1 and 22:20 should be interpreted in the light of Acts 26:10.

(3) At this period the Sanhedrin was incompetent to order the execution of a capital sentence. This point is still too controverted to provide a solid argument. The Sanhedrin

certainly had the right in theory and, given the Jewish attitude towards the Romans, it seems probable that it also claimed it in practice when it felt that it could get away with it. In A.D. 62 during the interregnum between the death of the procurator Festus and the arrival of his successor Albinus, the high priest Ananus "assembled the sanhedrin of judges and brought before them the brother of Jesus called Christ, whose name was James, and some others. And when he had formed an accusation against them as breakers of the law, he delivered them to be stoned" (Josephus, *Antiquities* 20:200).

(4) Finally, it is pointed out that Acts nowhere else speaks of Paul as having persecuted the church in Jerusalem or its environs. This is certainly correct, but the argument from silence is nullified by Gal 1:22 which unambiguously implies that Paul had in fact persecuted the believers in Judea.

In contrast to such unconvincing arguments the context of 26:10b can be shown to be solidly historical:

(1) In Acts 26:10a Paul's authority as a special prosecutor is said to derive from 'the chief of priests'. Both the NT and Josephus agree that this term designated the group that effectively controlled the Sanhedrin. Their role would have been comparable to that of the 'inner cabinet' in many democracies today, and their approval would have been a prerequisite for any executive action.

(2) The procedure used to winkle out undeclared Jewish-Christians in Acts 26:11a is highly plausible, for the deeply committed will not act against their consciences. Precisely the same technique was used by the Jews in the Birkat ha-Minim, and by Pliny in Asia Minor (*Letters*, Bk. 10, n. 96).

(3) The reference to 'outside cities' (Acts 26:11b) does not mean 'cities in countries outside Palestine', as the RSV translation 'foreign cities' would seem to imply. Since, 26:10-11a concern Paul's activities in Jerusalem, the most natural interpretation is 'cities outside Jerusalem', of which there were a number in Judea alone. It is much more reasonable to assume that Paul must have carried out minor

missions in the area adjacent to Jerusalem before being approved (Acts 9:2) to seek out the believers in the synagogues of a city as important as Damascus.

If the context of Acts 26:10b is so securely rooted in known facts and valid assumptions, the historicity of Paul's membership in the Sanhedrin emerges as solidly probable.

Such being the case, Paul was not only a pupil of Gamaliel I but also a junior colleague. He would have grown into a relationship with his master which permitted a freedom of intercourse denied to a mere student. Inevitably, he would have been privy to the discussions of the other Pharisaic members of the Sanhedrin, most of whom would have been present at the trial of Jesus. I find it impossible to imagine that the figure of Jesus of Nazareth was not evoked in the debates that must have ensued as soon as the Christian presence in Jerusalem began to make itself felt. Despite the theological overtones of Luke's account in the first chapters of Acts, there can be little doubt but that he accurately reflects the reaction of the Jewish authorities to the appearance of another splinter group. A very similar situation had developed nearly two hundred years earlier when the Essenes first came on the scene, but now the threat was much more serious because the 'faith' (Gal 1:22) of this new group was different; they were proclaiming that the Messiah had in fact come. This makes it even less probable that the concern of the authorities was limited to the phenomenon. There must have been a deep preoccupation with its roots, namely, the claims of Jesus. To combat the problem the Pharisees would have had to know exactly what was going on, and Paul would have been a partner in this dialogue.

This brings us to the most important question: what did the Pharisees know about Jesus? To answer, we cannot simply go through the gospels and combine all the episodes in which the Pharisees are mentioned, because on many occasions 'Pharisee' functions as a symbol for opposition to Jesus which in reality may have come from a variety of sources; this is particularly true for the gospels of Matthew and John. Hence, stringent precautions against anachronism must be taken, the control being what we know of the interests and concerns of the Pharisees from other sources. If this is done, a rather curious picture emerges.

The Pharisees knew Jesus as a teacher with disciples (Mk 2:18). Despite his lack of formal training (Jn 7:15), he risked being taken as one of their number. This created a danger to their authority which was based on ostentatiously strict observance of the Law. Hence, their criticism of his association with 'sinners' (Mk 2:16; Lk 7:36; 15:2), of his relaxed attitude towards 'work' on the sabbath (Mk 2:24; 3:6; Lk 6:7; 14:1; Jn 9:13), and of his neglect of the rules of ritual purity (Mk 7:1). Yet, they must also have known that on some issues he was more rigorous than they, notably as regards divorce (Mk 10:2).

From such data the Pharisees could hardly have failed to draw the conclusion that Jesus was acting as if he enjoyed a privileged position as regards the Law, and this could only be construed as a claim to a special relationship with God. Obviously, that was the heart of the matter, which makes it all the more strange that the Pharisees are never represented as confronting this issue directly. The closest we get to a confrontation is their request for a sign (Mk 8:11), but we catch a hint that they saw the problem in terms of messianism in the assertion, reported by the disciples, that Elijah must come first (Mk 9:11), and another one in their insistence on Jesus' Galilean origins (Jn 7:52), for they expected a Davidic Messiah (Mt 22:42). Thus, whatever its historical value, the question of the high priest during the trial of Jesus, "Are you the Christ, the Son of the Blessed One?" (Mk 14:61), must have articulated precisely what was running through the minds of the Pharisaic leaders. This view is supported by the fact (see above) that Josephus, who claimed to be a Pharisee, knew that Jesus was reputed to be the Messiah.

Finally, it is also probable that the Pharisees were aware of the Christian claim that Jesus had been raised from the dead. The fact that this was a consistent element in the earliest Christian preaching lends credibility to the basis of

Mt 28:11-15; the Pharisees were maintaining that the disciples had stolen the body, an attitude that is explicable only if they were aware of what believers maintained.

Thus, despite the fanaticism of Paul's repudiation of Jesus and all that he stood for, any reminder of Jesus would have set up the following associative resonances: (1) a claim to Messianic Sonship with its connotations of mission and obedience; (2) rejection of the absolute authority of the Law; (3) resurrection. At first sight this may seem to be a very meagre result to a rather laborious inquiry. The contrary is in fact true, because in these overtones evoked by the name of Jesus lie the seeds of two of the key ideas that shaped the whole theology of Paul, namely, the unique Sonship of Jesus, and the merely relative value of the Law.

Paul's Conversion Experience

Paul himself tells us very little about this event, and the only clue he gives as to its meaning for him is his assimilation of the experience to the post-resurrection appearances of Jesus (1 Cor 9:1; 15:8). Obviously, we need concern ourselves only with what have been termed 'recognition Christophanies' because these were in effect re-conversion experiences; the disciples had to accept anew the Risen Lord. Such narratives exhibit a very clear pattern which is most evident in the appearance to Mary Magdalene (Jn 20:11 and 16) and to the Eleven (Jn 20:19-20), but which can also be detected in the more developed stories (Lk 24:13-35, 36-43). The four component elements are: (1) absence of any expectation on the part of the disciple(s); (2) an initiative of Jesus who (3) gives a sign of his identity; (4) recognition of Jesus by the disciple(s).

Paul no more expected to encounter the risen Jesus than did the disciples, even though, as a Pharisee, he was committed to belief in the resurrection, and they had heard Jesus' prediction. Equally, Paul presents Jesus as having taken the initiative; "he appeared to me" (1 Cor 15:8), and, of course, the story ends with his acceptance of Jesus. The parallel appears to break down as regards the third element which is the critical one, viz. the sign of identity given by Jesus. Paul could not have 'recognized' him in precisely the same way as the other disciples because he had never seen him in the flesh. However, we can be sure that Paul had a mental image of Jesus. The intense anger directed against Christians must have encompassed their leader as the one who had led some of his people astray. The stress thus produced would have interfered with the Apostle's normal rationality and would have heightened his susceptibility to anything associated with the focus of his emotion. On account of his mental condition Paul was in fact much more vulnerable than is normally conceded, a factor that greatly reduces the seeming paradox of his radical and immediate shift of allegiance. When something happened, and here we touch the edge of mystery, the two images fused, and Paul's world was turned upside down.

The key factor, as in the case of the other disciples, was the conviction that a dead man had been raised, that the crucified Jesus was alive again. This indisputable fact transformed Paul's value-system. If one of the three resonances that the name of Jesus set up his Pharisaic mind was true, then the other two immediately appeared in a totally different light. No longer were they the blasphemous pretentions of a madman but utter truth. If Jesus had been raised from the dead, then his claim to be the Christ and Son of God could not be denied, and his attitude towards the Law must reflect the will of God.

In other words, Paul's encounter with the living Jesus on the Damascus road gave him a fundamental insight into the person and mission of Jesus and, at the same time, opened to him the possibility of salvation for the gentiles, for if the Law had relative value, then it was not the only way to God. In a very real sense, therefore, what were to be the two major axes of his theology came into Paul's possession at the moment of his conversion. Vague and embryonic as they were at this stage, they were nonetheless deeply embedded in his mind and heart. We are now in a position to comprehend what Paul meant when he wrote, "The gospel preached by me is not man's gospel, for I did not receive it nor was I taught it, but it came to me through a revelation of Jesus Christ" (Gal 1:12). It was not as if Jesus shot new ideas into his mind. The encounter gave him a radically new perspective on ideas which he had hitherto rejected; ideas which he had not learned through the concern of a master to instruct his mind, but ideas which he had heard of in passing as examples of prideful error. Thus, 'he did not receive it from man, or was he taught it'. The experience of the living Christ enkindled in him the truth he unknowingly possessed.

The Christian Tradition

As we have just seen, the independence asserted in Gal 1:12 is justified on the level of Paul's basic theological intuitions. It is certainly not true as regards the full range of his initial knowledge about Jesus, for after his conversion he lived in Christian communities before undertaking missionary work. He was in touch, therefore, with the gospel tradition in its formative stage and some of his fellow-believers may have been eye-witnesses of parts of the earthly ministry of Jesus.

The earliest date we can establish in the life of Paul is his escape from Damascus when it was controlled by the Nabataean king Aretas (2 Cor 11:31-32). In all probability this occurred in late A.D. 37, and the episode is to be identified with the departure from Damascus mentioned in Gal 1:17-18, because there is no hint that Paul ever returned to that city again. At this point Paul had lived in Damascus for 'three years' (Gal 1:18), a round number which, in terms of the way the ancients reckoned years, could mean a minimal sojourn of as little as eighteen months. The earliest that Paul could have taken up residence in Damascus is the autumn of A.D. 34, and the latest would be sometime in the spring of A.D. 36. Prior to that he had been in 'Arabia' for an unspecified time immediately subsequent to his conversion (Gal 1:16-17). The importance of these dates becomes apparent once it is recognized that the more probable date of the crucifixion is April 3, A.D. 33, because we are forced to conclude that Paul's conversion took place within two years of the death and resurrection of Jesus. In other words, he joined the church at a time when memories of Jesus were still vivid and before the stories about him had become stereotyped.

Paul himself does not tell us what he did during his time in Damascus. Luke, however, informs us that he preached Jesus as Son of God and Messiah (Acts 9:20-22). In itself nothing is more probable, but valuable confirmation of the value of Luke's tradition is supplied by what we have seen above regarding Paul's Pharisaic background as crystal-lized in the high priest's question, "Are you the Christ, the Son of the Blessed One?" (Mk 14:61). If Paul's concern was 'to prove' that Jesus was the Christ his argument must have taken the form of a demonstration that Jesus was the fulfill-ment of prophecy. In this case, the sayings of Jesus would have been much less important than his person and deeds, for the Old Testament speaks only of what the Messiah would accomplish. Hence, we can infer that Paul must have been concerned to accumulate as much information as pos-sible about the earthly ministry of Jesus. There is no basis for the rather common opinion that Paul was completely disinterested in the historical Jesus.

In this perspective it might appear natural to translate Gal 1:18 as "I went up to Jerusalem to get information from Kephas". This meaning for *historêsai* is certainly not impossible, because the basic connotation of the verb is 'to inquire, to examine', but it is equally certain that Paul did not intend this meaning because his purpose in Gal 1-2 is to establish his independence of the Jerusalem church. The demands of the context are fully met by the common trans-lation which implies that Paul's goal was to get to know Peter. The implication is that Paul was aware of Peter's position—the title 'Kephas' alone proves this—and I find it impossible to imagine that Paul had never inquired why Peter held his office and where he got his title. Whether this happened in Damascus or Jerusalem is irrelevant in comparison with the hint that Paul was aware of the tradition behind Mt 16:13-20, with all that it implies about community and structure.

A very strong case can be made in favour of the hypothesis that Gal 2:7 embodies the essential content of Paul's first meeting with Peter. If this is correct, we are given a valuable clue to another dimension of Paul's personality; by the time of his arrival in Jerusalem he was already conscious of his apostolic vocation to the gentiles. I have no hesitation in seeing this as the natural outgrowth of his reflection on the implications of Jesus' attitude towards the Law. However, it would be a little unrealistic to imagine that Peter and Paul spent all their time together thrashing out their spheres of ministry (Gal 2:7). Paul's must have been as interested in Peter's relationship to the historical Jesus as he was in the way he preached the risen Christ. The fact that Peter's reminiscences might already have begun to take on a stereotyped form is less significant than the fact that Paul was for two weeks in contact with one of Jesus' closest companions and one of the prime sources of the gospel tradition.

To sum up this brief survey of Paul's contacts with the Christian tradition at the beginning of his missionary career we can say, (1) that he had been in a position to learn a lot about the historical Jesus from prime sources, and (2) that he would have been interested in the person and deeds of Jesus and not merely in his sayings.

It is surprising, therefore, that the letters tell us so little of what Paul must have known. Jesus was a Jew (Rom 9:4-5) of the line of David (Rom 1:3) who had a mother (Gal 4:4). He was betrayed (1 Cor 11:23) and crucified (1 Cor 2:2, and passim), as a result of which he died and was buried (1 Cor 15:3-4). Then God raised him from the dead (1 Cor 15:5 and passim). However, we must recall that Paul's epistles are not systematic expositions but responses to specific problems that arose in the communities for which he was responsible.

The letters, moreover, were addressed to formed believers who were considered to have assimilated the basic kerygma. Paul was under no obligation to repeat everything, and his occasional utterances concerning aspects of the earthly life of Jesus are related to the needs of specific situations.

Another point to be kept in mind is the fact that the historicity of Jesus is fundamental to Paul's theology. The disciple who wrote Ephesians caught his master's approach exactly when he presents Jesus as the truth of Christ (Eph 4:21). There was a tendency in some of the Apostle's communites to separate the Christ of faith from the Jesus of history. We find Paul resisting this attitude in his insistence that the Lord of Glory was the crucified Jesus (1 Cor 2:6), and in his stress that the Colossians had received Christ 'as Jesus the Lord' (Col 2:6). The hypothesis that Paul might have emphasized this point when it was denied is explicitly excluded by his condemnation of anyone "who preaches a Jesus *other than the one we preached"* (2 Cor 11:4). The italicized phrase clearly indicates that a portrait of the historical Jesus formed part of Paul's oral preaching; the use of 'Jesus' unqualified underlines the reference to the earthly ministry. I find it impossible to assume that he limited himself to a presentation of the death and resurrection, not only because of its intrinsic improbability but because it is contradicted by the letters themselves (cf. above). If Paul believed himself capable of representing 'the life of Jesus' (2 Cor 4:10) he must have had a very clear idea of the comportment of Jesus which manifested his authentic humanity.

How much Paul knew of the sayings of Jesus is a very controverted issue. Those who claim that the teaching of the historical Jesus had no influence on Paul are opposed by others who assert that it formed the primary source of his ethical instruction. The truth probably lies between these two extremes.

There are only two direct citations of words of Jesus in the letters, the prohibition of divorce (1 Cor 7:10-11) and the directive concerning the support of pastors (1 Cor 9:14), but the most recent studies devoted to these texts tend to show that Paul knew not just the saying but the context in which it appears in the synoptic tradition. This is not the place to develop this point, and one example must suffice. The theme of support of pastors appears in Lk 10 and it has been shown that this chapter is linked to 1 Cor 9 by a whole series of common terms: an 'apostle' who is ('to sow' and) 'to reap' has the 'right' to a 'reward' for his 'preaching the good news' because a 'workman' has the right 'to eat' and 'to drink'. The contracts are too numerous to make coincidence an acceptable explanation, particularly since the same type of contracts are to be found in other blocks of material. It should also be noted that the two dominical sayings that Paul quotes did not end up as part of a collection of sayings (such as the hypothetical Q source) but as part of a source which also contained accounts of deeds of Jesus.

It has also been pointed out that, although Pharisaism was essentially an urban movement and Paul a cityman, the Apostle uses an unusually high proportion of metaphors which reflect an agrarian culture (Rom 1:13; 6:21; 7:4-5; 15:28, 1 Cor 3:6-9; 9 (passim); 15:36-44; 2 Cor 9:6-10; Gal 5:22; 6:7-9; Phil 1:22; 4:17). The most convincing explanation is that he was familiar with the language of Jesus' parables, because the contacts are too specific to be explained by common dependence on the Old Testament.

Hence, contemporary Pauline scholarship is inclined to consider that Paul had a rather extensive knowledge of what became the synoptic tradition. It is characteristic of his personality, however, that he never draws on this material as an authoritative source. His method was not to drive by means of an authoritarian use of proof-texts, but to lead by the persuasive force of truth calmly presented. His familiarity with the developing Christian tradition concerning the ministry of Jesus is revealed only by the way it has conditioned his mode of expression, but the perspectives on the humanity of Jesus that it embodies permeate his thought. His reflections on the meaning of Christ for the church and the world are rooted in the reality of Jesus of Nazareth.

Suggested Readings

E. Schürer, *The History of the Jewish People in the Age of Jesus Christ, II* (revised and edited by G. Vermes, F. Millar and M. Black), Edinburgh: Clark, 1979, § 26 (Pharisees).

J. Jeremais, *Jerusalem in the Time of Jesus,* London: SCM, 1969, ch. 11 (Pharisees).

R. Jewett, *A Chronology of Paul's Life,* Philadelphia: Fortress, 1979.

A.J. Huldgren, "Paul's Pre-Christian Persecutions of the Church: Their Purpose, Locale and Nature,"*Journal of Biblical Literature* 95 (1976) 97-111.

G. Lohfink, *Paulus vor Damaskus,* Stuttgart: Katholisches Bibelwerk, 1965 = *La conversion de saint Paul,* Paris: Cerf, 1967.

J. G. Gager, "Some Notes on Paul's Conversion," *New Testament Studies* 27 (1981) 697-704.

D. G. Dungan, *The Sayings of Jesus in the Churches of Paul,* Philadelphia: Fortress, 1971.

D. Stanley, "Pauline Allusions to the Sayings of Jesus," *Catholic Biblical Quarterly* 23 (1961).

J. Murphy-O'Connor, "Pauline Missions before the Jerusalem Conference," *Revue Biblique,* Jan. 1982.

II
CHRIST THE CRITERION

Christ is at the center of the Christian faith. Paul accepted this fully so that, for him, Christ was the beginning and end, not merely of salvation, but of everything. His whole perspective on reality was conditioned by his vision of Christ. Specifically, his understanding of what humanity could and should be was rooted in his understanding of the humanity of Christ.

How Humanity Should Be Understood

As we shall see in more detail in a moment, we are conditioned to think of Christ in terms of ourselves. He is human and we are human, and it is natural to move from the known (ourselves) to the unknown (Christ). Thus, in the some 60,000 biographies of Jesus written during the 18th and 19th centuries, the portrait of Jesus that emerges is conditioned principally by the subjectivity of the author who creates a hero in conformity with his own aspirations. In consequence, Jesus appears variously as an idealist, a rationalist, a romantic, a socialist, etc. It is not surprising, therefore, that Paul's converts should have been tempted to do likewise. We are fortunate that they did, because this forced Paul to draw attention to the change of perspective that should follow on acceptance of Christ:

> Christ died for all, that those who live might live no longer for themselves, but for him who for their sake died and was raised. Therefore, from now on we know no one *kata sarka*. Even though we once knew Christ *kata sarka* we know him so no longer. Therefore, if anyone is in Christ he is a new creation; the old things have passed away, they have become new (2 Cor 5:15-17).

I have left the phrase *kata sarka* in Greek because its meaning has been the subject of a long debate. Theoretically, it can be understood either as an adverb 'in a fleshy way' qualifying the verb 'to know,' or as an adjective 'in the flesh' qualifying the proper noun 'Christ'. Which meaning did Paul intend? Some understand him to intend the adjective, because this would then mean that Paul had actually encountered Jesus during the days of his earthly ministry. It has even been claimed that Paul was the rich young man who refused the act of faith (Mk 10:17-22)! This position has now lost virtually all its supporters. When Paul uses *kata sarka* as a adjective he gives it a different position in the sentence (cf. Rom 4:1; 9:3; 1 Cor 1:26; 10:18). More importantly, however, if we make *kata sarka* an adjective when it refers to Christ, we make nonsense of the preceding phrase where it also appears, because it then must be translated "We know no one in the flesh", i.e. we have no human contacts. A reading of any of the letters shows this to be absurd. Hence, *kata sarka* must be understood as an adverb qualifying 'to know'.

What Paul is saying, therefore, is that he once knew Christ 'in a fleshy way'. He had possessed an inferior type of knowledge about Jesus. All this can mean in the light of what he says about his persecution of the church (Phil 3:6) is that he at one time shared the estimation of Jesus common among his contemporaries, namely, that he was an heretical teacher and a turbulent agitator whose activities had with justice brought him to the scaffold. This, Paul now recognizes, was a false judgement which he has abandoned. How this happened is not our concern here.

What is important is that he has also abandoned a similar way of judging others: "From now on we know *no one* in a fleshy way". His intention, obviously, is to encourage others to do likewise. Why he should insist will become clearer if we digress for a moment to examine the type of situation he had in mind. In his previous letter to the Corinthians he was forced to write:

> I brethren, could not address you as spiritual men, but as men of the flesh, as babes in Christ . . . . For while there is jealousy and strife among you are you not of the flesh and walking according to men? For when one says 'I belong to Paul', and another 'I belong to Apollos', are you not men? (1 Cor 3:1-4)

'Walking' is a common Semitic idiom for a pattern of behaviour, and in Paul's lexicon 'according to man' means 'according to the common estimation' (Rom 3:5; 1 Cor 9:8; 15:32; Gal 3:5). By accepting jealousy, strife and party factions as part of their habitual pattern of behaviour the Corinthians were simply conforming to the common estimation of what was normal. Such things were taken for granted as an integral part of human existence. That was the way the world lived, and there was no justification for being either shocked or surprised. The presence of such attitudes within the community was taken for granted by the Corinthians. Paul's reaction is to criticize such acceptance as childish immaturity, because they should have recognized that they now have a standard which frees them from the tyranny of the 'common estimation' in determining what pattern of behaviour is appropriate for the human creature. He does not spell out precisely what this standard is, and consequently had to return to this point in the passage of 2 Cor with which we have been dealing.

This time there is no ambiguity. The statement "From

now on we know no one in a fleshy way" is prefaced by a particle meaning "therefore" which makes it the consequence of "Christ died that all those who live might live no longer for themselves". Such altruism is in flat contradiction to the egocentricity that the Corinthians took for granted. Christ's pattern of behaviour is the standard by which Christians must judge the quality of life of others. Consequently, if anyone is "in Christ" he must judge in a new way. "The old things have passed away, they have become new" means that the judgement has been renewed in accepting a new standard or point of reference, namely, "the love of Christ" by which Paul himself is now constrained (2 Cor 5:14). Paul does not exaggerate when he speaks of this as a "new creation".

A False Approach

What has just been said highlights the supreme importance of Christ in Paul's anthropology. We cannot have an authentic understanding of humanity unless we first know Christ. The contemporary approach to Christology, however, is exactly the reverse, as two citations, the first from a Catholic and the second from an Episcopalian, will illustrate:

> To know how human Christ is, we must first set down in a summary way at least what it is to be a man. It is, evidently, to be born and grow up loved or unloved; to distinguish oneself (one's Ego) from the surrounding world; to be taught language and to imbibe attitudes; to come to an awareness of oneself and of one's task and mission in life, and to be free to fulfil it; to struggle to fulfil one's mission, for struggle is the concomitant of freedom; to commit oneself to God in the struggle and the dark. This is not to be taken as an exhaustive list of the specifically human aspects of man's life, nor is it being suggested that these aspects are separable from the rest. I

am merely pointing to an obvious fact: if we are to take as genuine the Church's profession that Jesus is truly man, the aspects just outlined must be taken into consideration. (P. de Rosa, *Christ and Original Sin,* London, 1967, 43).

We may ask, however, whether we can speak significantly of the humanity of Christ unless we *do* regard him as having been 'a man like other men' . . . . He must have learned as we learn and have grown as we grow. His joys must have been human joys and his sorrows the immemorial sorrows of men like ourselves. He must have known loneliness, frustration, anxiety, just as we do. He must have felt temptations to doubt and fear. He would have loved others in the way men love their fellows — more, we shall say, but not differently. He too would have shrunk from death, the breaking of familiar ties with beloved things. His knowledge of God, for all its sureness and its peculiar intimacy, would have been the kind of knowledge it is given men to have of their Creator and Father. If all this were not true, would we be able to say that he was truly man? For the real marks of a man are not his shape and appearance, or the way he walks, but the way he feels and thinks in his heart, the way he knows himself, others and God. (J. Knox, *The Humanity and Divinity of Christ,* Cambridge, 1967, 63, 68).

That the issue of Christ's humanity should have been raised in this way is a tremendous advance on those studies of Pauline theology which either ignore the problem completely, or deal with it inadequately. The former take it for granted that we all know precisely what the distinctive characteristics of human nature are. The latter attempt to prove the humanity of Jesus by asserting that he was born, grew hungry and tired and died. It is difficult to decide whether the condescension of the first group or the naivete of the second is the more lamentable. Characteristics that we share with the animal kingdom tell us nothing of the *humanity* of Christ, and while we may have our own ideas of what humanity is, what guarantee do we have that it corresponds with that of Paul?

The criteria outlined by Knox and de Rosa are of tremendous value when we deal with specific incidents in the life of Jesus. They permit us to see the Baptism as the beginning of Jesus' progressive discovery of the meaning of his mission. They force us to see the Temptations and the Agony in the Garden as moments of real decision when Jesus had to struggle to remain faithful to his understanding of what his Father demanded of him. In other words, they constrain us to take the humanity of Jesus seriously.

In this, we can perceive a reaction against a tendency to undervalue the humanity of Jesus which had been prevalent in the church for many centuries. The reality of this humanity was affirmed as a matter of principle, but the way in which it was presented often amounted to a de facto denial. Thus, for example, Clement of Alexandria wrote at the end of the second century:

> Christ ate, not for the sake of the body, which was kept together by a holy energy, but in order that it might not enter into the minds of those who were with him to entertain a different opinion of him . . . . But he was entirely impassible, inaccessible to any movement of feeling, either pleasure or pain.

This was intended to emphasize the perfection of Jesus' humanity, but it only succeeds in making it so totally other that the human dimension disappears. The tendency that is here illustrated was given great impetus in the fourth century by the advent of Arianism, a heresy which insisted that Jesus was no more than a man used as an instrument by the Word, the Second Person of the Trinity. In response the church was led to stress the divinity of Christ. Because of the limitations of the human mind, these two aspect of Christ — humanity and divinity—are in tension, and the inevitable result is that one aspect is given prominence. The other, in consequence, recedes into the background. Ever since the time of Arius this has been the lot of the humanity of Jesus. There was never any outright denial, but his humanity was seen in the light of his divinity, and as a result was accorded a perfection that took it out of the orbit of mankind as we know it. Thus, it was claimed that the knowledge of Jesus was not subject to the limitations that we experience, and that his body felt the force of suffering but without experiencing pain. Only in this century has there been an effort to restore the balance by emphasizing the humanity of Jesus. To some this has appeared as a denial of his divinity. This is in fact not the case. It is an effort to be faithful to the *two* aspects of the tradition of the church concerning Jesus. Both Knox and de Rosa are worthy representatives of this contemporary theological task, but since a move away from falsehood is not necessarily a step towards the truth, we must look a little more closely at the criteria they put forward.

The principle that underlies their presentation is explicitly stated by Knox: if Jesus is not like us he is not a man. The next step is to look at contemporary humanity with the object of abstracting the common denominators which are then predicated of Jesus. At this point two questions need to be asked. Are Knox and de Rosa faithful to this method? Is the method in itself such as to be capable of producing the desired result?

The answer to the first question must be in the negative. Indifference to the needs of others is more common than love. Jealousy and possessiveness are just as widespread as loneliness and frustration. In other words, a whole series of features of contemporary humanity are left out of account. What Knox and de Rosa give us is not an objective view of humanity as it is, but a biased view. In place of a complete list of characteristic features, they offer us only a *selection*. The principle on which the selection is based is never explained, but if we look for its justification we find the answer to the second question. Certain features of contemporary humanity were left aside because they were felt to be inappropriate to Jesus. Knox and de Rosa were aware that the object of their observation is a *fallen* humanity, and as a result they did not include those elements which seemed to them to belong to fallen human nature. How they know which is which can never be explained. Objective observation of contemporary humanity can never result in a portrait of humanity as such. The best it can produce is a portrait of fallen humanity which is inapplicable to Christ, because he was without sin (Rom 1:4; 2 Cor 5:21; Jn 8:46; 1 Jn 3:5; Heb 4:15; 1 Pt 2:22). The phenomenological approach, therefore, its vitiated in its very essence. It can never tell us what authentic humanity is, because its subject matter is inauthentic humanity. In consequence, any attempt to discern the distinctive features of the humanity of Christ in terms of our actual humanity is foredoomed to failure.

The Divine Intention

If the route of empirical observation is closed to us, have we any alternative way to determine the constituent element of authentic humanity? Fortunately, we have. The fact of creaturehood means that we can say that true humanity is the mode of existence that the Creator intended his human creatures to have. But the only means of access to the divine intentions is, as Paul insists, through "the things that have been made" (Rom 1:20). Hence, in order to discover how God intended humanity to exist we have to look at the figure of Adam. Prior to the Fall, Adam was exactly what God intended humanity to be. He is not merely the first man, but man as such.

This insight did not originate with Paul. Jewish tradition, represented by Philo and the intertestamental literature, believed that Adam prior to the Fall was the perfect embodiment of the divine intent for humanity. Concern with this point followed from the belief of Jews that there is a correspondence between the Beginning and the End. Consequently, what they hoped would come about in the definitive kingdom of God was said to have been present prior to the Fall. They could not imagine that certain characteristics that made life miserable on this present earth would find a place in the eschaton. Thus, ugliness, sickness, weakness of intellect and will were denied to the renewed humanity of the future. Since Adam must have been what the blessed will be some day, the opposites of these defects were then predicated of him. Philo begins his exposition of the qualities of Adam with these words:

> It seems to me that this first man born of earth, the leader of all our race, was engendered excellent in both body and soul, and that he greatly differed from those who came after by the supereminent perfection of these two constituents of his being. He was, in truth, beautiful and good. (*De opificio mundi,* n. 136).

Philo then explains the physical perfection of Adam, before turning to a detailed presentation of his intellectual qualities. He touches on these topics in others of his works, and by assembling all the evidence the following portrait emerges. Adam's size was greater than that of our contemporaries. His senses were more perceptive; his eyes in particular were capable of seeing everything in heaven and on earth. He moved in the world in full confidence, and was never prey to fear. He lived in peace because there was no threat of war, and his happiness was without shadow. His intellect and will were strengthened by the divine spirit which had been breathed into him in abundance, and as a result the paths of virtue appeared as great highways, so that he earnestly endeavoured in all his words and actions to please God. Adam, therefore, was "superior to the men of today and to all of those who preceded us, because we are born of men, but he came forth from the hands of God. The better the cause, the more perfect the product" (*De op. mundi,* n. 140).

In this presentation Philo incorporates the insights of his predecessors and anticipates those of his successors. It is, therefore, typical, and the very language used is a clear indication of what is going on. We are not dealing with facts but with the very human desire for a better world. We are faced, not with history, but with prophecy. The portrait of Adam, therefore, is nothing but a mental construct developed by fallen humanity, and there is not the slightest guarantee that it conforms to the divine intention.

Hence, for Paul, a new creation was necessary to restore to humanity an authentic exemplar of the divine intention. There had to be a perfect individual who would be all that God desired humanity to be, and Paul found him in Christ. He, as the Last Adam, was the visibility of God's intention. He was what Adam was created to be.

This comes to the fore in the outline of the history of salvation that Paul presents in Rom 7:7 — 8:4. This is an extremely complicated passage, but while scholars diverge significantly in their interpretation of detail there is general agreement on two points: (1) The "I" who speaks in this text is not Paul, nor any typical young Jew, but humanity; (2) The religious history of humanity is divided into three stages. The consensus is maintained with regard to two of the three phases of the history of salvation: the second (7:14-24) is concerned with humanity under the dominion of the Mosaic Law, whereas the third (7:25 — 8:4) deals with the benefits brought by Christ. The first phase, however, remains a bone of contention. There are those who maintain that it concerns humanity in the period between the Fall and the promulgation of the Mosaic Law, but this view is open to serious objections, and lacks solid support in the text. If one reads 7:7-13 without any preconceptions as to the meaning of the term 'law', one is immediately struck by the number of parallels with the situation, described by Gen 3, prior to the expulsion from the Garden of Eden. Then all humanity was summed up in the persons of Adam and Eve. The Pauline "I" has the same extension. They lived in virtue until God gave the commandment "You shall not eat of the fruit of the tree which is in the midst of the garden, neither shall you touch it lest you die" (Gen 3:3). This commandment promised life (Rom 7:10), but its very existence excited forbidden desires (Rom 7:7). Sin (Rom 7:8) or the Serpent (Gen 3:4-5) used the opportunity provided by the commandment to incite humanity to sin (Gen 3:6; Rom 7:8), and so brought death into the world (Gen 3:19; Rom 7:9). Both passages, therefore, present the same elements in the same order: command - desire - sin - death. The first stage of the history of salvation must, in consequence, be considered to be the period prior to the Fall. Thus, we have the sequence:

1. Humanity before the Fall (7:7-13).
2. Humanity between the Fall and Christ (7:14-24).
3. Humanity after the advent of Christ (7:25 — 8:4).

The first and third stages are linked by a common denominator, since both are characterized by 'life'. Stage 1: "I was once *alive* apart from the law" (7:9); Stage 3: "The law of the spirit of *life* in Christ Jesus has set me free" (8:2). Stage 2, on the contrary, is radically different, because it is characterized by 'death': "Wretched man that I am! Who will deliver me from this body of *death*?" (7:24). The suggestion of this careful structure is that the 'life' which Adam enjoyed before the Fall is restored in the person of Christ. We shall have to investigate the precise meaning of 'life', and its correlative 'death', later. All that concerns us at this point is the clear evidence that, for Paul, Christ was in fact what Adam was destined to be. The 'life' that Adam lost is once again represented in the world, and in it the divine intention for humanity becomes manifest.

This conclusion is confirmed by another passage in which Paul writes:

> In their case the god of this world has blinded the minds of the unbelievers, to keep them from seeing the light of the gospel of the glory of Christ, who is the image of God. For what we preach is not ourselves, but Jesus Christ as Lord, with ourselves as your servants for Jesus' sake. For it is the God who said, 'Let light shine out of darkness', who has shone in our hearts to give the light of the

knowledge of the glory of God on the face of Christ (2 Cor 4:4-6).

This text has three specific contacts with the Creation narrative. The most obvious is the presentation of Christ as "the image of God" (Gen 1:27), and the God in question is identified as the Creator of light (Gen 1:14-18). The third is the affirmation that Christ possessed "the glory of God". This element is not found in Genesis, but according to Jewish tradition Adam possessed "glory" before the Fall. In the *Apocalypse of Moses* (composed before 70 AD) Adam, after having eaten the apple, cries to Eve "O wicked woman! What have I done to thee that you have deprived me of the glory of God?" (21:6). Christ, therefore, has what Adam lost. He is the New Adam who perfectly embodies the authentic humanity that was the goal of God's creative act.

One final text associates 'image of God' and 'creation' as predicates of Christ. According to the hymn in Col 1:15-20, Christ is "the image of the invisible God, the first-born of all creation" (1:15). The terminology of this hymn is cosmic, but humanity is at the center of the author's thought because it alone can be the instrument of change of the rest of creation. What did the author have in mind in proclaiming Christ as "the first-born of all creation"? The parallel attribute of "image of the invisible God" is a clear indication that his attention was focussed on the humanity of Christ. This humanity was not pre-existent; it came into being only at a given moment in history (Gal 4:4). The phrase can only mean that God was thinking of the humanity of Christ when he formed Adam. This seems so paradoxical as to be meaningless, but once we recognise that the category of exemplar causality was furnished by the Wisdom literature (Prov 3:19; 8:22, 30), the author's mental process becomes clear. In order to create Adam, God must have had an idea of perfect humanity. For Christians, that perfect humanity was realized only in Christ. Christ, therefore, was conceived to represent the divine intent which came to historical expression in the creation of Adam.

The conclusion to be drawn from the three texts that we have been discussing is that Paul's anthropology has a Christological basis. In order to find the true and essential nature of humanity he did not look to his contemporaries but to Christ, for he alone embodied the authenticity of humanity. It was inevitable, therefore, that Paul should insist that the humanity of Christ was the standard by which the humanity of other creatures should be judged.

Authentic Humanity

In presenting Christ as the model of authentic humanity, Paul must have had in mind certain specific features which distinguished the humanity of Christ from that of others. Our task now is to determine what these were.

If we except the mention of the Last Supper (1 Cor 11:23-25) the only 'event' of the life of Christ to which Paul draws attention is his death. It is in this act, therefore, that we should expect to find the distinguishing features of Christ's humanity. Death, unfortunately, is not a simple idea, but can be understood in different ways. In some cases death is merely the negation of existence, a passage from being to non-being which renders any further achievement impossible. But this is not true in all cases. The death of a convicted murderer who willingly submits himself to a dangerous medical experiment redeems his blameworthy past. The death of an alcoholic who, in a crowded street, smothers an exploding grenade with body gives meaning to a wasted life. In both these instances death is *the* achievement of a lifetime, because the self is exalted and affirmed in the supreme act of renunciation. Paul would certainly include the death of Christ in this category because he consistently underlines that it was as death 'for others' (Rom 5:8; 14:15; 1 Cor 8:11; Gal 2:20; etc.). But there is still another perspective from which death can be viewed. It can be seen as highlighting the dominant characteristic of a lifetime. That this was also in Paul's mind is suggested by the formula he created, "the dying of Jesus" (2 Cor 4:10), which evokes life as culminating in death and carries the connotation that the two are homogeneous. Consequently, he can proclaim that "Christ died for all in order that those who live might live no longer for themselves" (2 Cor 5:15). The pattern of behaviour that Christians are to imitate (1 Cor 11:1) is thrown into high relief in the death of Christ which focused to a sharp clarity the fundamental option of his life.

As we saw in the first chapter, Paul knew quite a lot about the tradition of the earthly ministry of Jesus which was eventually committed to writing in the Synoptic Gospels. At first sight this makes it all the more surprising that Paul found the death of Christ most revealing of his humanity, because so many incidents could have been used as illustrations, particularly since he wanted believers to live as Christians, and not merely to die as Christians. His reason for acting as he did becomes evident when we recognize that for Paul Jesus did not have to die. This idea appears in the first strophe of the Philippian hymn:

> He who being in the image of God,
> did not use to his own advantage his right to be treated as a god,
> but he emptied himself,
> taking on the condition of a slave (Phil 2:6-7).

The background against which the thought of this strophe becomes clear is provided by a text which we have already encountered: "God created man in incorruption, and made him in the image of his own eternity" (Wis 2:23). The Sage, as we have seen, interpreted the Genesis narrative to mean that death was no part of God's original intent for humanity; it entered the world only as a punishment for sin. For Paul, and the other theologians of the New Testament, Christ was absolutely free of all taint of sin (Rom 1:4; 2 Cor 5:21; Jn 8:46; 1 Jn 3:5; Heb 4:15; 1 Pt 2:22). This absolute purity gave him the right to the incorruptibility which, according to the divine intention, was to be the privilege of humanity. In Paul's world only the gods were thought to live for ever. Accordingly, the right to the privilege of incorruptibility was effectively the right to be treated as god. Christ, however, did not turn this situation to his own advantage. He did not demand the treatment that his condition merited. On the contrary, he gave himself over to a mode of existence that was not his by accepting the condition of a slave, a condition that involved suffering and death. The formula "He emptied himself", and its correspondent in the next strophe, "He humbled himself", emphasise that Christ made a choice. There was no question of an acceptance of something that was by nature inevitable. Once this perspective is grasped it becomes clear why Paul should see the death of Christ as the key to the distinctive element of his humanity.

The act of dying, however, derives its meaning from the motive that inspired it. In the case of Christ, Paul saw this motive as complex. In harmony with the Gospel tradition he recognised that Jesus was motivated by the will of his Father. Hence, we find such statements as, "He did not spare his own Son but gave him up for us all" (Rom 8:32), with a corresponding emphasis on the 'obedience' of Christ (Rom 5:19; Phil 2:8). In this, however, God was acting out of love, "While we were yet helpless, at the chosen moment, Christ died for the ungodly. Why, one will hardly die for a righteous man - though perhaps for a good man one will dare even to die. But God shows his love for us in that while we were yet sinners Christ died for us" (Rom 5:6-8). This rather tortuous formulation is due to an effort to insinuate that even though the decision was God's it was also Christ's. This dimension comes to clear expression in another series of texts, "The life I now live in the flesh I live by faith in the Son of God who loved me and gave himself for me" (Gal 2:20; cf. 1:4; 2 Cor 8:9). Since the 'and' here is explicative, the text presents the self-giving of Christ as an expression of love. What then is love? The best answer is that provided by John Macquarrie:

Love, in its ontological sense, is letting-be. Love usually gets defined in terms of union, or the drive towards union, but such a definition is too egocentric. Love does indeed lead to community, but to aim primarily at uniting the other persons to oneself, or oneself to him, is not the secret of love and may even be destructive of genuine community. Love is letting-be, not of course, in the sense of standing off from someone or something, but in the positive and active sense of enabling-to-be. When we talk of 'letting-be', we are to understand both parts of this hyphenated expression in a strong sense — 'letting' as 'empowering', and 'be' as enjoying the maximal range of being that is open to the particular being concerned. Most typically, 'letting-be' means helping a person into the full realization of his potentialities for being; and the greatest love will be costly, since it will be accomplished by the spending of one's own being. (*Principles of Christian Theology*, London, 1966, §52, p. 310).

In this brilliant exploitation of the Old Testament insight that love is power (Ps 62:11-12) we see that love is the most profound form of creativity open to a creature. The distinctive characteristic of authentic humanity is a creativity which effectively opens new horizons of being to others. The validity of this insight is confirmed by a brief analysis of the Old Testament concept of "image of God" which Paul predicates only of Christ (2 Cor 4:4; Col 1:15).

The Image of God

In the Genesis narrative the Priestly writer thrice defines humanity as made in "the image of God" (Gen 1:26-27; 5:1-3; 9:6). What precisely he intended to convey by this phrase has been a matter of intense debate, and it seems unlikely that full certitude will ever be attained. All agree that the phrase is intended to distinguish humanity from the rest of creation. Human creatures are bound up with the world in which they live, move and have their being, but they are not part of it. The biblical view of man, therefore, is opposed both to the Greek attempt to classify him within a unified reality as a rational animal, and to the contemporary scientific view which considers him as an unusually complicated phenomenon of nature. Helpful as this is, it fails to respond to the question: what did the Priestly writer see man as having in common with God? A way to the answer is provided by another question: What do we know about God from that section of Genesis in which the phrase appears? Two elements immediately stand out. He is Creator and Law-giver. This suggests that humanity's resemblance to God should be sought in the form of some sort of creativity which has an ethical dimension. Some slight confirmation for the creativity aspect is provided by the one act that is performed before the Fall, because Old Testament scholars understand the naming of the beasts (Gen 2:19-20) as a creative act since a new form of relationship comes into being, and thereby a new possibility of existence is offered to the animals. Seen in this perspective the dominance of humanity over the beasts (Gen 1:28) takes on a new dimension: it is parallel to that of God because also based on a creative act.

Paul, however, did not read Genesis in isolation from the body of traditional interpretation that had grown up around it. Hence, in order to be able to perceive what he had in mind when using the phrase we must briefly survey the different interpretations that were current in his day.

An appropriate starting point is provided by Sirach. Written in Hebrew in Palestine towards the beginning of the 2nd cent. BC, it was translated into Greek by the author's grandson in 132 BC. The fact that fragments were found both at Qumran and Masada show that its teaching had a wide extension. It offers an extensive interpretation of the Creation narrative:

> (1) The Lord created man out of the earth,
> and turned him back to it again.

> (2) He gave to men few days, a limited time,
> but granted them authority over the things upon the
> earth.
> (3) He endowed them with strength like his own
> and made them in his own image.
> (4) He placed the fear of them in all living beings,
> and granted them dominion over beasts and birds.
> . . . . . .
> (7) He filled them with knowledge and understanding,
> and showed them good and evil.
> (8) He set his eye upon their hearts
> to show them the majesty of his works.
> (10) And they will praise his holy name,
> to proclaim the grandeur of his works.
> (11) He bestowed knowledge upon them,
> and allotted to them the law of life.
> (12) He established with them an eternal covenant,
> and showed them his judgements.
> (13) Their eyes saw his glorious majesty,
> and their ears heard the glory of his voice (Sir 17:1-13).

The parallelism of v. 3 shows that here image is conceived in terms of power. It is a question, therefore, of a capacity for action; as God is in heaven so is humanity upon earth. The context, however, severely circumscribes this creative dimension and inhibits any exaggeration which would make man a little god. This power is the basis of humanity's authority over the rest of creation (v. 2) but this is not the most important aspect. This power displays itself in the choice consequent on the knowledge of good and evil (v. 7). Thus far we are within the framework of the Genesis narrative, but the latter part of the citation (v. 11-13) shows that the author has imposed a radically new perspective on Genesis. The allusions to the 'law' and the 'covenant' show that he is thinking, not of humanity as such, but exclusively of Israelites. It is they alone who are "the image of God". And the rest of humanity? Sirach gives no explicit answer, but the logic of his position would force him to agree with a

Jewish author who wrote towards the end of the 1st cent. AD, "As for the other nations which are descended from Adam, you have said that they are nothing" (4 Ezra 4:55). Such arrogance is understandable only if we assume that the author views humanity from a strictly moral perspective. The Israelites are different because they alone have been graced by the gift of the Law which lights the creative choices that all must make. What the predication of "image of God" conveys, in consequence, is the capacity for ethical behaviour.

While remaining within the same basic framework the book of Wisdom, composed in Alexandria in the second half of the 1st cent. BC, takes a different line:

> God created man in incorruption,
> and made him in the image of his own eternity,
> but through the devil's envy death entered the world,
> and those who belong to his party experience it (Wis 2:23-24).

In opposition to Sirach who believed that God gave to men only "a few days, a limited time" (17:2), the Sage did not believe that death was inevitable. It was not part of the divine intention that the human creature should die as do animals and plants. He deduced this from Gen 2:17 and 3:3 which present death as a punishment for disobedience. The body, however, was "perishable" (Wis 9:15) since it was "made from earth" (Wis 15:8). Hence, he claimed that prior to the Fall the human creature was endowed with the privilege of incorruptibility, a divine gift which inhibited the natural tendency of the flesh towards dissolution. This made humanity in a sense immortal, and this parallel with the eternity of God (Gen 31:33; Is 40:28) justified the assertion that it was the "image of God".

Death, in consequence, nullifies the image of God. Those who die cannot be "in the image of his eternity". For the Sage, however, all did not die because he distinguished between 'real' death and 'apparent' death. Only the wicked truly died; death was the negation of their entire existence to the point that not even their memory remained (Wis 4:19; 5:14). The just, on the contrary, only seemed to die (Wis 3:2-3), whereas in fact they lived for ever (Wis 4:17; 5:15). This difference is due to the fact that the just possess wisdom which is the root of all virtue and the assurance of immortality (Wis 6:17-21; 8:13-17). Inevitably, such wisdom was conceived in relationship to observance of the Mosaic Law (Wis 6:18).

It would seem therefore that with respect to Sirach, the Sage imposes a further limitation on the application of the idea of image of God. Whereas the former would apply it to all bound by the covenant, the latter would apply it only to those Israelites who actually obeyed the Law. In other words, whereas Sirach relates image of God to capacity for action, the Sage relates it to action itself. It is not those who are capable of observing the Law who are the image of God, but those who in fact observe it.

This line of thought is taken a step forward if we note that the Sage predicates 'image of God' of another reality:

> She (= Wisdom) is a reflection of eternal light,
> a spotless mirror of the working of God,
> and an image of his goodness.
> Though she is but one, she can do all things,
> and while remaining in herself she renews all things.
> In every generation she passes into holy souls
> and makes them friends of God. (Wis 7:26-27).

Here we encounter the common theme of the Sapiential literature that Wisdom has a role in creation (cf. Prov 3:19; 8:22, 30), but with a new nuance. It belongs to the creative function of Wisdom to offer human beings the possibility of a new mode of being, namely, that of being "friends of God". It is Wisdom which enables them to pass from the state where they are liable to real 'death' to the state where they possess 'life' and the assurance of immortality. How does this happen in practice? The Sage's answer can be deduced from his assertions that "a multitude of wise men is the salvation of the world . . . . Therefore be instructed by my words and you will profit" (Wis 6:24-25) and "the beginning of wisdom is the most sincere desire for instruction, and concern for instruction is love of her" (Wis 6:17). Wisdom, therefore, is mediated by those who possess it. But it is precisely these who exist "in the image of his eternity". They exercise a creative function in offering to others a new possibility of existence. The suggestion of Genesis that "image of God" carried the connotation of creativity in an ethical dimension has been taken up by the Sage, but in such a way that the implications are sharply focused.

The critical contribution of the author of the Book of Wisdom was to relate "image of God" not to human existence as such (as Genesis does), nor to a particular religious group (as Sirach does), but to a specific quality of existence. This point is also echoed by Philo (20 BC - 54 AD). Philo's anthropology is extremely complex, and a detailed summary is out of place here. He reserves the predication of "image of God" for the Logos, an intermediary between God and humanity. Of the latter he will say only that it was made "according to the image" of the Creator. Strictly speaking humanity is *an* image of *the* image which is the Logos. The divine imprint is manifest in the intellect, but some use their intellect to follow the royal way of Wisdom, whereas others do not.

> In consequence, there are two types of men, those who exist by the reasoning divine spirit, and those who live by blood and the pleasure of the flesh. The second is moulded of earth, the first is the faithful imprint of the divine image. (*Quis rer. div.* n. 57).

Thus, while all are potentially the image of God, Philo reserves this notion to those who manifest a particular quality of existence. As in the case of the Sage his criterion is based not on a theoretical view of humanity as such, but on experience of a lived pattern of behaviour.

This brief summary provides some idea of the complex of notions that had surrounded the concept of "image of God" at the time of Paul. Despite the diversity of interpretations there is, nonetheless, a certain common ground that we must take for granted in determining what Paul meant by the phrase. In the first place, the predication of the phrase "image of God" was made critically. It was not applied indiscriminately to all talking beings who walked upright on two legs. The suggestion is that not all human creatures lived up to the standard desired by the Creator. We can be sure, nonetheless, that in everyday speech Paul's contemporaries used "image of God" as casually and unthinkingly as we often do. Then, as now, it was comforting to think of oneself as dignified by such an impressive phrase.

Paul's lack of sympathy for such illusory comfort is evident in the highly selective way in which he uses "image of God". He never applies it to himself or any of his contemporaries. In 1 Cor 11:7 it is designed to evoke Adam before the Fall, as the notion of "glory" (whose meaning we shall see at the end of the next chapter) clearly indicates. Precisely the same concept is used to underline that Christ is the New Adam in 2 Cor 4:4, "the glory of Christ who is the image of God". As regards believers, Paul will say only that "we are being changed into his image from glory to glory" (2 Cor 3:18), i.e. he holds out the hope that one day we may *become* the "image of God".

Paul's usage, therefore, reveals his dissatisfaction with a definition of humanity (represented by Sirach) based on capacity or potentiality alone. We must assume, in consequence, that he would range himself with the Sage or Philo. There is nothing in his epistles, however, which would suggest that he habitually thought in the highly intellectual categories of Philo. Where there are contacts between the Apostle and the great philosopher, the former is in reaction to ideas that can be associated with the latter. By exclusion, then, we have arrived at the position that Paul probably followed the line opened by the author of the Book of Wisdom, a conclusion that is confirmed by the widespread influence of this book in the Pauline epistles. The title "image of God" is justified only when the creature is also a creator. It is as offering a new possibility of existence to others that the human creature is truly God's image. Even though his approach is purely speculative John Macquarrie's great insight brings him to a point where he faithfully expresses Paul's intention:

> The full meaning of the claim that man is made to the image of God can be better conveyed in the contemporary language of 'existence'. What distinguishes man from other creatures is that he 'exists', and to exist is to have an openness which is perhaps the best clue to the mysterious affinity of God and man. Just as God opens himself into the creation and pours out being, and therefore has 'letting-be' as his essence, so man is most truly himself and realizes his essence in the openness of an existence in which he too can let be, in responsibility, in creativity, and in love. (*Principles of Christian Theology*, § 35, p. 212)

Historical Reality

While Paul may have been influenced by the Book of Wisdom, his understanding of the distinctive characteristic of authentic existence is derived, not from a theoretical approach to human nature, but from his contemplation of an historical individual, Jesus of Nazareth. What he saw revealed in him became the norm that he used in judging all others.

This point must be emphasised because it is the only evidence we have that the creativity which characterises authentic existence is *really possible*. Had Jesus not demonstrated such love under the conditions of normal life there would be no guarantee that it was not a utopian illusion, beautiful in theory but impossible in practice. Deep down we all believe that what humanity can do is what humanity has done. Even though we knew that it was theoretically possible to reach the moon, a lingering doubt remained until Armstrong actually walked on its surface. To stand on the top of Mount Everest was recognized as a real possibility only when Hillary and Tensing reached the summit. The fear of what might happen to the human body if it ran a mile in four minutes was banished only when Bannister did it. What happened when such breakthroughs were made? A different mental attitude was immediately generated. Individuals were released from the inhibition of the impossible. Those who held back, perhaps subconsciously, because of a fear that what they were striving for was incapable of achievement were called forward by the success of others such as they. A new energy was released by the demonstration of a higher standard.

To propose as the criterion of authentic humanity a love which continuously reaches out to empower others could be as unrealistic as a suggestion to imitate the exploits of Superman, if we did not know that at least one individual had demonstrated this possibility. Because he lived under the same historical conditions of time and space as we do, the mode of existence displayed by Jesus Christ remains a perpetual challenge to an attainable standard.

Suggested Readings

J.W. Fraser, "Paul's Knowledge of Jesus: II Corinthians V.16 Once More," *New Testament Studies* 17 (1970-71) 293-313.

S. Lyonnet, "History of Salvation in Romans 7," *Theology Digest* 13 (1965) 35-38.

W. Pannenberg, *Jesus - God and Man,* London: SCM, 1973, ch. 5.

C.K. Barrett, *From First Adam to Last,* London: Black, 1962.

R. Scroggs, *The Last Adam,* Oxford: Blackwell, 1966.

J.D.G. Dunn, *Christology in the Making,* London: SCM, 1979, ch. 4.

J. Murphy-O'Connor, "Christological Anthropology in Phil 2:6-11," *Revue Biblique* 83 (1976) 25-50.

J.M. Miller, "In the 'Image' and 'Likeness' of God," *Journal of Biblical Literature* 91 (1972) 289-304.

III
JESUS CHRIST AND GOD

The implication of the previous chapter is that what made Jesus unique for Paul was the perfection of his humanity; he was and is the only perfect man. What then of his divinity? Does not Paul claim that Jesus was pre-existent, that he was the Son of God, and that he was to be identified with Wisdom? And are not all these pointers to a belief in his divinity? Such questions deserve an answer, not least because they evoke significant aspects of Paul's Christology. My concern, however, is to prevent any misunderstanding of these issues from distorting or negating the concept of Jesus Christ as the New Adam which is the most fundamental aspect of Paul's Christology. The challenge of his person, on which Paul insists, is difficult to face, and we have to be aware of the facility with which our fallen nature will discover ways of avoiding it.

A number of considerations are fundamental to the discussion which follows. The issue is not the divinity of Christ as such. John unambiguously affirms that Jesus was God and, in my opinion, so does Matthew though in a much more indirect way. The divinity of Christ, therefore, is part of the formal teaching of the New Testament and it is not my intention to question it. The point at issue here is an historical one: did *Paul* think of Jesus in terms of 'divinity'?

In striving to answer this question we must keep in mind that Paul stands very close to the beginnings of Christian theological reflection. We have seen that he knows a significant amount of the material later incorporated into the synoptic gospels. It is universally recognized that there is no evidence of a belief in Jesus' divinity in the early strata of the gospel tradition. Thus, there are no grounds for reading Paul with the presumption that the Christians with whom he came in contact believed in the divinity of Christ. We cannot assume a view of Jesus that became current only much later in the history of the church. Paul was not a disciple of John!

We must also remember that Paul was a trained rabbi. The monotheism of his people was not something that he had inherited unreflectively, but something that he had consciously studied. It was a belief to which he was deeply committed. Denial would have been the ultimate heresy. And this is precisely how the affirmation of Christ's divinity would have appeared, the concept of God broadened to include *two* persons! It is difficult for us now to appreciate the magnitude of the rupture with Jewish tradition that this implied. It could not have happened, particularly at the early stage that Paul represents, without an explosion that would certainly have left much more definite traces in his letters than the incidental and ambiguous allusions which are the most that anyone has ever claimed to find.

The thrust of these observations is to underline that a sound methodology demands that supposed references to the divinity or pre-existence of Christ in the Pauline letters be critically examined in order to determine what they really do say, and not naively interpreted in the light of unfounded preconceptions.

The Crux of Romans 9:5

In all of the Pauline corpus there is only one passage which could possibly be interpreted as a formal affirmation of the divinity of Christ, namely, Rom 9:5. Unfortunately, however, this verse can be interpreted in a number of different ways, depending on the way it is punctuated. The two principal ones are to be found in the RSV, one in the text the other in a footnote:

> A. They are Israelites . . . to them belong the patriarchs, and of their race, according to the flesh, is the Christ, who is God over all, blessed for ever. Amen.
>
> B. They are Israelites . . . to them belong the patriarchs, and of their race, according to the flesh, is the Christ. God, who is over all, (be) blessed for ever. Amen.

According to A, Paul affirms that Christ is God over all. According to B, he says only that Christ is of the Jewish race, the reference to God being a doxology, a spontaneous outburst of praise.

Which punctuation is correct? Paul himself provides no answer because the earliest manuscripts containing this verse have no punctuation. Thus, we are reduced to weighing the available grammatical and contextual evidence. The verse has occasioned so much discussion because the evidence points in different directions.

Nothing in the grammar of the verse is opposed to punctuation A, and those whose ear is attuned to the rythm of Greek find that the verse reads more naturally if it is allowed to flow on continuously to the Amen. It is further pointed out that punctuation B involves a joyful doxology which is out of harmony with the apostle's sorrowful mood in this section of the letter.

Such arguments in favour of punctuation A are countered by others derived from the immediate context. Rom 9:5 is the climax of a paragraph in which Paul evokes the privileges of Israel. These privileges were the gift of God, and just previously Paul had evoked the love of God. "(Nothing) will be able to separate us from the love of God in Christ Jesus our Lord" (Rom 8:39). Here God and Christ

are quite clearly distinguished. The latter is the manifestation of the love of the former, just as the privileges were the
manifestation of God's providential care. That Paul's
thought continues to move within the same framework is
strongly suggested by Rom 9:3 which also makes a distinction between Christ and God, "I could wish that I myself
were accursed and cut off from Christ for the sake of my
brethren." Paul could not desire to be cut off from God.

If the verses before v. 5 clearly distinguish God from
Christ, the same is true of those which follow. In v. 6 we
read, "It is not as though the word of God has failed." This is
a reference back to the 'promises' in v. 4, and quite obviously
the reference is to the Father, as is the case in all subsequent
mentions of 'God' (9:8, 11, 14, 16; and in particular 9:20
where 'God' = the Creator). In none of these texts would it be
natural to interpret 'God' as meaning Christ. The consistency of this usage is a strong argument against punctuation
A, for sound methodology demands that the sense of a
polyvalent verse be determined by the context; the probable
meaning is that required by the context.

Throughout the section 9:1-5 Paul's attention is focused
on the Father. The multitude of his gifts, culminating in the
sending of Christ, serves to highlight the fidelity of Israel. It
is entirely natural that the Apostle should experience great
anguish when he contemplates the sin of his people. But this
is only one side of the coin, for it is equally understandable
that the listing of God's gracious acts should provoke a
spontaneous outburst of praise. The word-order of v. 5
lifted Paul's mind to the notion of providence, and thence to
the Father and his blessedness. A fuller version of the same
doxology appears in Rom 11:36, "For from him and
through him and to him are all things. To him be glory for
ever". Note the same order, providence followed by glorification. On balance, therefore, the evidence favours punctuation B, and the probability of this punctuation is
strengthened by the fact that no other passage in Paul's
letters necessarily implies that Christ is God. In fact, Paul
explicitly states that Christ is subordinate to God, "When all

things are subjected to him, then *the Son himself will also be subjected to him* who put all things under him, that God may be all in all" (1 Cor 15:28). Rom 9:5, then, presents Christ as God's gift without in any way asserting his divinity.

Son of God

Of the 16 passages in which Paul calls Jesus 'Son' two stand out because the title is qualified by an adjective. "Sending his *own* Son in the likeness of sinful flesh and for sin, he condemned sin in the flesh" (Rom 8:3); "He who did not spare his *own* Son but gave him up for us all, will he not also give us all things with him?" (Rom 8:32). The intention of these texts is to underline the unlimited generosity of God's love, and this type of statement makes sense only if Paul understood Jesus to stand in a special relationship to God. The problem, then, is to determine the nature of the relationship.

There is wide-spread agreement that two Pauline references to the Son are derived from the earliest kerygma: "The gospel concerning his Son, who was descended from David according to the flesh, and constituted Son of God in power according to the spirit of holiness by resurrection of the dead" (Rom 1:3-4); "To wait for his Son from heaven, whom he raised from the dead, Jesus who delivers us from the wrath to come" (1 Thess 1:10). A detailed exegesis of these much-debated texts is out of place here, but two points hardly need demonstration. Neither of these passages hints at pre-existence, on the contrary, both associate the sonship of Christ with *resurrection.* There is a faint hint that resurrection is here considered as a reward for the way in which Christ exercised his sonship.

This interpretation is strengthened by two further passages which present his sonship in terms of mission. Rom 8:3 has already been cited; the second passage is Gal 4:4, "When the fullness of time had come, God sent forth his

Son, born of woman born under the law, in order that he might redeem those under the law, in order that we might receive adoption." 'Sending' in both these texts has no reference to pre-existence; the verb is regularly used in both Old and New Testaments for the commissioning of a human agent in view of a particular task. Though sharing the disadvantages of humanity ('born of woman, born under the law'), Christ accomplished his saving mission, thereby manifesting the obedience which, in the Hebrew thought-pattern that Paul inherited, was the constituent of true sonship; "The Son of God, Jesus Christ ... was not 'Yes' and 'No', but in him it was (always) 'Yes'. For as many as are the promises of God in him (is) the 'Yes'" (2 Cor 1:19-20). This fidelity was acknowledged by God in raising Christ.

In view of what we have seen concerning Paul's relationship to the synoptic tradition, it seems likely that he derived his teaching about the 'sending' of 'the son' from the preaching of Jesus. The only gospel text in which the sending of a Son is mentioned is Jesus' parable of the dishonest tenants (Mk 12:1-12), a text that is linked to Gal 4:4-7 by the further themes of eschatology ('last' [eschaton] Mk 12:6; 'in the fullness of time' Gal 4:4) and of heritage (Mk 12:7; Gal 4:7). So many contacts would appear to preclude coincidence as a adequate explanation, and so it would be unwise to read more into the Pauline text than can be inferred from the earliest synoptic tradition.

A further pointer in this direction is provided by Paul's definition of the spirit of the Son in terms of "Abba" (Gal 4:6; Rom 8:15). His use of an Aramaic term reflects his dependence on the synoptic tradition of Jesus' own words. By his use of 'Abba' Jesus expressed his sense of intimate sonship (Mk 14:36), but at the same time the term proclaimed the revelation of God as Father, not only of Jesus himself, but also of those to whom he would communicate his sonship (cf. Lk 11:2; 22:29). The suggestion is that such sonship is constituted by a response modeled on that of Jesus. Paul will call it "the obedience of faith" (Rom 1:5). It is because we are sons of God through faith and baptism

(Gal 3:26-27) that we instinctively address God as 'Abba' (Gal 4:6; Rom 8:15), just as Jesus did. Since we have put on Christ we can use his distinctive term when we call on God.

The idea of 'adoption' that Paul employs in speaking of our sonship (Gal 4:5; Rom 8:15, 23) cannot be pressed to prove a radical difference between Christ's sonship and ours, because Christ belonged to a people one of whose privileges was 'adoption' (Rom 9:4). Once again, this places Paul's understanding of Jesus as Son of God firmly within a Jewish context whose monotheistic presuppositions must inhibit us from interpreting that sonship in terms of community of nature. For Paul Jesus was the Son in a unique way because he fulfilled the demands of sonship in a way paralleled by none other.

Lord

A different approach to the problem of the divinity of Christ has been developed on the basis of Paul's use of the title 'Lord' for Jesus. In the LXX 'Lord' is the normal substitute for the Hebrew 'Yahweh', and this usage appears in the scripture quotations in Rom 4:8; 9:29, etc. Paul applies to Jesus texts of the OT where 'Lord' designates God (e.g. Rom 10:13). This he could only have done because he believed Jesus to be divine.

This line of argument has rightly been dismissed as simplistic, because Paul did not derive the title from the OT; it was already current in the church he joined, as we can deduce from the credal formulae of Rom 10:9 and 1 Cor 12:3. The term 'Lord' is not a synonym for God, It was used commonly in the secular world to connote a relationship of power. It did not define the status of an individual taken in isolation, but evoked his mastery over a group or sphere of life. It was perfectly applicable to the Creator, but was not limited to him. The fact that the first Christians looked up to Christ as their master, an attitude which began during his earthly life as a teacher but which took on an infinitely deeper dimension in their experience of him in the post-paschal period, is sufficient explanation of their use of 'Lord' in his regard. They looked up to him as to a superior on whom they depended.

The basis of lordship is power, and the power enjoyed by Christ is that of giving or withholding the gift of life. Prolonged into the future this power will make him the universal judge (2 Thess 1:5-10; Rom 2:16). In the OT dominion over life is, of course, a divine attribute (Dt 32:39); it belongs to God by nature. For Paul, this power did not belong to Christ by right; it had to be given him, and this gift is consistently presented as a reward for the fidelity with which he executed his mission. "To this end Christ died and lived in order that he might be Lord both of the living and of the dead" (Rom 14:9). "Therefore, God has highly exalted him and bestowed on him the name that is above every other name . . . that every tongue might confess that Jesus Christ is 'Lord' " (Phil 2:9-11). The power of lordship is given to Christ for a specific purpose, and when it is accomplished, that power will be surrendered (1 Cor 15:20-28). In the thought of Paul, 'church' and the 'lordship' of Christ are intrinsically linked; his power is operative in and through the Christian community. When, in the plan of God, the time of the church comes to an end of the Parousia, the lordship of Christ will cease.

Wisdom

1 Cor 10:4 is often treated as the most formal expression of Paul's belief in the pre-existence of Christ. Referring to the rock from which the Israelites drank during the Exodus (Num 20:7-11), he says, "The rock was Christ." Previously he had written that Christ is the wisdom of God (1 Cor 1:24), and Jewish tradition represented by Philo had asserted "The flinty rock is the wisdom of God" (*Legum Allegoriae* 2:86). This, it is claimed, provides a neat chain of equations: the rock = wisdom = Christ. Since the rock preexisted the life of

Christ, so he must have existed before his human birth. It is considerations such as these which have inspired the widespread hypothesis that the idea of pre-existence came to Paul through speculation on Wisdom and its relationship to Christ.

There can be little doubt that Paul was influenced by the sapiential tradition, but I doubt very much that it exercised the dominant role that some have postulated. It is becoming progressively clearer that his involvement with this tradition was not something that he consciously chose because he saw its value in elucidating the mystery of Christ. It was forced upon him because of developments in the community at Corinth. A group of believers were convinced that they possessed a speculative wisdom which gave them direct access to God. In consequence, they though of themselves as a spiritual elite. They no longer needed Paul and his teaching; instruction was necessary only for those on a much lower spiritual plane. Despite his sensitivity, Paul could perhaps have lived with this situation, but a further consequence obliged him to react vigorously. Christ had become irrelevant for these so-called Christians. His humanity and his fate were the antithesis of the immaterial and eternal Wisdom who was their mother and guide. This attitude was very close to the type of theology associated with Philo. Because the rock in the desert provided nourishment, he could see it as a symbol of the speculative wisdom which, from his point of view, sustained the souls of the enlightened.

Paul could not share this perspective. He was convinced that Jesus Christ was the only mediator between God and humanity (1 Cor 8:6; 1 Tim 2:5); he was the revelation of God's demand and the model of humanity's response. Paul was sufficiently realistic to recognize that he could not wipe from the minds of the Corinthians ideas that they had already assimilated. Hence, he had to redefine Christ in a way that would bring about a change in their way of thinking. The only possible solution was to insist that Christ was "the power of God and the wisdom of God" (1 Cor 1:24; cf.

1:30). In his person he was both the manifestation and the means of God's plan of salvation. If the Corinthians wished to concern themselves with Wisdom they should focus on Christ crucified, for wisdom is no longer expressed in words or deeds (1 Cor 1:22) but in a person whose bodily existence was integral to his mission.

If such was Paul's attitude, we have no right to suppose that he accepted Philo's understanding of the rock from which the Israelites drank. On the contrary, it is much more probable that he was consciously modifying that interpretation by insisting that the rock was not wisdom, but Christ. The past tense was forced on him by the fact that the rock was not a reality of the present. The chain of equations designed to establish the pre-existence of Christ in 1 Cor 10:4 is an illusion; it never existed in Paul's mind.

The controversy with the Corinthians added a new dimension to Paul's thought without modifying it in any fundamental way. Jewish tradition found it meaningful to talk of God's wisdom. Given the vitality of Jewish monotheism it is most improbable that they conceived his Wisdom either as a divine being or as a divine hypostasic. It was a way of expressing the involvement of a transcendent Creator with his creation; it was a consolation to believe that there was a divine plan behind the meaningless chaos of the phenomena. It was the only antidote to the pessimism engendered by contact with reality. Once his attention had been drawn to this perspective, Paul would immediately have seen the relevance to his own situation. It was Christ who gave meaning to his life; through him everything fell into place. No longer was Wisdom merely spoken about as enshrined in the Law (Sir 24), it was present in power. Jewish wisdom speculation did not lead Paul to think of Christ in other than human terms. On the contrary, the fact of Christ provided the key to a correct understanding of the way God's Wisdom worked in the world.

To sum up. Son, Lord, and Wisdom are used in the Pauline letters, not to suggest a super-human dimension in Christ, but to highlight different facets of Christ's mediation between God and his creatures. Wisdom emphasises that God has a plan for humanity. Son shows that plan to be inspired by love. And Lord guarantees the power necessary to bring it to completion. All three aspects are unified in him who displays the creativity of the New Adam.

Suggested Readings

J. Knox, *The Humanity and Divinity of Christ,* Chicago: Cambridge University Press, 1967.

R.E. Brown, "Does the New Testament call Jesus God?," *Theological Studies* 26 (1965) 545-573; reprinted in his *Jesus God and Man,* London: Chapman, 1968.

B.M. Metzger, "The Punctuation of Rom 9:5," in *Christ and Spirit in the New Testament. Studies in Honour of C. F. D. Moule* (ed. B. Lindars and S. S. Smalley), Chicago: Cambridge University Press, 1973, 95-112.

J.D.G. Dunn, *Christology in the Making,* London: SCM, 1979, chs. 2 and 6.

J.A.T. Robinson, *The Human Face of God,* London: SCM, 1973.

IV
THE DIVISION WITHIN HUMANITY

When illuminated by the authenticity of Christ's humanity the world appears as divided into two camps. Paul has many labels for these groups. The contrast between the 'Old Man' and the 'New Man' (Rom 6:6; Col 3:9-10) comes immediately to mind. His most fundamental description, however, is the contrast between 'life' and 'death'. Some are 'alive', and others are 'dead'.

'Life' and 'Death'

One of the difficulties in understanding Paul is created by his penchant for using the same term with very different meanings in various contexts. The terms with which we now have to deal provide a case in point, because he uses the nouns 'life' and 'death' (and the corresponding verbs) in three distinct senses.

The first meaning of 'life' is normal one of everyday existence, as is illustrated by the statement "While we live we are always being given up to death for Jesus' sake" (2 Cor 4:11; cf. Rom 8:38; 1 Cor 3:22). This text also reveals the corresponding meaning of 'death' as the termination of earthly existence. In this sense, Paul's use of 'life' and 'death' is exactly parallel to our contemporary usage.

The second meaning of 'life' is eternal life. Normally Paul employs the full expression 'eternal life' (Rom 2:7; 5:21; 6:22-23; Gal 6:8), but on two occasions he abbreviates this to 'life' (Phil 4:3; 2 Cor 5:4). It is quite clear from the context that it is a question of a heavenly life after physical death in both instances. Corresponding to this concept of eternal life is a series of texts in which 'death' functions as an abbreviated formula for the negative eschatological judgement that will be pronounced on sinners (e.g. Rom 6:21; 7:5; 8:13). Both 'life' and 'death' in this sense are consistently presented as realities of the future.

The third meaning of 'life' and 'death' is the most difficult to determine. The one point that is clear is that it is to be distinguished from the other two. When Paul says "You who were dead . . . God has made alive" (Col 2:13), it is evident that it cannot be question of physical life and death, because 'death' is predicated of those who are physically alive, and those who are alive physically are said to be 'made alive' in another sense. It is equally obvious that it cannot be question of eternal life and death, because these are realities of the future, whereas the 'life' and 'death' of which this statement speaks are realities of the past and of the present. Of course, there is a relationship between the 'life' and 'death' with which we are concerned here and eternal life/ death, because it is only those who are 'alive' in this sense who will attain eternal life. Hence, we could say that 'life' in this third sense is 'eternal life in an embryonic form' (as many scholars do), but this would be a purely verbal solution, an apparent answer but not a real one. All that 'embryonic eternal life' can signify is a potentiality for eternal life. What concerns us is the condition in which that potentiality is rooted.

Traditionally, 'life' and 'death' in this third sense have been understood by theologians and by exegetes influenced by dogmatic considerations to mean 'spiritual life' (= grace) and 'spiritual death' (= absence of grace). At a further remove the difference has been expressed in the form: 'life' =

supernatural life, whereas 'death' = natural life.

We can concede immediately that there is at least one point of contact between the Pauline distinction between 'life' and 'death', and the theologians' distinction between 'supernatural' and 'natural'. Paul insists that it is impossible for humanity to move unaided from the state of 'death' to that of 'life', and the theologians make precisely the same point with regard to the movement from 'natural' to 'supernatural'. Is this sufficient to permit us to assume that Paul's meaning is identical with that intended by the theologians? What we have already seen in previous chapters would suggest that it is not.

When dealing with the survey of the history of salvation in Rom 7:7 — 8:4 (above p. 43) it was noticed that Paul predicates 'life' of Adam prior to the Fall (Rom 7:9). Adam as he came forth from the hands of the Creator was precisely what God intended him to be. This was his 'natural' or 'normal' condition. All that Adam possessed prior to the Fall was natural to humanity. This natural state was recreated in Christ (Rom 8:2), and we have seen Paul's insistence that Christ is the norm of humanity. These observations make it clear that Paul and the theologians see what is 'natural' from different perspectives. The theologians take the fallen state of humanity as its natural condition, and in consequence are forced to consider the 'life' brought by Christ as a supernatural gift. Paul, on the other hand, since he begins, not from humanity as it actually is, but from the divine intention sees the unfallen state as the natural condition of humanity. The restoration of that state in Christ is a gift, but for him nothing supernatural is involved. Christ in his humanity is precisely what God intended from the beginning, no more and no less. 'Life' in the Pauline sense, therefore, is not a grace that raises human nature to a higher level, but simply human nature in its perfection.

What, then, does Paul mean by the corresponding term 'death'? Far from being the natural state of humanity, as the theologians claim, our preceding observations permit us to

affirm immediately that it denotes an un-natural state. If
'life' is the Pauline word for the normative condition of
humanity, then 'death' is intended to evoke an abnormal
condition. If those who are 'alive' are truly human, then
those who are 'dead' are sub-human.

The Existentialist Approach to Humanity

The suggestion that Paul considered a great segment of
the human race to be sub-human is so strange that it
demands further explanation. We have to ask why he
adopted this view, and the answer becomes clear once we
recognize that his approach to humanity approximated very
closely to that of contemporary existentialism. At first sight
it might appear anachronistic to claim that Paul's philosophy was that of the 20th century, but it is now admitted
that existentialism has its roots in the very beginning of
human reflection. Paul was not a Heideggerian, nor was he
a follower of Kierkegaard or Sartre, but his basic approach
to human nature was parallel to theirs, and in consequence
the categories that they have developed are of great assistance in enabling us to grasp what he was driving at.

The existentialist starting-point is phenomenological. It
starts with reality as observed, but not all the segments of
reality have the same value. The basic distinction is between
things and persons. Things are those realities which can be
grouped into a class without doing any violence to the
individual units. Thus to know one golf-ball is to know all
golf-balls. From the knowledge of the behaviour of one
golf-ball the performance of all other golf-balls in identical
circumstances can be predicted. If golf-ball A hit with force
X in wind condition Y flys in a certain trajectory, all other
golf-balls hit with the same force in the same wind conditions will fly in precisely the same trajectory. This is not
true of persons. To know individual A's reaction in a given
situation is no basis for a prediction concerning individual
B's reaction in precisely the same situation. The reason for

this is that a person enjoys a more complex type of being than a thing. His being is subject to modification in a way that the being of a thing is not.

The existentialist approach, therefore, concentrates on the person rather than on nature in general, and is so impressed by the difference between persons and things that it refuses to define the person in any way which might seem to bring it into relation with the non-human world. This happens when, for example, the person is defined as a rational animal, because this definition makes the person just a species within a generic category which includes things. In this existentialism is more faithful to the biblical view which, in defining the human creature as "the image of God", operates a radical cleavage between the person and the rest of created reality. This, we should expect, would also be the approach of a pastor such as Paul was, because his concern is with persons and not with things.

In its observation of the person the existentialist approach recognizes that the individual is continuously changing. Every new situation means an experience whose consequence is change. An individual who has gone through a war, or a severe illness, or a love-affair is not the same person afterwards as before. Hence, existentialism is forced to define the person, not in closed static terms, but in an open-ended fashion which takes account of this fact of experience. Modifications, however, are introduced by a lived situation only insofar as the implications of the situation are consciously assimilated and then accepted or rejected. Reflection and choice are essential. Existentialism, in consequence, defines the person as possibility determined by decision. More graphic words are supplied by a 15th century scholar, Giovanni Pico della Mirandola, who depicts God as saying to man, "Thou, like a judge appointed for being honorable, art the molder and maker of thyself; thou mayest sculpt thyself into whatsoever shape thou dost prefer." (*Oration on the Dignity of Man,* tr. A.R. Caponigri, Chicago, 1956, pp. 4-5). The person is an entity which can give itself different orientations by means of the choices it makes. As a result of such decisions the person can exist in different ways.

The type of decision that a person can make is limited by the structure of his being. No human being can jump off the top of a twenty story building without any equipment and decide to fly to the ground. Equally no one can decide to see through a brick wall. On the other side of the fundamental division in reality, no animal can decide to write a book. Hence, the existentialist affirms that each type of nature is made up of a fixed range of possibilities. The scope allotted to the person is much greater than that assigned to an animal, but it is not infinite.

This range of possibilities serves as the criterion by which the existentialist judges the decisions the person makes, for not all decisions are of the same value. Some decisions make the person authentic, they create his true identity, whereas others make the person inauthentic, because in them the true self is lost. In other words, the person exists authentically if his decisions actuate the possibilities given with his being. If he fails to actuate those possibilities he exists inauthentically.

Up to this point all the existentialists would be in substantial agreement, although their forms of expression would differ widely. But the moment one asks, what precisely are the distinctive possibilities given with human nature? the consensus breaks down. To a Christian this is hardly surprising, because the humanity that is the subject of the phenomenological analytic is defective. It is not human nature as such, but fallen human nature. In refusing to admit this, the philosophers launch themselves into descriptions of authenticity whose variety is indicative of their subjectivity and whose content betrays despair rather than hope.

Paul, however, was exempt from this sorry situation. Through his understanding of revelation as focused in the humanity of Christ he was convinced that creativity vis-a-vis others was the distinctive possibility of human nature. The human creature was brought into being precisely in order to exercise a power-laden love which would enable others to be creative in the same order of being. Those who fail to actuate this possibility do not exist as God intended them to exist. In this precise frame of reference they can be said to be non-existent. This is a very close approximation to what a Semite would understand by death. Death was not annihilation, but the antithesis of the vitality and movement that characterised the living. The dead were just shades or shadows of their former active selves. For Paul, those who did not love were nothing like what they could and should be, and he simply carried this notion to the limits of realism by proclaiming them 'dead'. It is also probable that by his choice of this term Paul intended to insinuate that those who have opted for inauthenticity cannot unaided change their status; the dead are powerless to help themselves.

If the truly human are those who have actuated the capacity for creative love that is built into their being, then those who fail to actuate this potentiality are non-human, or sub-human. An instinctive reaction against this conclusion is inevitable. It is said that it smacks of Nazi philosophy. The objection is raised that it appears to reduce the majority of the human race to the level of 'things'. This in fact is not the case, because built into their being is the permanent possibility of *becoming* authentically human. This is never true of 'things' because only persons have the capacity to modify their mode of being. All these expressions of the reaction carry the aura of sane respectability, but the reaction is not really rooted in an attitude of charity towards others. It is based on fear of the challenge that immediately confronts us if the conclusion is accepted. It is comforting to think that all who walk upright on two legs and talk are human, and to believe that humanity is a given. It is disconcerting and disturbing to discover that humanity is in fact something to be achieved, and that the only way to this goal is a continuous creative effort directed towards others. This demand frightens us, and we strive to transmute our fear into something socially acceptable by taking a stand on the dignity of man.

Paul's attitude condemns our complacency, and explains the tremendous urgency that he felt in his apostolate. To bring the creative love of God in Christ to others was not a gratuitous extra. It was the only way to restore to persons the dignity of authentic humanity. He saw no distinction between Christianity and humanism, because the only way to be authentically human was through Christ. In order to move from the sub-human state of 'death' to 'life' the person has to be the recipient of the creative love of Christ, and that possibility is grasped only by those who exercise that same creativity for the benefit of others.

Likeness

Once we appreciate that human nature can exist in two distinct modalities (which Paul terms 'life' and 'death') it becomes possible to understand what the Apostle was trying to convey when he suggests a difference between Christ and the rest of the human race. This comes to the fore in two passages: "God . . . (sent) his own Son in the likeness of sinful flesh" (Rom 8:3), and "Having become in the likeness of men, and being found in shape as a man" (Phil 2:7).

In both these texts there seems to be a curious hesitation about saying bluntly that Jesus was a man. In the Docetic heresy these texts were given great prominence because they appeared to support the claim that Jesus was not truly man; he merely possessed the appearance of a man without really being one. That this was not Paul's intention is clear from his statements that Jesus was "born of a woman" (Gal 4:4), that he was "descended from the race of David according to the flesh" (Rom 1:3), and that he possessed "a body of flesh" (Col 1:22).

There is a nuance in these last two texts which indicates the true direction of Paul's thought. They speak of 'flesh' whereas the passage using 'likeness' speaks of 'sinful flesh'. Now 'flesh' is an ambiguous term in Paul's lexicon. It can be either a neutral description of the physical dimension of human existence, or it can connote a negative value-judgement regarding the quality of that existence. When Paul says that Jesus had "a body of flesh", or that he was a Jew "according to the flesh", he is simply evoking the physical dimension of his existence. 'Sinful flesh' on the other hand clearly implies a negative value-judgement, and Paul's point is that while sharing the facticity of human existence, Jesus did not fall under the value-judgement attaching to that existence on account of human sin.

Support for this interpretation is furnished by 2 Cor 5:21: "For our sake God made him to be sin who knew no sin". In order to understand this statement correctly we have to refine our concept of sin so that it comes into line with that of Paul. To us sin has nothing to do with 'humanity', because all too often we understand sin in a strictly legalistic context. It is an illegal act which draws upon us the wrath of the legislator (God), and makes us liable to punishment. If the act has any effect on our persons it is the role it plays in the creation or reinforcement of a bad habit. For Paul the effect of sin was much more profound. "If I do what I do not want, it is no longer I who do it, but Sin which dwells within me" (Rom 7:20). Sin is the alienation of the authentic self. It is the rejection of the humanity for which the human creature was made, or as Paul more graphically puts it, "the wages of Sin is death" (Rom 6:23), i.e. the effect of sin is to produce non-existence in the sense explained in the previous section. At this point, but on a much deeper level, we rejoin the idea of sin as alienation from God which is intregral to the Christian view. John Macquarrie formulates the relationship with his customary clarity:

> So far as man is fallen away from his true self, he is fallen away from the being which the Creator has given him. He is, therefore, denying God and rebelling against God, whose command is life — that is, the authentic existence for which man was created (Rom 7:10). Alienation from God follows from alienation from the authentic self. (*An Existentialist Theology*, London, 1965, p. 109).

From Paul's perspective, therefore, to say that Jesus did not sin whereas others did, is equivalent to saying that Jesus did not exist in the same way as they. His use of the phrase 'in the likeness of' is fully justified because Jesus was 'alive' whereas others were 'dead'. John Knox hesitates to go this far and is inclined to find Paul in error because "sin . . . belongs so inseparably to actual humanity", by which he means that sin is "something in the actual nature of mankind itself". In effect, therefore, by saying that Jesus was sinless Paul "finds himself introducing, perhaps without intending to or even knowing that he was doing so, a hint of the flesh's unreality" (*The Humanity and Divinity of Christ*, pp. 50-52). This, of course, does not follow at all. Knox has driven himself into an impass because of his failure to distinguish between the ontological and the ontic levels of human nature, and to assume that Paul is speaking of the ontological level when in fact he is concerned only with the ontic level. The ontological level is constituted by the range of possibilities that make up human nature, and on this level Jesus is absolutely identical with all others of the human race. The difference with which Paul is concerned comes on the ontic level, the domain of real existence in which those possibilities appear as actualised or not actualised. Sin, however common it may be, is not implied in the ontological structure of human nature. It is merely one of the options open to the human creature. Once this is recognized, it becomes immediately evident that it is possible to have a perfect individual, i.e. one whose real existence is not disordered by sin. Had Christ not been 'different' we could never have been convinced that the mode of existence evidenced by the world was not the only option open to humanity.

Humanity and Resurrection

At this point it becomes possible to deal with another assertion made by Knox which reflects a rather wide con-

sensus among Pauline scholars. He maintains that "Jesus
became the New Man at the resurrection" (op. cit., p. 84).
The immediate implication of this view is that during his
lifetime Jesus did not exhibit the perfection of humanity.
This is never clearly stated, but the subtle insinuations are
numerous. It is obvious that Knox's view is conditioned by
his assumption (noted above) regarding the sinlessness of
Jesus, and in view of what has been said we can by-pass this
point. In part, however, Knox's position is based on the
Pauline affirmation that Christ gained something by his
resurrection. The Apostle claims that Christ was "constituted Son-of-God-in-power" (Rom 1:4) and that he
"became a life-giving spirit" (1 Cor 15:45). If the suggestion
that Christ attained perfect humanity only as the consequence of his resurrection is to be rejected, then an alternative explanation must be proposed for these statements.

The texts which present Christ as the embodiment of
authentic humanity are too clear to be ignored, and we have
seen that for Paul this authenticity comes to its clearest
expression in the death of Christ. The problem, then, is to
explain how Paul could speak of an augumentation of
power after the resurrection. The answer is to be found in
the convergence of a number of lines of thought.

The very concept of resurrection involves both loss and
restoration. This is clearly formulated in one of the earliest
Jewish statements concerning the meaning of resurrection,
"The creator of the world, who fashioned the generation of
man and devised the generation of all things, will in mercy
give back to you again both your spirit and life, since you
now forget yourselves for the sake of his laws" (2 Macc
7:23). Every resurrection, therefore, is in a very real sense a
gain.

It must also be kept in mind that the only Jesus that Paul
knew was the Risen Christ, and it is not going beyond the
limits of reasonable possibility to presume that Paul saw a
difference between what Jesus achieved during his earthly
ministry and what he achieved in the post-paschal period.
This probability is reinforced by what we know of his con-

tacts with the church in Jerusalem (Gal 1:18-19; 2:1-10). The growing community of Jerusalem, to say nothing of Paul's own successes, would have stood out in salient contrast to the Eleven and the women who had committed themselves to Jesus during his lifetime. The natural inference to be drawn from these facts was that there had been an augmentation in Christ's 'life'-giving power, and this would have appeared as inevitable to one habituated to thinking in the Old Testament pattern of humiliation and reward, a pattern that is clearly exhibited in Phil 2:6-11 and 1 Tim 3:16.

The turning-point in this evolution could only have been the resurrection, and here it must be recalled that Paul makes no radical distinction between the death and resurrection of Christ, "For this purpose Christ died and came to life that he should be Lord both of the dead and of the living" (Rom 14:9; cf. 4:25; 2 Cor 5:15). Within the framework of semitic thought the resurrection was necessary if the 'life'-giving love which had been focused to its highest intensity in the dying of Jesus was to be permanently effective.

These three lines of though converge to show how Paul could speak as he did. They reveal that there is no intrinsic contradiction between what has been said regarding the death of Christ as the supreme expression of the dominant attitude of his life, and the concept of resurrection as the restoration of that humanity through the resurrection with its 'life'-giving power augmented. One final point must be underlined. If it is possible for other human beings to achieve authentic humanity within the framework of a sinful world, there is no reason to deny that Christ could have done, and did in fact do, the same prior to his resurrection. It is to this aspect that we must now turn.

The Glory of God

We have already had occasion to note that, according to Jewish tradition, "the glory of God" was a quality that Adam lost as a consequence of his sin (above p. 44). This directs our attention to a series of texts in Paul which do not always receive the attention that is their due.

Speaking of those who are 'dead' Paul says, "All have sinned and fall short of the glory of God" (Rom 3:23). Those who are 'alive', on the contrary, are classified as "the image and glory of God" (1 Cor 11:7). The strangeness of this language is somewhat alleviated when we recognize that the genitive can have two quite distinct meanings. On the one hand, it can be a subjective genitive and in this case 'glory of God' would mean the glory *belonging to* God. This is the normal sense in the Old Testament where the phrase denotes the visible concomitants of the divine presence. On the other hand, the genitive can be objective and in this case 'glory of God' would mean the glory *given to* God. Only this latter sense suits the context of the texts with which we are concerned.

This is particularly clear in Rom 3:23 which can only mean that sinners are incapable of giving glory to God. The Old Testament provides a close parallel, "A son glorifies his father, and a slave his master. If then I am a father, where is my glory? And if I am a master, where is my fear?, says the Lord of hosts to you, O priests who despise my name" (Mal 1:6). A son gives glory or, as we would say, honours his father by respect manifested in obedience. Through their disobedience the priests of Israel refused to God the honour that is his due. The prophet is thinking within the framework provided by the prescriptions of the Mosaic Law. This is not true of Paul, who never presents the Law as a criterion. Those who are 'dead' are ontically *incapable* of giving honour to God.

The capacity to give honour to God is restored only through faith (Rom 3:21-22), and it is significant that the *Apocalypse of Moses* equates 'glory' with 'righteousness' (20:1-2). It is only as restored in Christ that humanity is not merely the "image" but also "the glory of God" (1 Cor 11:7). By this double formulation Paul is possibly reacting against the idea, prevalent in some Jewish circles, that the idea of "image of God" was related primarily to potentiality. He adds the notion of "giving glory" precisely to avoid this interpretation. A defective product reflects no credit on its maker. The human creature, however, honours its Maker when it is what the Creator intended it to be. 'Glory', therefore, is a synonym for 'life' understood in the sense of authentic humanity.

As we might have expected Paul predicates 'glory' primarily of Christ (2 Cor 3:18; 4:4; 2 Thess 2:14), because he is *the* exemplar of authentic humanity. He is the first human creature since the Fall to give perfect honour to the Creator simply by being what he was, and because of him other individuals can acquire this status. To the Thessalonians Paul says, "To this God called you through our gospel, so that you may obtain the glory of our Lord Jesus Christ" (2 Thess 2:14). The purpose of the gospel is to permit the human race to achieve authentic humanity. Since the Thessalonians have accepted this call, they are already in possession of authenticity. This possession is real but inchoative and progressive, as Paul points out to the Corinthians, "We all with unveiled face contemplating the glory of the Lord are being changed into the same image from glory to glory" (2 Cor 3:18). Here we have the association of 'image' and 'glory' that also occurs in 1 Cor 11:7, but the thought is deepened insofar as Paul underlines the relationship between the authentic humanity of Christ and that of the believers. Acceptance of the humanity of Christ as the model and standard is the beginning of the process, and this is what Paul intends to suggest by the allusion to contemplation. But contemplation alone is not sufficient. A real change must take place. They must be "conformed to the image of his Son" (Rom 8:29), and such conformity takes place only through imitation: "You became imitators of us *and of the Lord*" (1 Thess 1:6); "Become imitators of me, as I am an imitator *of Christ*" (1 Cor 11:1). It is a question of a mode of being, a pattern of behaviour, as Paul expressly emphasises, "I beg you, become imitators of me. My purpose in sending Timothy to you . . . was to remind you of *my ways in Christ*" (1 Cor 4:16-17). To the extent that their behaviour expresses the creative love that distinguished the humanity of Christ, the believers possess 'glory'. They are a credit to their Creator.

Paul's concern with reality (as opposed to mere theory) is evident in the phrase 'from glory to glory'. The perfection of humanity is inaugurated by the act of conversion, but is not thereby fully possessed. Paul recognizes that believers can and must grow in love (Phil 1:9), and since love is the touchstone of authenticity any increase in love means an increase in authenticity. The Apostle was forced to this conclusion by his experience of the communities for which he was responsible. The decision for 'life' is an absolute rejection of the mode of being that he calls 'death,' but on the level of practical living there is very often an overlap because the attitudes and behaviour patterns characteristic of 'death' are not eradicated by a single contrary decision. Real authenticity, in consequence, is a matter of continuous struggle, and in a later section we shall have to discuss the conditions that make victory possible.

* * * * * *

At this point two questions naturally arise. What are the structures of 'death', and what are the structures of 'life'? In other words, what are the concrete manifestations of the two modes of being open to the human creature? The two parts which follow present Paul's response to these questions. The details that come to light in confronting these questions will clarify what has already been said, but it seems appropriate to try and synthesise here the insights that we have thus far gleaned.

To be human is to be a creature, and thus necessarily to exist in a relationship of dependence on the Creator. Human creatures, however, are not fixed in their being as an animal is. There is no automatic progression to the mode of being willed by the Creator. The being of human creatures is such that they can give themselves different modes of exis-tence. They become what they choose to become, and that choice lies between two fundamental options, 'life' which is authentic humanity and 'death' which is a spurious humanity. Adam once possessed authentic humanity but lost it, and, until Christ, all shared his loss. True humanity again entered the world in the person of Christ, and so must be the basis of any genuinely Christian anthropology. What was distinctive in the humanity of Christ was a creative love which fully realized the divine intention in creating human beings in the image of God. The reality of this love, whose power Paul experienced in his own person, forced the Apostle to realize that this possibility built into human being was not given any place in his contemporaries' understanding of what it meant to be human. Their vision was limited by the behaviour patterns that they were able to observe, and in consequence they accepted as normal attitudes that were in radical contradiction to the creativity that Paul saw in Christ. His awareness of the historicity of the humanity of Christ enabled him to replace the criteria of his contemporaries with a new vision of what the human creature could and should become. He was convinced that he was not proposing a utopian ideal because one man had in fact lived and died in this way. He realized that in order to be as Christ was the human creature needed to be empowered, but such power was made available in the love of Christ. The only way to the form of humanity desired by the Creator lay in surrender to this love.

Suggested Readings

J. Nélis, "L'antithèse littéraire *zoe-thanatos* dans les épitres pauliniennes," *Ephemerides Theologicae Lovanienses* 20 (1943) 18-35.

R. W. Thomas, "The Meaning of 'Life' and 'Death' in the Fourth Gospel and in Paul, "*Scottish Journal of Theology* 21 (1968) 199-212.

John Macquarrie, *An Existentialist Theology*, London: SCM, 1965, ch. 2.

—————, *Existentialism*, New York: World Publishing Co., 1972, ch. 3.

J. Coppens, "La gloire des croyants d'après les lettres pauliniennes," *Ephemerides Theologicae Lovanienses* 46 (1970) 389-392.

PART 2
SOCIETY

V
SIN AND THE WORLD

A book with the title *Pagan and Christian in an Age of Anxiety* gives the impression that it might be a plea for concerted action in the face of the numerous anxiety-producing problems that confront our generation, the arms race with its propensity for nuclear war, food shortages, racial uprising. Its author, E.R. Dodds, is in fact an historian and his concern is with the first three centuries of our era. He has little difficulty in showing that, from the 1st century AD on, a deeply pessimistic view of humanity pervaded the different cultures of the Eastern Mediterranean. There was a profound sense that something had gone wrong which, when allied to the assumption of human responsibility, produced wide-spread guilt-feelings. Since these were focused on no specific object they gave rise to a sentiment of futility, a vague conviction that human activity had no real meaning, that it was 'absurd' in the sense of Camus who took Sisyphus as the symbol of mankind — a mythical hero condemned to spend his days rolling a boulder to the top of a hill only to see it ever slip from his grasp and crash back to the bottom.

The Jews recognized the same problem but because they believed in a God who controlled history their response was one of resigned hope. Their hope in the advent of a Messiah gave them the strength to carry on, but they were as pessimistic as their Gentile neighbours as to the possibility of any change in the human condition arising from within the historical situation. Only God could create a new world in which humanity would be as the Creator desired.

Paul, therefore, did not need the figure of Christ to make him aware that the human situation was distorted and twisted. That awareness was communicated to him by the two cultures with which he came in contact, and conditions in the port cities in which he worked were hardly conducive to a favourable view of human nature. His conviction that humanity had fallen had nothing to do with Christ. However, his analysis of this fallen state is related to his understanding of Christ in two ways. First, the possibility of existence revealed in the humanity of Christ provided him with a tool which enabled him to select and highlight the key factors which contributed to the actual condition of humanity. Where others saw so much wrong that they did not know where to start, he was able to establish a hierarchy in the causes which produced the conditions which he observed. Second, the perspective afforded him by Christ forced him to range the Jews with the rest of humanity, and to deny the privileged position that they claimed for themselves.

Humanity As 'Dead'

We have already had occasion to speak of Paul's survey of the history of salvation in Rom 7:7 — 8:4, but then our concern was with the first and third stages which showed the relationship of Adam and Christ to 'life' (cf. p. 43). The second stage (Rom 7:14-24) describes very graphically the situation of humanity before the advent of Christ, and it is to this that we now turn because it reveals the key structural elements of the state of 'death'. In reading this passage it must be kept in mind that the "I" represents, not a single individual, but humanity. It is a literary device to produce a more dramatic picture. Consequently, the passage cannot be understood as an exercise in psychological introspection. Paul is concerned with the stresses and strains of fallen human existence.

Those who are 'dead' are presented as being in a state of unbearable tension. They exist at the focal point of radically conflicting tendencies. It is not as if two different parts of the human personality were at war with each other, a superior part (symbolised by 'inner man', 'mind', 'will') opposed to a lower part (symbolised by 'flesh', 'sin'). Rather, we have on the one hand, the desire of humanity for authenticity, the inclination of a created being to be what its Creator intended. 'Willing' is directed towards 'life'. This instinct, however, is overridden by a stronger orientation which results in a 'doing' that leads to 'death'. "I do not do the good I want, but the evil that I do not want is what I do. Now, if I do what I do not want, it is no longer I who do it, but Sin which dwells within me" (Rom 7:19-20). All the striving of humanity culminates in the loss of its true identity; the "I" is no longer; the self has been totally alienated. Humanity has the sensation of being no longer in control of its own destiny. Paul's insistence on this point is remarkable, for the last part of the verse just quoted is merely a repetition of v. 17, "It is no longer I who do it, but Sin which dwells within me". The futility of human endeavour is highlighted by the miserable bewilderment of the words "I do not understand my own actions" (v. 15). Humanity feels itself condemned to a sort of slavery; it has been "sold under Sin" (v. 14). The picture is a frightening one. The human race appears as a society of puppets manipulated by a force which Paul terms Sin.

The question that arises from this description is: what is Sin? But before we attempt an answer, it is worthwhile underlining how accurately Paul sensed the malaise affecting humanity, and how relevant his description is for our own day. The nameless anxiety that permeates our world is rooted in the hopeless feeling that things have gone too far to ever be brought back under control. Developments have been too swift and too wide ranging for the human nervous system to cope with successfully. The sense of being manipulated by forces that cannot be accurately specified has given rise to a frustrated restlessness whose manifold expressions — violent revolution, use of drugs, mental illness — only intensify the sense of loss.

Sin And The World

The statement that "all men, both Jews and Greeks, are under (the power of) Sin" (Rom 3:9) immediately suggests that by Sin Paul means something other than the personal sins of individuals. This impression is confirmed by a whole series of passages where the Apostle attributes personal activities to Sin. It "came into the world" (Rom 5:12) like an actor coming on stage, and "reigns" there (Rom 5:21; 6:14) as a brutal tyrant who "enslaves" humanity (Rom 6:6, 17, 20; Gal 3:22) or who buys it into its service (Rom 7:14). Sin pays wages (Rom 6:23) to those who submit to its law (Rom 7:23).

Sin, therefore, is a symbol. But for what? The first possibility that springs to mind is that Sin is but another name for Satan of which Paul sometimes speaks (Rom 16:20; 1 Cor 5:5; 7:5; 2 Cor 2:11; 11:14; 12:7; 1 Thess 2:18; 2 Thess 2:9). This hypothesis, however, has nothing to recommend it. Not only does Paul never make this identification, but the language he uses when speaking of Satan is quite different to that he employs when speaking of Sin. More significantly, when he speaks of Satan it is always relative to those who are already believers, and he never evokes this figure to explain the condition of humanity prior to Christ.

The clue to what Paul had in mind is provided by the relationship he establishes between Sin and human responsibility: "Therefore, as Sin came into the world through one man and death through sin, so also death spread to all inasmuch as all sinned" (Rom 5:12). The thought of this verse is extremely condensed, and is complicated by the fact that Paul here uses 'death' in two senses. The primary meaning is that of inauthentic existence, but associated with this is the physical death which is its consequence. Moreover, Paul is making two distinct statements: (1) Adam was responsible for the inauthentic mode of human existence in the world ('death') because of a personal decision opposed to the will of his Creator ('sin') which had wide implications for all the other members of the human race ('Sin'). (2) All the members of the human race are responsible for the inauthentic mode of their own existence ('death') because they have fulfilled the requisite condition, namely, personal decisions opposed to the will of their Creator ('sin').

The fact that Paul juxtaposes these two statements entitles us to suppose that there is some relationship between them, but the nature of this relationship is not specified beyond the fact that the two cases are similar ('as . . . so also'). Yet, the situation of those who came after is not identical with that of Adam, because he introduced into the human condition something that was not there before. From the letter of the text this is all we can glean. A somewhat clearer vision is provided if we recognize the background out of which Paul is writing.

The first and perhaps most crucial point is that Paul in his first statement makes a choice among the explanations for the origin of evil that were current in his day. These were three in number. According to the first, which was based on Gen 6:1-4, evil came into the world as a consequence of the unnatural intercourse that rebellious angels had with women. The second, on the basis of Gen 8:21, maintained that God had built an 'evil inclination' into the structure of human existence. The third, of course, is the story of the fall in Gen 3. The first two theories have a feature in common which distinguishes them from the third. They place the responsibility for evil outside the human race by attributing it either to angels or to God. This is in radical contrast to the Paradise narrative which presents the origin of evil as the consequence of a human decision whose freedom is underlined by the conditions under which it takes place. The purpose of the paradise myth is to stress that the original error took place within the historical framework of humanity, and the truth of the myth is not dependent on Adam and Eve being actual figures of history.

Thus, by his evocation of the Fall, Paul consciously committed himself to the position that humanity was responsible for its own sorry condition. It could not avoid that responsibility by imputing blame to any force outside itself. At the time of Paul, however, there were various opinions regarding the relationship between Adam and his descendants. It is easy to illustrate this by means of two citations from Jewish works composed in the second part of the 1st century AD:

2 Baruch	*4 Ezra*
For though Adam first sinned, and brought untimely death upon all, yet of those who were born from him, each one of them has prepared for his own soul torment to come, and again each one of them has chosen for himself glories to come...Adam is, therefore, not the cause, save only of his own soul, but each one of us has been the Adam of his own soul (54:15-19).	A grain of evil seed was sown in the heart of Adam from the beginning, and how much fruit of ungodliness has it produced unto this time (4:30). O Adam, what have you done! For though it was you who sinned, the fall was not yours alone but ours also who are your descendants (7:118).

The difference between the two is obvious. For *4 Ezra* the human race is a plant sprung from rotten seed, and in consequence shows the defects of its origin. It labours under the burden of an inherent infirmity productive only of ungodliness. This is precisely what is denied by *2 Baruch* which insists that each one is capable of chosing in the same freedom that Adam enjoyed.

Paul does not identify with either of these positions. He

could accept neither the automatism of *4 Ezra* nor the naivete of *2 Baruch*. In opposition to the former he gave importance to individual human decisions, and he denied the assumption of the latter that the sin of Adam introduced no modification into the human situation. The link between Paul's two statements in Rom 5:12 is provided by v. 19 of the same chapter, "Through the disobedience of one man all were constituted sinners". This presumes a causal link. The question, then, is: how does this cause operate? It is in answering this question that we discover what Sin is.

The answer is suggested by Genesis. The point of Gen 3 is that at some point in the history of humanity a false decision was made. From then on, according to Gen 4-11, things went downhill at an ever increasing pace. The picture is one of geometric progression of evil. As the human race spread wickedness became progressively more endemic. The immediate impression is that sinners influenced one another. Children were conditioned by the attitudes of their parents, and displayed behaviour patterns modeled on those of their ancestors, which in turn were passed on to their descendants.

We have evidence from 1 Cor 3:1-4 (cf. above p. 35)that Paul thought in these categories, because the point of this passage is Paul's disagreement with the way of looking at themselves as humans that the Corinthians had inherited. Thus, it seems highly likely that Paul conceived Sin as a massive disorientation of society or, more specifically, as the corroding pollution of a corrupt environment. His precise perspective has been expressed by H.H. Rowley even though he was not dealing with Paul's thought:

> We are all in large measure the creatures of our age, reflecting the Zeitgeist of our day. And that Zeitgeist (= spirit of the time) is not something that exists outside all living individuals, nor merely in a large number of separate individuals. It inheres in the totality of the whole, and is operative in greater or lesser measure in each. It characterises our day, yet it is not born of our day alone. It is

generated in the stream of life that binds the former
generations to ours . . . But if we are more than separate
individuals, if we are members of a wider whole that
embraces the past as well as the present, that gathers into
the stream of its life each one of us, and that operates
through us, then a potent force of evil may be in the
stream of life, derived from individuals, but transcending
individuals, though found in varying degrees in individuals. (*The Relevance of Apocalyptic*, London, 1944, p.
151).

The causal pressure that Paul had in mind is that exercised
by the pressure of inherited attitudes. No one exists in a
neutral situation. All individuals are born into a society
which marks them. This society is a product of its past and a
cause of the future. Those who are marked cooperate,
because by acting in conformity with the conditioning they
have received they reinforce those attitudes which descend
to the next generation with increased potency.

It is very easy to reduce these generalities to concrete
terms. In a society in which various forms of dishonesty are
considered acceptable behaviour they become virtues which
are inculcated as a matter of course. In a society which puts
a premium on independence and self-sufficiency everything
concurs to impress the individual with the desirability of
these attitudes. In a society which measures success by the
ability to acquire material goods everyone will desire such
possessions. This list could be continued indefinitely. The
accepted value-system of a society exercises a tremendous
pressure, as can be attested by anyone who tries to hold out
against it. What everyone does cannot be wrong, and those
who protest are held up as objects of ridicule. Only the very
strong can think of opposing any resistance. The majority
simply acquiesce and most frequently are not even conscious of how they are manipulated.

Who is doing the manipulating? No answer can be given,
for no one cause or even complex of causes can be singled
out to bear the responsibility. There is no dictator who can
be blamed. The sensation is that of being caught in a tightly

packed crowd swept by a motion of panic. It moves blindly and all are carried along in the grip of irresponsible forces. It is easy to see how this sense of being swayed by a force beyond human control could be transmuted in the mind of simple people into a belief in a supernatural evil power. It is an explanation which alleviates the burden of bewilderment and hopelessness. Paul, as we have seen, refuses this option. The intelligence that seems to be directing humankind on the path of evil is simply the collective thrust of a multitude of individual decisions spread over centuries. For him the assignation of blame was of less importance than a correct delineation of the problem, because his concern was with finding a solution.

If Sin is the inexorable pressure of a false value-system that permeates society, then it is not simply 'in the world', it *is* the 'world'. Paul can use this term to mean the created universe in general (e.g. Rom 1:20), but he does so only very rarely since material reality was only incidental to his central concern. In the vast majority of cases 'world' means the sphere of inter-personal relations. The 'wisdom of the world' (1 Cor 1:20) is the speculations of humankind, just as the 'refuse of the world' (1 Cor 4:13) are those held in contempt by their fellows. The 'world' that God reconciles (2 Cor 5:19; Rom 11:15) is the 'world' that he will judge (Rom 3:6). The distinctively Pauline usage appears in the question, "Why do you live as if you still belonged to the world?" (Col 2:20), since 'world' here is clearly humankind in its inauthentic orientation. It is, in other words, "the present evil age" (Gal 1:4). Hence, Paul can talk of the 'spirit of the world' which leads to a misunderstanding of the human condition (1 Cor 2:12), and — like Sin — can attribute to it such human qualities as wisdom (1 Cor 3:19) and grief (2 Cor 7:10). Since human beings must live 'in the world' (1 Cor 5:9-10) they cannot avoid immersing themselves in 'the affairs of the world' (1 Cor 7:32-34), and in consequence are swept along by the orientation of the society to which they belong. As Bultmann graphically phrases it: "The eerie fact is that the 'kosmos', the world of men, constituted by that which the individual does and upon which he bestows his care, itself gains the upper hand over the individual. The 'kosmos' comes to constitute an independent super-self over all individual selves." (*Theology of the New Testament I,* London, 1965, p. 256). This, of course, is also true of Sin because it is question of the same reality.

Human Responsibility

When Sin is understood as the massive disorientation of a whole society which expresses itself in a false-value system, its relationship to 'sinning' becomes much clearer. 'To sin' is to ratify that value-system by acting in conformity with it. We must now confront the delicate question of responsibility with regard to such actions. To do so takes us deeper into Paul's vision of the 'world' that he had to change.

There is plenty of evidence to show that Paul held individuals responsible for their inauthentic decisions. The very use of the word 'sin' to describe such decisions points in this direction, as does his references to the wrath of God (Rom 1:18; 9:22; Col 3:6). Such wrath is provoked by 'transgressions'. The Jews transgress the explicit Law of Moses, and the Gentiles transgress the law written on their hearts (Rom 2:12-15). They are, in consequence, "vessels of wrath made for destruction" (Rom 9:22). This type of language presumes culpability which is the correlative of responsibility. Only those who are truly responsible can be considered culpable.

Responsibility, however, implies freedom of choice. Those "who do evil" (Rom 2:9) can be blamed only if they are free to do good. Here we touch the nub of the problem because, for Paul, those who have not committed themselves to Christ in faith are not free; they are 'enslaved' to Sin which 'reigns' over them. Paul insists over and over again that only those who are 'in Christ' are free. What this means is that only believers are in a position to effectively choose the good. The logic of Paul's perspective is that all others are incapable of choosing the good. This, moreover, is the only consequence that can be drawn from the key element of his theology, namely, that authenticity is possible only through Christ. Humankind is justified only by faith (Rom 1:16 and *passim*), and Bultmann has perfectly grasped Paul's point in writing that "It is only as one who is righteous before God that man is what he should and can be" (*Existence and Faith,* London, 1964, p. 178).

Thus, we have in Paul two lines of thought which do not converge and which in fact contradict one another. In one series of texts human beings who belong to the 'world' are considered culpable, whereas in a second series of texts it is clear that they cannot be considered culpable because they are not free.

In order to define the problem more precisely we have to digress a moment to examine the notion of moral responsibility. Heidegger's distinction between ontological possibility and ontic possibility is here of great utility. An ontological possibility is one that is given with a partcular type of nature. Thus, for example, rational thought is an ontological possibility for humans but not for animals. Equally, unaided flight is an ontological possibility for birds but not for humans. Ontological possibility is but another name for theoretical possibility. It refers to what is theoretically possible for a given nature, and so refers to being as such. Ontic possibility, on the other hand, refers to a being in a concrete situation and in specific circumstances. Obviously ontological and ontic possibilities are closely related. Nothing that is ontologically impossible can be an ontic possibility. However, what is ontologically possible may be ontically impossible due to circumstances either imposed or chosen. Thus, while remaining theoretically possible, rational thought may become ontically impossible for a particular individual because of severe brain damage. Such an accident makes rational thought really impossible. Previous choices can also limit the ontic realization of an ontological possibility. It is ontically impossible for a speaker at a public meeting to take a bath there and then. It will become really possible only when he gets home.

Freedom is an ontological possibility for all human beings. It is built into the very structure of their nature. It is something that can never be taken away without destroying human nature. The deprivation of freedom, therefore, takes place on the ontic level of real existence. All human beings are theoretically free, but in practice some are not. Real freedom is ontic freedom, and individuals can be deprived of it only through circumstances which make genuine choices impossible. Such limitation may be physical, as in the case of those committed to prison. All their decisions are made for them. The limitation may also be economic, as in the case of those so poor that they have no choices.

In our understanding responsibility and culpability are related, not to the ontological freedom that is given with human nature, but to ontic freedom. Take, for example, the situation of a man in prison who, looking out through the bars, sees a sadistic pervert molesting a child. He is morally obliged to come to the aid of that child. Can he be blamed if he does not do so? Obviously not, because he has no freedom to act in this way. Serious illness provides a parallel example. A paralytic cannot be held responsible for any failure to fulfil an obligation that involves movement. In both these situations the reality of freedom is destroyed by circumstances, and in consequence culpability cannot be imputed.

These examples have been chosen deliberately in order to sharpen our perception of the situation of humanity that Paul had in mind, and to avoid a possible equivocation. Paul was not interested in freedom of thought, i.e. what some authors term 'inner freedom'. This is nothing else than the liberty to think idealistically about what might be. His concern was with the translation of thought into action, with the living out of an authentic decision. As we saw when discussing Rom 7:14-24, he was fully prepared to concede that those who did not know Christ might have a perception of the truth, but it was equally clear to him that they were unable to act on that insight: "I can will what is right but I cannot do it" (Rom 7:18). Paul could not have blamed the pagans for neglecting the possibility of knowing God through the things he created (Rom 1:20) unless some had in fact arrived at such knowledge (e.g. Aristotle). His point, however, is that they did nothing about it: "Although they knew God they did not honour him as God" (Rom 1:21). That his thought moves consistently on the level of action is evident also in his statement: "There will be tribulation and distress for every human being who *does evil,* the Jew first and also the Greek, but glory and honour and peace for everyone who *does good,* the Jew first and also the Greek" (Rom 2:9-10). In this, of course, he is in perfect harmony with the Old Testament for which the only knowledge of God that had any value was that which displayed itself in obedience, and with the teaching of Jesus who said, "What do you think? A man had two sons, and he went to the first and said, 'Son, go and work in the vineyard today'. And he answered, 'I will not'; but afterward he repented and went. And he went to the second and said the same, and he answered, 'I go, sir', but did not go. Which of the two did the will of his father? They said, 'The first'." (Mt 21:28-31). In a vision of authenticity centered on creativity, only actions count. For Paul, those who did not know Christ could not choose a pattern of behaviour in which this creativity was displayed. The pressure of Sin was too great to permit it. In limiting freedom Sin also destroyed responsibility and culpability.

A Dilemma

It seems, therefore, that Paul wants to have his cake and eat it. This forces us to confront two questions. Why does he impute culpability when his perspective excludes it? Faced with the contradiction in his thought, which line must we follow?

In part the answer to the first question must be that Paul was thinking of humanity in general, and not of specific individuals. On this level it was natural that he should think in terms of responsibility because, as we have seen, the explanation of the human condition that he accepted (the Paradise version) insisted that humanity was responsible for its own situation. No outside agency had made it what it was. The consequence of the historic decision was that humanity existed in a state contrary to that willed by the Creator. To this extent, therefore, the situation governed by Sin could be described as one of generic responsibility and generic culpability. It seems highly likely that Paul was also influenced, perhaps unconsciously, by the attitude of his people towards non-Jews who were assumed to be deliberately and maliciously perverse in their refusal to accept the light of the Law. "Each of the inhabitants of the earth knew when he was transgressing, but My Law they knew not by reason of their pride" (2 Baruch 48:40; cf. 4 Ezra 7:24, 72-73). The combination of these two aspects would explain why he should have given the impression that *individuals* were personally responsible.

The assertion that individuals are personally responsible is not as essential to Paul's theology as the assertion that individuals cannot be personally responsible for their inauthentic state. Hence, in answer to the second question we must follow the latter line. The fundamental reason for this is that, for Paul, Christ is the key to authenticity. If those who do not know Christ are free to choose authenticity without any reference to him, then Christ is not necessary for salvation. If Christ is the source of authenticity then those who do not know him have no choice. Their ontological freedom cannot flower into ontic freedom without him. To say that it can is equivalent to saying that justification is possible without faith. To maintain that those without Christ are 'sinners' in the strict sense is to destroy the very foundation of Pauline theology.

But, it may be objected, does not the refusal to consider fallen humanity 'sinners' destroy another element of Paul's theology, namely, the sacrificial character of the death of Christ? Here we must be very careful. Paul does in fact say that "Christ died for our sins" (1 Cor 15:3), and that he was "put forward as an expiation by his blood" (Rom 4:25). This, and the many allusions to the 'blood' of Christ (Rom 3:25; 5:9; 1 Cor 10:16; 11:27; Col 1:20), is certainly sacrificial language. But Paul only once explicitly presents the death of Christ as a sacrifice, "Our passover has also been sacrificed, even Christ" (1 Cor 5:7). At first sight such language would appear to insinuate the culpability of individuals but this is precisely the point at which we must tread warily, and not take it for granted that we know what Paul means.

The first point to be noted is that Paul makes very little use of sacrificial ideas relative to Christ. This is surprising given his Jewish background because, prior to the destruction of the Temple, sacrifice was the central unifying element in Jewish life. One would have expected Paul to have made far greater use of a category with which he was so familiar. Hence, if he did not do so, it can only be because he was conscious that the category of sacrifice was not entirely satisfactory to bring out the full meaning of the death of Christ.

In the second place it must be noted that in Paul's hands the Jewish notion of sacrifice has undergone a transformation. We have already had occasion to note that the death of Christ was voluntary. For Paul, he did not have to die. Hence, even though Paul did not himself formulate the letter to the Ephesians, it renders his thought exactly in writing, "Christ loved you and gave himself up for us, an offering and a sacrifice to God for an odour of a sweet smell" (Eph 5:2). Christ is both the offerer and the offering, the priest and the sacrifice. The assertion that Christ loved and gave himself up for us is parallel to Gal 2:20, and this, we have seen, is the key element in Paul's understanding of Christ's death. The idea of sacrifice is introduced, not for itself, but in order to underline the *value* of Christ's death. It places it in the supreme category of religious values. In the process, of course, the traditional Jewish understanding of sacrifice is broken apart because under no circumstances in the Jewish system could the priest be himself the victim. It follows naturally that if the notion of sacrifice has been transformed, then the corresponding notion of culpability has also been modified.

Once this is recognized, it becomes possible to relate Paul's notion of sacrifice to the generic culpability of humanity in the sense noted above. The death of Christ did for humanity what the sacrifices of the Law did for sinners within its system. The identity of this proportion explains Paul's use of sacrificial language, but proportional identity does not demand that the component elements be identical. 'Sacrifice' changes its meaning when applied to Christ, and 'sin' changes its meaning when applied to humanity. 'Sinners' are those who are under the dominion of Sin. Just as sacrifice released the Jew from his sin, so the death of Christ broke the bonds of Sin which bound humanity.

To claim that those under the power of Sin are not responsible for their 'sins' is not to obviate the need for redemption. Those enslaved to Sin, who are forced to accept a false value-system, are in a sub-human condition. They lack freedom which is the dignity of authentic humanity, and the influence of Sin is so all-pervasive that none can escape. A new divine creative act was necessary to change that situation, and the channel through which that power became operative was the authenticity of the humanity of Christ. His love focused in his death brought 'life' where there had been only 'death'.

In this chapter we discovered that, for Paul, the root cause of the inauthenticity of humanity was the domination of Sin. Because its state originated in a free decision, humanity is in a condition of objective culpability. Its mode of existence is the contrary of that willed by the Creator. The influence of that original decision is perpetuated in an ever-intensified form by the false value-system of society. By acting in conformity with the conditioning they have received, individuals ratify the disorientation of their 'world'. They are not, however, subjectively culpable because they lack freedom of choice due to their enslavement to Sin.

Suggested Readings

R. Bultmann, "Romans 7 and the Anthropology of Paul,"
in *Existence and Faith. Shorter Writings of R. Bultmann*
(ed. S. Ogden), New York: Meridian, 1960, ch. 7.

———, *Theology of the New Testament,* London: SCM,
1965, §25-26 (Sin and World).

J. Macquarrie, *An Existentialist Theology,* London: SCM,
1965, §14 (Fallenness).

———, *Principles of Christian Theology,* London: SCM,
1966 §40 (Sin).

H. Haag, *Is Original Sin in Scripture?* London: Chapman,
1967.

L. Sabourin, "Original Sin Reappraised," *Biblical Theology
Bulletin* 3 (1973) 51-81.

T.A.Barrosse, "Death and Sin in St. Paul's Epistle to the
Romans," *Catholic Biblical Quarterly* 15 (1953) 438-59.

VI
ALIEN BEING

Thus far we have considered only the fact of inauthenticity and its root cause, and so we must now turn to an examiniation of the concrete manifestations of this mode of being as they are revealed in the Pauline letters. In the world humanity is confronted with two radically different types of reality, things and other people. Humankind has to react to both, and it is from the decisions controlling such reactions that authenticity or inauthenticity evolve. For the sake of clarity we shall deal with the relationship to things in this chapter, and in the next concern ourselves with the relationship to persons. In both I intend to make use of Heidegger's analysis of contemporary humanity because it provides a framework which highlights the salient elements of Paul's thought both by confirmation and by contrast. Heidegger's language is more comprehensible to us than is Paul's and they complement each other to a great extent, because both were concerned to describe the world as they saw it. All observers, however, see what they are conditioned to see. Their vision is controlled by their initial assumptions. Paul's presuppositions differed from those of Heidegger, and in consequence there is a difference in their respective visions of reality. The consequences of this will be evident in the next chapter.

In the sense in which it is used in this chapter a 'thing' is any non-human reality whether animate or inanimate. Heidegger defines it as 'being-to-be-used', and this definition harmonizes perfectly with the biblical perspective because, according to Genesis, God gave humanity dominion over the rest of creation (Gen 1:26, 28; 2:19-20). All non-human reality, therefore, has an instrumental character; it is at the service of humanity. It does not exist for itself, but for humanity. This is obvious in the case of tools fashioned for a specific purpose, such as a pen or an automobile. But the sun can be used for heating, and the stars are used in navigation. Nature is used for recreation, and also as a source of raw materials. In the plan of creation all non-human realities have essentially a utilitarian value. This does not mean, of course, that we can wantonly abuse non-human reality. The obligation to respect it, however, does not derive from the nature of the thing itself, but from the possible use that others, particularly succeeding generations, may derive from it.

Human beings can make themselves authentic or inauthentic through the type of decision that they make with regard to things. An authentic decision is one which recognizes that a thing is inferior to a person and which gives it the utilitarian value appropriate to its nature. An inauthentic decision is one which elevates a thing to a position of superiority with respect to the person, because this perverts the intention of the Creator. If authenticity with regard to things is expressed in the relationship "I — it", inauthenticity reverses this relationship to "It — I". As an instrument a thing is essentially a means. Its utilitarian value is denied if it is treated as an end in itself. This occurs when a thing is desired for its own sake, when it is made a matter of ultimate concern. Those who concentrate their whole being on, for example, the acquisition of wealth or social status in effect define themselves in terms of things. They alienate their true selves by making themselves part of a lower order of being. They become immersed in the world of things. Here we perceive another facet of the sub-human mode of existence that Paul calls 'death'.

Covetousness

Things can acquire dominion over human beings only if they are intensely desired. It is not surprising, therefore, to find Paul assigning 'covetousness' (*epithumia, pleonexia*) as one of the fundamental attitudes of inauthentic humanity. It is a concrete expression of 'acting according to the flesh' (Rom 13:14; Gal 5:16-17, 24), and so is typical of 'the old man' (Col 3:5) dominated by the power of Sin. It is through 'covetousness' that the orientation of a false value-system takes possession of individuals, "Do not let Sin reign in your bodies to obey its lusts" (Rom 6:12).

The critical position that this attitude occupies in Paul's thought is evident from his sketch of the history of salvation in Rom 7. In the first stage (Rom 7:7-13) which concerns the situation of Adam in Paradise we find the words, "I should not have known what it is to covet if the law had not said, 'You shall not covet' " (v. 7). The Fall, in his perspective, was due to 'covetousness', an attitude whose radical character is underlined by the fact that no object is specified. What Paul had in mind is well brought out in C.K. Barrett's commentary on this verse, "Desire [= 'covetousness'] means precisely the exaltation of the *ego* which we have seen to be of the essence of sin. Regardless of his place in creation, and of God's command, man desires, and his desire becomes the law of his being. Through 'covetousness' things take possession of their possessors. They imagine that they dominate them, but in fact they are dominated by the objects of their overweening desire. Instead of being governed by God, as the authentic Creator-creature relationship demands, they are governed by 'covetousness'. It implies an anxious self-seeking whose unrestricted longing for possessions sets aside the intention of the Creator."

Paul was led to this insight which postulates 'covetousness' as one of the fundamental attitudes of fallen humanity by his awareness of the importance of this theme in the Exodus narrative, one of whose stages was called "the Graves of Covetousness, because there they buried those who coveted" (Num 11:34). After evoking the experiences of the Exodus, he concludes, "These things are warnings for us, that we should not be covetors of evil things as they coveted" (1 Cor 10:6). It seems likely that he was also influenced by the Jewish classification of the gentiles as 'those who covet'. This idea is found in the Palestinian Targum on Ex 20:17, "My people, children of Israel, you shall not be covetous nor companions nor partners with those who covet." In this passage 'those who covet' are the pagans, fallen men par excellence from a Jewish point of view, as a text from the Babylonian Talmud demonstrates, "Why are idolators covetous? Because they did not stand at Mount Sinai. For when the serpent came upon Eve he injected covetousness into her. As for the Israelites who stood at Sinai, their covetousness departed; the idolators who did not stand at Sinai, their covetousness did not depart" (Shabbath 145b-146a). Paul's vision of the human condition is undeniably more realistic, but the importance of this text is that Paul also identifies 'covetousness' with idolatry (Col 3:5).

Apart from one remark, "Why not rather be defrauded?" (1 Cor 6:7), and passing references to theft (Rom 2:21; 1 Cor 5:11; 6:10), Paul does not demonstrate any great concern about material goods, but 'thing' also englobes such intangible realities as social status (2 Cor 11:21f; Phil 3:4f) and knowledge (1 Cor 1:22; 8:1; 2 Cor 10:5; Col 2:8), as well as the more obvious vice of gluttony (Rom 16:18; "Their god is their belly", Phil 3:19). In the ultimate analysis 'covetousness' is the assertion of self through the medium of things (2 Cor 10:8; Gal 6:3) with the ultimate object of acquiring human glory (1 Thess 2:6; Gal 1:10). It is to serve "the creature rather than the Creator" (Rom 1:25), and thus the equivalent of idolatry. The exact antithesis is provided by Paul's statement of his own attitude, "I seek not what is yours but you" (2 Cor 12:14).

The concrete expression of 'covetousness' is 'anxiety' or 'care' for 'the things of the world' (1 Cor 7:33). The underlying idea is perfectly brought out in the statement of the Sermon on the Mount, "Do not lay up for yourselves treasures on earth, where moth and rust consume and where thieves break in and steal, but lay up for yourselves treasures in heaven, where neither moth nor rust consumes and where thieves do not break in and steal. For where your treasure is, there will your heart be also" (Mt 6:19-21). Such 'care' has its roots in 'fear' (Rom 8:15) which is occasioned by the instinctive awareness that something has gone wrong with the human situation and by the recognition that what is possessed may be lost. To 'care' in this way is to be committed to the thing as an end in itself; one's whole being is focused upon it. Hence, Paul's exhortations, "I want you to be free from care" (1 Cor 7:32); and "Have no care about anything" (Phil 4:6).

External Religious Observances

A certain attitude towards religious observances is one of the more subtle expressions of an inauthentic decision regarding things. Paul asks the Colossians, "Why do you live as if you still belonged to the world?" (Col 2:20). This is a question that Heidegger would have understood without any difficulty because it implies his distinction between being 'in the world' and being 'of the world'. To be 'in the world' is one of the givens of human existence (1 Cor 5:9). There is no alternative to the situation in which one is forced to encounter both things and persons. To be ' of the world', on the other hand, is but one of the two options open to humanity, and it means acceptance of "a yoke of slavery" (Gal 5:1), i.e. submission to the dominion of Sin. In the case of the Colossians, they were in danger of becoming part of an alien world of being because their minds were set, not on 'the things that are above', but on 'the things that are on the earth' (Col 3:2). Paul is not concerned with the attention to mundane matters which is essential to everyday living. Beneath these general statements lies a reference to a specific problem of perennial actuality:

> If with Christ you died to the elements of the world, why do you live as if you still belonged to the world? Why do you submit to regulations, 'Do not handle, Do not taste, Do not touch' — referring to things which all perish as they are used — according to human precepts and doctrines? These have indeed an appearance of wisdom in promoting rigour of devotion and self-abasement and severity to the body, but they are of no value in checking the indulgence of the flesh. If then you have been raised with Christ, seek the things that are above, where Christ is seated at the right hand of God. Set your minds on things that are above, not on things that are on earth (Col 2:20 — 3:2).

Although this passage contains a number of elements which are still a matter of lively discussion among exegetes, the main point is clear. Paul condemns a ritualism involving, not only ascetic practices, but the calendar which determined the liturgical feasts (Col 2:16-17).

Obviously what concerns Paul is not these practices in themselves but the importance that the Colossians attached to them. He must have had reason to believe that the community was giving to these external observances a position that conflicted with their essentially utilitarian value. It would seem, therefore, that the Colossians showed a tendency to make such practices a criterion of their state before God. They thought of them, not as aids to Christlike living, but as the touchstone of authenticity. In thus perverting the finality of these observances, the Colossians perverted themselves because they were in fact defining themselves in terms of things. They were committing themselves once again to inauthenticity. Their attitude had become that of those under the power of Sin.

Obedience to Law

Colossae was not the only community to have problems with 'things' of this nature. Paul found himself obliged to make the same criticism of the Galatians:

> Now that you have come to know God, or rather to be known by God, how can you turn back again to the weak and beggarly elements whose slaves you want to be once more? You observe days, and months, and seasons, and years! I am afraid that I have laboured over you in vain (Gal 4:9-11).

This situation is much more significant than that of the Colossians, because what is at issue here is not heterodoxy of an indeterminate type (Col 2:22) but the Law of God. The situation in Galatia need be evoked only briefly. The Galatians were converted by Paul but, possibly because of their celtic origins, found themselves ill at ease in their new mode of existence. The guidelines given by the Apostle in order to get them started in working out a pattern of behaviour appropriate to authentic existence left so much to their own discernment that they could not face up to the responsibility. In consequence, they were predisposed to give a hearing to the Judaizers, Jewish Christians who could not accept that salvation was through Christ alone. They insisted that in addition the Mosaic Law must be observed. It was, after all, given by God himself, and so must have a permanent validity. Paul's reaction to this attitude is outlined in Galatians and more completely articulated in Romans, and at first sight his position seems to be self-contradictory.

On the one hand, his respect for the Law is evident not only in his formal statement that "whatever was formerly written was written for our instruction that by steadfastness and the encouragement and exhortation of the Scriptures we might have hope" (Rom 15:4; cf. 1 Cor 10:6), but also in the extent to which he employs its directives in his own ethical teaching (e.g. Rom 7:7; 12:19-20; 13:9; 1 Cor 9:9; 2 Cor 8:15; Gal 5:14). He states unequivocally that "the Law is holy, and the commandment is holy and just and good" (Rom 7:12) because it promised life (Rom 7:10). But on the other hand, he can qualify the Law as "a law of sin and death" (Rom 8:2), and as a tyrant which holds humanity captive (Rom 7:6).

The resolution of this tension is suggested by Paul himself when he writes, "As far as I am concerned the commandment which was ordained to life proved in fact to be ordained to death" (Rom 7:10). The implication of this verse is that the original purpose of the Law had been perverted. Bultmann notes, "Paul does not criticize the law from the standpoint of its *content,* but with respect to its *significance* for man" (*Existence and Faith,* London, 1964, p. 159). In other words, Paul's objection to the Law was not based on what it said but on what the Jews had made of it. His criticism bears on a human attitude towards the Law.

The importance of the Law for the Jews needs no emphasis, but one can admit this without being fully aware of the reverence in which it was held. An appreciation of this point is essential if we are to grasp Paul's position accurately, and it is finely illustrated by a quotation from the article "Torah" in the recent *Encyclopaedia Judaica:*

> There is an ancient tradition that the Torah existed in heaven not only before God revealed it to Moses, but even before the world was created . . . . It was one of the very few real dogmas of rabbinic theology that the Torah is from heaven (Heb. *Torah min ha-shamayim*; Sanh. 10:1, et al.; cf. Ex 20:22 [19]; Deut. 4:36); i.e. the Torah in its entirety was revealed by God. According to the *aggadah,*1, Moses ascended into heaven to capture the Torah from the angels (Shab. 89a, et al.). In one of the

oldest mishnaic statements, Simeon the Just taught that
(the study of) the Torah is one of the three things by
which the world is sustained (Avot 1:2). Eleazar ben
Shammua said, "Were it not for the Torah, heaven and
earth would not continue to exist" (Pes. 68b; Ned. 32a). It
was calculated that "the whole world in its entirety is only
1/3200 of the Torah" (Er. 21a; cf. TJ, Pe' ah 1:1, 15d).
God Himself was said to study the Torah daily (Av. Zar.
3b, et al.).

Obviously, the most striking statement in his summary is
the last one from *Avoda Zarah:* "There are twelve hours in
the day; during the first three the Holy One sits down and
occupies Himself with the Torah". Precisely the same teaching appears in the Jerusalem Targum on Dt 32:4: "For three
hours does He occupy Himself with the Torah". *Bereshith
Rabbah* goes a step further, "Just as the Most High deeply
mediates upon the mysteries of the Torah, so does He also
fulfil its precepts" (c. 49). To what extent this type of statement may antedate the 3rd century AD, when they are first
attested, can only be a matter of conjecture. The tendency
which they represent was certainly operative at the time of
Paul if we recollect the attitude towards the Law exhibited
by Ps 118, and the identification of divine Wisdom with the
Law on which Sir 24 insists. There can be little doubt that
W.D. Davies accurately depicts the situation in the 1st century AD in writing:

> As the gift of Yahweh and as the ground plan of the
> Universe it [the Law] could not but be perfect and
> unchangeable; it was impossible that it should ever be
> forgotten; no prophet could ever arise who would change
> it, and no new Moses should ever appear to introduce
> another Law to replace it. (*The Setting of the Sermon on
> the Mount,* Cambridge, 1964, pp. 157-158).

Such reverence for the Law was founded in the belief that
it expressed the fulness of the divine mind in a definitive

form. God and the Law were inseparable, because the Law gave permanent and immutable form to the divine will and purpose for humanity. Paul himself articulates this attitude:

> But if you call yourself a Jew and rely upon the law and boast of your relation to God and know his will and approve what is excellent, because you are instructed in the law, and if you are sure that you are a guide to the blind, a light to those who are in darkness, a corrector of the foolish, a teacher of children, having in the law the embodiment of knowledge and truth — you then who teach others, will you not teach yourself? (Rom 2:17-21).

According to the common opinion this passage levels only the accusation that the Jews did not in fact observe the Law which they held in such high esteem (cf. Rom 2:21-24). This, however, is but the second and least important point. His major criticism is that they have made of the law something on which to 'rely' and of which to 'boast'. These are two of the most damning terms in Paul's lexicon and they bear on the assumption that the Law expresses the will of God and is, in consequence, a sure guide to 'what is excellent' (literally: 'the things that really matter'), and a valid criterion of one's relationship to God. This assumption was, for Paul, the root of the inauthenticity of that section of humanity governed by the Law.

In the last analysis this is due to his recognition of the fact that exaggerated respect for the Law produced blind obedience. In practice the Law became more important than the Lawgiver, and so a 'thing' became *the* matter of ultimate concern. By stressing complete submission to the Law as the goal of human existence the Jews in effect defined themselves in terms of a 'thing'.

Such an attitude could be made to look extremely respectable. After all it was *God's* Law! The truth, however, was not so complimentary. According to the plan of the Creator humankind was given responsibility both for itself and for the rest of creation, a responsibility that was to be exercised in creativity. But the complexity of reality was too frightening, the burden of responsibility was felt to be too great, and in the face of this fear the precise concrete detail of the Law provided a refuge and a sense of security. Humans could turn their gaze from reality and focus it exclusively on the Law. For the consequent sense of release they paid dearly. The Law provided a refuge only by preempting the right of decision. Through exaggerated reverence the human obligation to make genuine choices was ceded to the Law. The Law decided and the creature submitted.

Something more than submission is necessary for authenticity, as all child-psychologists recognize. Parents can irremediably stunt a child's evolution towards maturity by making all the real decisions, by taking all the risk out of life. This image is not irrelevant, because Paul does in fact depict the Jews as children under the 'custodianship' of the Law (Gal 3:24). The Law was intended to supervise conduct, to guide towards maturity in freedom, but because of the Jews' attitude towards it, it kept them 'confined' and 'under restraint' (Gal 3:23). Excessive respect manifested in absolute obedience destroys freedom which is the indispensible condition of authenticity and clarity by St. Thomas Aquinas in his commentary on 2 Cor 3:18:

> Whoever acts of his own accord acts freely, but one who is impelled by another is not free. He who avoids evil, not because it is evil, but because a percept of the Lord forbids it, is not free. On the other hand, he who avoids evil because it is evil is free.

The accuracy of this insight into Paul's mind is confirmed by what the Apostle himself says in the epistle to Philemon. "Although I have enough confidence in Christ to command you to do what is fitting, yet for love's sake I prefer to appeal to you" (Philem 8). The point at issue is quite clear. Paul wants Philemon to do what is fitting with regard to his runaway slave Onesimus, i.e. not to assert his legal right to punish him but to treat him as a brother and send him back to Paul. It is a question, therefore, of the performance of an act of charity. The problem, then, is: why does Paul refuse to command such an act? The answer is provided in v. 14: "I preferred to do nothing without your consent in order that your good act might not be by compulsion but of your own free will". In other words, Paul's concern for Philemon's authenticity made him refuse to make a decision that should be the latter's, and this is what would have happened had he issued a command which Philemon would have understood as a binding precept.

The case of Philemon is not an isolated one, and the consistency of Paul's attitude is shown in the case of the collection for the poor of Jerusalem. After complimenting the Corinthians, he tells them bluntly, "Excel in this gracious work also" (2 Cor 8:7). The verb has the force of an imperative; the form of the statement is that of a command. But in the very next verse he hastens to add, "I say this not as a command". His reason? "Each one must do as his heart chooses, not reluctantly or under compulsion" (2 Cor 9:7).

Given this perspective it becomes perfectly evident why the works of the Law were without value. Because the Jews believed that they were obliged to act as the Law commanded they were acting under compulsion. Authenticity, on the contrary, must be freely chosen. It cannot be achieved in any other way. By their profession of reverence for the Law, the Jews hid from themselves the challenge of their humanity. They gave the Law an authority which aided and abetted their flight from responsibility and so, inevitably, "the commandment which was ordained to life proved in fact to be ordained to death" (Rom 7:10).

A paradoxical consequence of exaggerated reverence for the Law was that it was drawn into the orbit of 'covetousness'. It was desired, not for what it should be in relation to the Creator, but for what it seemed to be in relation to creatures, namely, as something on which they could 'rely' (Gal 3:10) to make them 'alive' (Gal 3:21). Its very existence encouraged creatures to presume a certain autonomy over against the Creator, and thereby to 'boast' (Rom 2:23). They were conditioned to formulate their own concept of authenticity in preference to that willed by the Creator (Rom 10:3). The result was the tragic situation that Paul outlines in Rom

7:14-24 (cf. above p. 90).

It is not difficult to catch the undertone of relief with which Paul proclaims, "Christ is the end of the Law, that every one who has faith may be justified" (Rom 10:4). The authenticity of the humanity of Christ puts an end to the period of confused striving when every upward effort only succeeded in miring humanity ever deeper. The way to authenticity, to be as God intended, is through the free decision of faith inaugurating an existence modeled on that of Christ (1 Cor 11:1).

Contemporary Applications

Christians know themselves to be no longer bound by the Mosaic Law with which Paul was so concerned. This can blind us to the fact that his basic principle remains valid with respect to any law. To give blind obedience to any authoritative directive is to place oneself in a state of inauthenticity, because to do so is to surrender one's freedom in an endeavor to escape responsibility.

The ambiguity of all law, both religious and civil, is that it is both necessary and destructive. Without some rules no human grouping can survive for very long. A legal framework enshrines the values that make continuity possible. A society without order is a contradiction in terms. Law, however, is pointless unless it is obeyed, and those responsible for a society, in order to facilitate their task, inevitably tend to insist that something be done simply because it is the law. Ignorance is no excuse for non-compliance, and sanctions are enforced against those who do not conform. In the end the law assumes a definite autonomy over against those whom it was designed to serve, and thus becomes a means of escape for those too lazy to think for themselves. They are satisfied to think of their 'duty' and refuse to look closely at the situation in which they must react creatively. Established custom, needless to say, has the force of law in this type of development.

The actual situation in the domain of civil law has been finely described by Peter G. Hodgson:

> Recent analyses of the 'corporate state' or bureaucratic-technological society have pointed out that the social world in which we live is highly legalistic; however, law serves no longer primarily as an instrument of justice and delimitation of power but as the value-free medium which permits the bureaucratic system to function smoothly and to maintain a high degree of institutional control. Laws are enacted primarily to satisfy the exigencies of administration rather than to protect the rights of individuals. Because of its external, impersonal, and often dehumanizing effect, law has a profoundly alienating impact on millions of citizens. For oppressed peoples everywhere in the world, law is experienced not merely as alienating but also as oppressive. The poor and powerless know that the law is both constructed against them and enforced against them. The role of the law first in legitimating the institution of slavery, then in enforcing patterns of segregation and discrimination, is a shameful episode in the history of American jurisprudence. Racist societies tend to be highly legalistic (e.g. the antebellum slave-holding states and present-day South Africa) because law provides a means both of social repression and of sublimating guilt feelings for the injustices perpetrated. (*New Birth of Freedom*, Philadelphia, 1976, p. 190).

The relationship between inauthenticity and submission to a law that should be recognized as evil needs no emphasis. The point was made with extreme clarity at the various trials of Nazi war criminals. On Paul's principle, however, unquestioning obedience to a good law is productive of inauthenticity. Common consent would suggest that the laws of the church are good laws, and it is precisely here that we touch the kernel of the problem.

No one would deny that the prohibition of murder is a

good law. It prohibits something that is incompatible with the positive creativity that is of the essence of authenticity. What then of the case of the German citizens who conspired to murder Hitler? Those who believe in the absolute supremacy of law can only say that they were wrong. Those more attuned to the lesson of Christ's life will recognize it for what it was, an effort to embrace responsibility. Past history, however, provides only pale examples, and in this particular instance the rightness of the conspirators' attempt has been proclaimed so widely that it is taken for granted. But was Idi Amin so different from Hitler? Might we be tempted to use the commandment 'Thou shalt not kill' as an excuse to avoid responsibility?

The purpose behind the law prescribing attendance at Sunday mass is certainly good. It is entirely fitting that creatures should worship their Creator regularly. But what of the situation of those who go to mass on Sunday purely and simply because it is laid down? In this hypothesis they go exclusively because of fear of committing sin. Not only do they get nothing out of it, but they end up so frustrated and annoyed that they are hardly capable of a civil word as they exit. Think of those emotionally committed to the pre-Vatican II latin liturgy who force themselves to a folk mass because it is the only one within reach. Do they differ from the Colossians or the Galatians? Paul would certainly answer in the negative. Their preoccupation with a 'thing' condemns them to inauthenticity.

The goodness of other church laws is more open to question, for example, the law restricting ordination to males. But the more fundamental issue concerns the role of positive law within an authentic community which, for Paul, is necessarily a Christian community. It would seem to be a logical inference from Paul's position that by enacting binding legislation the church contributes to the inauthenticity of its members. John Knox has perfectly grasped the Pauline perspective:

> But, it may be asked, is Paul's rejection of the law as binding on the believer so radical as this? Is not the 'law'

> he rejects simply an external code, a list of thou shalts and thou shalt nots, in particular the code of Judaism? Whatever may seem to be implied in some of his practical teaching, I feel sure that in his 'theory' of the Christian life Paul went much further than this. Although undoubtedly he is frequently referring to the Jewish law, one cannot deny the presence — often, if not always — of a more radical, more inclusive reference. . . . Law, as such, is no longer valid for the Christian. (*The Ethic of Jesus in the Teaching of the Church, London, 1962, p. 99*).

As we shall see, the precept of love is the only commandment that is binding on the authentic, and this is because it is demanded by the very nature of authenticity. This is not to say, however, that Paul must be considered as advocating a pure situation-ethic. This, as we shall see, is excluded by his understanding of the conditions under which authenticity becomes possible.

Suggested Readings

R. Bultmann, *Theology of the New Testament,* London: SCM, 1965, §27 (The Law).

B. Reicke, "The Law and This World according to Paul," *Journal of Biblical Literature* 70 (1951) 259-276.

H. Schlier, *Principalities and Powers in the New Testament,* Freiburg: Herder, 1961.

C.E.B. Cranfield, "St. Paul and the Law," *Scottish Journal of Theology* 17 (1964) 43-68.

J.A. Fitzmyer, "Saint Paul and the Law," *The Jurist* (1967) 18-36.

F.F. Bruce, "Paul and the Law of Moses," *Bulletin of the John Rylands Library* 57 (1974-75) 259-79.

E.P. Sanders, *Paul and Palestinian Judaism,* Philadelphia: Fortress, 1977, ch. 5 §4.

VII
EGOCENTRIC ISOLATION

The statement 'No one is an island' articulates the simple fact of experience that human existence is a web of interpersonal relationships. One cannot conceive of a human being in total isolation. Coming into existence necessarily implies a relationship to at least two other people. The process of education involves the association with many more. The possibilites of language and sex are a demand for complementarity, since each individual possesses only one part of a complete reproductive system and the purpose of language is communication with another. The amenities of daily life are dependent on the cooperation of a great number of individuals. My security depends on the police, my transport on bus drivers and motor mechanics, my recreation on movie makers, TV producers, and authors, my food on butchers and bakers. The list could be extended indefinitely. Hence, just as Aristotle described man as a 'social animal', so Heidegger insists that human being is necessarily a 'being-with-others'. In this encounter with other persons the individual is confronted with the choice between authenticity and inauthenticity.

Virtually all the existentialists are in agreement in seeing contemporary social existence as inauthentic. This is evi-

dent in the very terminology they use. The 'crowd' of Kierkegaard, the 'herd' of Nietzsche, the 'they' of Heidegger, the
'mass' of Jaspers are all highly suggestive of the uncompli-
mentary attitude of the philosophers which is rooted in the
awareness that the originality of the individual is lost in the
averageness of the multitude. No one will fail to recognize
the accuracy of Heidegger's analysis of the principal characteristics of contemporary existence as summarized by J.
Macquarrie:

> There is 'everydayness'. We have already frequently met
> the expression 'everyday existence'. This is technical term
> with Heidegger. It stands for a way of being dominated
> by unthinking habit, a mechanical following of the ways
> laid down for us in an established order. Then there is
> 'averageness', or mediocrity, which comes about as the
> result of a levelling tendency present in the use by all of
> facilities which make all alike, filling up forms, queueing
> for transport or entertainment are familiar examples . . .
> Publicity is another related characteristic of the deper-
> sonalized way of being. Whereas dread isolates the indi-
> vidual in his facticity and responsibility, in publicity he
> can forget himself and his responsibility, and so allay his
> anxiety, by identifying himself with the indeterminate
> impersonal multitude. Talking is the everyday way of
> speaking which, instead of disclosing anything as it really
> is, rather makes it become what the public says that it is.
> Corresponding to this baseless talking there is scribbling
> or popular literature which passes for writing. This scrib-
> bling really obscures the truth, but it becomes popular
> and authoritative because it tells people what they want
> to hear. Finally, there is curiosity. This is the desire to
> enter into experiences without taking the resolve to have
> them for one's self. The cinema affords imaginative entry
> into the gay luxurious world of Hollywood; the 'thriller'
> gives the reader the excitement of sharing in the deeds of
> daring of the hero without needing to leave his fireside;
> the sensational type of Sunday newspaper makes possible

vicarius indulgence in crime and adultery, even if the
reader professes (and himself believes) that he is horrified
by the stories which it reports. (*An Existentialist Theology,* London, 1964, pp. 91-92).

Existence is ruled by the faceless 'they' who is no one in
particular. 'They' ruin the economy. 'They' lower standards
of taste and morals. 'They' destroy the environment. 'They'
pursue the arms race. Individuals are not beings in themselves, but facets of the multiform 'they'. It was from this
standpoint that Sartre was able to proclaim that "Hell is
other people", and a popular song to chant that "Hell is in
hello".

It was inevitable that the existentialist concept of authenticity should be constructed in opposition to the general
pattern. If the inauthentic person is one who, in order to
relieve himself of responsibility, loses himself in the crowd,
then the authentic person, it is claimed, is the one who
emerges from the crowd, who breaks away from the mass by
having the courage to be different. The reaction to deper-
sonalization is to stress individualism. Hence, the phenomenon of the 'drop-out' of which Heidegger himself
furnishes a classical example in his retreat to isolation in the
Black Forest. The non-conformity of recent decades can
only be understood as a quest for authenticity. But there are
only a limited number of ways of being different from the
mass, and very quickly the effort to distinguish oneself
became subject to the tyranny of a different kind of conform-
ism. It was found to be impossible to separate oneself
from the crowd save by allying oneself with those who also
rejected the value-system of contemporary society. The
pressure of society was so great that it produced the paradox
that one could be 'unlike' only being 'like'. There is less
tolerance of diversity within non-conformist groups than in
society as a whole.

Experience, therefore, highlights the barrenness of a concept of authenticity based on radical individualism. It
should also force us to question whether the existentialist

analysis is in fact a completely accurate description of the human condition. What impresses the existentialists is the homogeneity of the mass, but is this really the whole picture? Paul certainly would not agree. As we saw, he had a very clear concept of authenticity as rooted in creativity. This implies a positive relationship to the other, and so where the existentialists see only collectivism he saw the lack of community. In consequence, he was much more conscious than they of the divisions within humanity, and he considered such divisions as the most obvious signs of inauthenticity.

Opposed Blocks

Paul's explicit statements that in Christ all social divisions have been abolished is sufficient to indicate that, for him, they belong to the inauthentic mode of human existence. "Here there cannot be Greek and Jew, circumcised and uncircumcised, barbarian, Scythian, slave, free man" (Col 3:11). "There is neither Jew nor Greek, there is neither slave nor free, there is neither male nor female" (Gal 3:27; cf. Rom 10:12; 1 Cor 12:13). This deceptively simple listing is not haphazard. It covers the whole of the then known world from religious, economic, geographical, and sociological points of view. The opposition 'male-female' immediately suggests that we have here something more than a neutral description. Even a brief outline of the attitudes of the period will make it clear that the oppositions carry overtones of hostility. We have to do, not merely with diversity, but with divisions.

The *Jewish attitude towards Gentiles* is accurately mirrored in Eph 4:17-18, "in the futility of their minds they are darkened in their understanding, alienated from the life of God, because of the ignorance that is in them", but much more graphically depicted in 4 Ezra, "All this I have spoken before you, O Lord, because you said that for our sakes you created this world. But as for the other nations which are descended from Adam, you have said that they are nothing, and that they are like unto spittle, and you have likened the abundance of them to a drop in a bucket"(4:55-56). According to the same author the fate of the Gentiles will be 'the pit of torment' and 'the furnace of Gehenna' (7:36-38), or alternatively he depicts them as subjected to a fiery stream which "burned them all up, so that suddenly nothing more was to be seen of the innumerable multitude save only dust of ashes and smell of smoke" (13:11). Not all the authors of the period were so venemous, but even the most beneign saw the salvation of the Gentiles only in terms of a penitent pilgrimage as depicted in Is 60: 3, "Nations shall come to your light, and kings to the brightness of your rising". Thus, for example, in the Sibylline Oracles we read:

> And then all the isles and cities shall say: How the Eternal loves these men [i.e. the Jews]. For all things work in sympathy with them and help them, the heaven and God's chariot the sun, and the moon. A sweet strain shall they utter from their mouths in hymns. Come, let us all fall upon the earth and supplicate the Eternal king, the mighty everlasting God. Let us make procession to His Temple, for He is the sole Potentate. And let us all ponder the law of the Most High God, who is the most righteous of all on earth. But we had gone astray from the path of the Eternal, and with foolish heart worshipped the works of men's hands, idols and images of men that are dead (III, lines 716ff.)

The choice for the Gentiles, therefore, was between destruction and unconditional surrender.

This arrogant assumption of the inherent superiority of one nation and its culture over all others could not fail to produce an equal and opposite reaction. In his *Contra Apion* Josephus records the irritation of such personages of the 1st cent. AD as Chaeremon (1:288), a Stoic philosopher who served both as tutor of Nero and as head of the great library of Alexandria, Lysimachus (1:304) an Alexandrian writer, and Apion (2:1) who taught in Rome during the reigns of Tiberius, Caligula and Claudius. Their spleen found expression in accusations designed to hold the Jews up as objects of ridicule. They did not break out of Egypt in the Exodus but were banished because they were afflicted with leprosy (1:299, 290, 308). The very etymology of the word 'sabbath' showed that they had a disease of the groin (2:21). Wherever they went they fomented sedition (2:68), and they all swore an oath to show no good will to any non-Jew (2:121). In their Temple they worshipped the head of an ass (2:80), and carried out unspeakable rites, "They would kidnap a Greek foreigner, fatten him up for a year, and then convey him to a wood, where they slew him, sacrificed his body with their customary ritual, partook of his flesh, and, while immolating the Greek, swore an oath of hostility to the Greeks" (2:95).

It is a question on both sides of generic attitudes which errupted into open violence only occasionally. But it is precisely this that is important for an understanding of Paul's global view. That individual Jews and Gentiles lived in mutual harmony and understanding is irrelevant to the general picture, because in times of crisis it did not hold out against the more fundamental attitude of hostility.

The same observation is also valid for the opposition between *male and female*. It is undeniable that in many respects both Jews and Greeks treated women as full equals, but their legal systems regarded women as subordinate and inferior to man and subjected her to various religious and social disabilities. If she was normally treated with courtesy and respect, this assumption of inferiority could at times surface into bitter cynicism. Demosthenes' famous remark, "Mistresses we keep for the sake of pleasure; concubines for the daily care of our persons; wives to bear us legitimate children and to be the trusted guardians of our households", could only have been made in a society which regarded women as having no more than a utilitarian value. The rabbis feared women as a distraction and a source of temptation. They were fundamentally unreliable (Shab. 33b) and endowed with four characteristics, greediness, curiosity, laziness, and jealousy (Gen. Rabba 45:5). Philo, who had a foot in both camps, wrote, "Progress is nothing else than the giving up of the female gender by changing into the male, since the female gender is material, passive, corporeal and sense perceptive, while the male is active, rational, incorporeal and more akin to mind and thought" (Quaest. in Ex 1:8). His point is to explain the difference between sense knowledge and intelligence, but the allegory he employs to clarify the distinction is a clear indication of the position of women in his society.

The inferior position of women was rooted in a radical misogyny, as is revealed in this summary of ancient proverbs by C.E. Carlston:

> Women, if we were to trust the ancient wisdom, are basically uneducable and empty-headed; vengeful, dangerous, and responsible for men's sins; mendacious, treacherous, and unreliable; fickle; valuable only through their relationships with men; incapable of moderation or spontaneous goodness; at their best in the dark; interested only in sex — unless they are with their husbands, in which case (apparently) they would rather talk. In short, women are one and all 'a set of vultures', the 'most beastly' of all the beasts on land or sea, and marriage is at best a necessary evil. (*Journal of Biblical Literature* 99 [1980] 95-96)

The examples he cites amply justify this vicious caricature. Proverbs, it must be remembered, were (and still are) understood to represent self-evident aspects of human experience.

Given the nature of society, women's proverbs concerning the opposite sex have gone largely unrecorded. It would be naive in the extreme to assume that none existed. The contrary is in fact indicated by the obviously male proverb reported by the 3rd cent. B.C. poet Philemon, "When a woman speaks to a woman in private a great treasure-house of evils bursts forth." Here we catch a hint that the hostility shown by men was fully reciprocated. Confirmation is furnished by the words that the 5th cent. B.C. playwright Sophocles places in the mouth of a woman:

> When we are young, in our father's house, I think we live the sweetest life of all, for ignorance ever brings us up delightfully. But when we have reached a mature age and know more, we are driven out of doors and sold, away from the gods of our fathers and our parents, some to foreigners, some to barbarians, some to strange houses, others to such as deserve reproach. And in such a lot, after a single night has united us, we have to acquiesce and think that all is well. (Tereus frag. 524).

It is hardly necessary to document the reciprocal attitudes of *slave and master*. At times there was a relationship of mutual trust and confidence, but the true position of the slave is highlighted by the chilling remark that, as time went on, "there was a tendency to give greater recognition to *de facto* personality" (*Oxford Classical Dictionary,* 996). In other words, there was a growing tendency to treat slaves as if they were persons. They had no personality save as an extension of that of their master. Their legal position was that of any material item of property, since the possession of rights belonged to the very definition of a free-man. It is calculated that in the cities slaves made up one-third of the population, and in the ultimate analysis they were simply used by the free. However, slaves may have felt towards their master, their attitude was certainly coloured by the desire for liberation. Resentment moved continuously within them. At times it spurted forth in flight, and at others it exploded in the suicidal outbursts of the slave revolts. The three greatest occurred in the two centuries prior to Paul's ministry, and in consequence the attitude of the free was always tinged by an element of suspicion and fear.

The final pair *'Barbarian' and 'Scythian'* has posed a difficulty to exegetes because it is not an expected antithesis, as are the other three groupings. It has been suggested that

Barbaria is occasionally used to describe the Somali coast
and part of Ethiopia. In this event the contrast would be
between northern and southern peoples, or even between
whites and blacks. Be this as it may, 'barbarian' was used by
both Jews and Greeks to mean 'outsider', i.e. anyone whose
difference in language, culture, and religion stamped him as
an unfortunate inferior. The Scythians, on the other hand,
were a specific racial group located round the Black Sea
whose crudity, excesses and ferocity made them the arche-
type of the 'barbarian'. Both terms, therefore, imply a
cruelly derisive contempt. Even if we knew what the Scythians thought of outsiders, it would certainly be impossible to
print it.

Paul with great realism saw his world as fragmented into
opposed blocks. It was a dung-heap of steaming resentment
in which the flies of fear, the maggots of mistrust, and the
worms of envy abounded. It would not be difficult to trans-
pose his categories to fit our situation. The same type of
corroding ill-will obtains between the developed nations
and the Third World, between the consumers and the producers, between the haves and the have-nots, between the
women's liberationists and the male chauvinists. In this
century wars have never been so numerous or so destructive.

Isolated Individuals

Paul, however, did not see only blocks of people opposed
to each other. He looked within the groupings and the
resulting picture is, if anything, even less pleasant. Our task
here is greatly facilitated by the fact that Paul himself occasionally drew up lists of the traits which, in his view, characterized those who existed inauthentically. These 'vice-lists'
appear in Rom 1:29-31; 13:13; 1 Cor 5:10-11; 6:9-10; 2 Cor
12:20-21; Gal 5:19-21; and Col 3:5, 8. All overlap to some
extent, and so the easiest way to begin is by drawing up a
simple alphabetical list:

1. Anger (2 Cor/Gal/Col).
2. Arrogance (Rom).
3. Arrogant (Rom).
4. Blasphemy (Col).
5. Carousing (Rom/Gal).
6. Conceit (2 Cor).
7. Contention (Rom/2 Cor/Gal/Col).
8. Contrivor of evil (Rom).
9. Covetousness (Rom/1 Cor/Gal).
10. Deceit (Rom).
11. Disobedient (Rom.)
12. Dissension (Gal).
13. Drunkenness (Rom/1 Cor/Gal).
14. Faithless (Rom).
15. Foolish (Rom).
16. Hating God (Rom).
17. Haughtiness (Rom).
18. Homosexual (1 Cor).
19. Idolatry (1 Cor/Gal).
20. Immorality (Rom/Cor/Gal/Col).
21. Jealousy (Rom/2 Cor/Gal).
22. Licentiousness (Rom/2 Cor/Gal).
23. Malignity (Rom).
24. Murder (Rom).
25. Obscene speech (Col).
26. Pederast (1 Cor).
27. Reviler (1 Cor).
28. Sect(arianism) (Gal).
29. Selfish ambition (2 Cor/Gal).
30. Senseless (Rom).
31. Sexual passion (Col).
32. Slander (Rom/2 Cor).
33. Sorcery (Gal).
34. Stealing (1 Cor).
35. Swindler (1 Cor).
36. Tale-bearer (Rom/2 Cor).
37. Unloving (Rom).
38. Unmerciful (Rom).

39. Unruliness (2 Cor).
40. Viciousness (2 Cor/Gal/Col).
41. Wickedness (Rom).

This list contains a mixture of abstract (e.g. 'malignity') and concrete nouns (e.g. 'reviler') which indicates that Paul is concerned with a real situation, albeit a typical one. Dispositions are considered to come to expression in action, and behaviour is treated as indicative of a deep-rooted attitude.

The technique of the 'vice-list' was common in the milieu in which Paul lived, and it is hardly surprising to find that, of the terms in the above list, some are found in lists of Jewish origin (nos. 1, 3, 4, 9, 10, 15, 17, 19, 20, 21, 22, 23, 24, 27, 30, 32, 33, 34, 35, 38, 40, 41), while others belong to popular Hellenistic tradition (nos. 9, 11, 14, 16, 18, 23, 26, 30, 31, 37). This dependence of Paul on the cultural setting in which he worked only serves to highlight the fact that the remaining 25% of the above list is attested only rarely, if at all, in comparable lists of the same period, namely, 'arrogance', 'carousing', 'conceit', 'contention', contriving evil', 'dissension', 'obscene speech', 'sect(arianism)', 'selfish ambition', 'tale-bearing', and 'unruliness'. These vices all have one thing in common; they make genuine community impossible. This in turn draws our attention to the fact that the vast majority of the items on the above list are of this type. Three concern religion (nos. 4, 16, 19), four sex (nos. 18, 20, 26, 31,), and a few others personal failings (e.g. nos. 13, 15, 30), but the rest are social vices.

This factor makes the Pauline lists stand out from other contemporary catalogues which are heavily weighted with individualistic vices, e.g. ignorance, tastelessness, awkwardness, pessimism, instability, etc. This difference is only one of emphasis, but it is extremely important for a correct understanding of Paul's perspective. The Apostle's contemporaries were not unaware of man's social nature. Both the Greek tradition of civic responsibility and the Jewish conviction of the solidarity of their race ensured that they gave some prominence to social vices. The individual, nonetheless, was primary. Philo, for example, presents his elaborate list of 160 vices (the great majority individualistic) as characteristic of 'one who loves Pleasure' (*De Sacrificiis Abelis et Caini,* n. 32). He was influenced by the Stoic tradition which was also at the root of the popular moral philosophy of the period. The Stoics believed that virtue is based on knowledge. Hence, only the wise can be virtuous. The four cardinal virtues characterize the wise, and from these Zeno, the founder of the Stoa, developed four cardinal vices as their exact counterparts, namely, 'folly,' 'excess', 'injustice', and 'timidity'. It is hardly unexpected, therefore, that the individual should be at the center of the picture. Society entered the scene only because the individual was forced to interact with it, and the belief was that society would improve insofar as individuals became progressively more virtuous.

Paul was not so naive, because he was extremely conscious of the power of a false value-system ('Sin') hostile to authenticity. His vision of the authentic nature of humanity made him much more sensitive than the existentialists to the factors that inhibit genuine communication. His 'vice-lists' betray that he saw the world as a place where individuals sealed themselves off from one another by attitudes which make community impossible. His catalogue suggests, not only failure to recognize the other, but an active repulsion of the other. It is the negation of an 'I–Thou' relationship.

Once again, there is a close correspondence between Paul's vision and a realistic assessment of contemporary society. Loneliness is endemic. The legitimate fear of being used or abused produces a fear of involvement. People can be robbed on the streets in broad daylight and no one will go to their assistance. People refuse to make friends with the people in the next house or apartment because there may be demands that they do not wish to meet. Doors are always locked, and preparations for a holiday are conducted in an atmosphere of trepidation. A miasma of suspicion reaches everywhere.

Suggested Readings

J.L. Daniel, "Anti-Semitism in the Hellenistic-Roman Period," *Journal of Biblical Literature* 98 (1979) 45-65.

A. Oepke, "Woman," in *Theological Dictionary of the New Testament,* 1:777-784.

R. Loewe, *The Social Position of Women in Judaism,* London: SPCK, 1966.

J.B. Segal, "The Jewish Attitude towards Women," *Journal of Jewish Studies* 30 (1979) 121-137.

S.B. Pomeroy, *Goddesses, Whores, Wives, Slaves: Women in Classical Antiquity,* New York: Schocken, 1976.

H. Kitto, *The Greeks,* London: Pelican, 1957, ch. 12.

Oxford Classical Dictionary, articles on "Slavery, Law of," and "Slaves".

S.S. Bartchy, *Mallon Chresai: First Century Slavery and the Interpretation of 1 Corinthians 7:21,* Missoula: SBL, 1973.

M.I. Finley, *Slavery in Classical Antiquity,* New York: Barnes & Noble, 1968.

Conclusion

Paul's understanding of the condition of inauthentic humanity is dominated by the concepts of Sin, Death, and the Law. All three are closely interrelated. Sin is the 'world' in the false orientation given humankind by the sin of Adam. This orientation is ratified and intensified by the attitudes of his descendants. Though theoretically free, all those born into a disoriented society have in reality no choice but to internalize its orientation. Their pattern of behaviour necessarily reflects the false value-system that they have received. They, therefore, exist in the state of Death which means that their mode of being is not that intended by the Creator.

For Paul, one of the most important manifestations of the power of Sin was an erroneous estimation of the role of the Law. All those born into the Jewish world of his day could not but assimilate the prevailing attitude of exaggerated respect for the Law which displayed itself in blind obedience. By handing over to the Law their inalienable obligation to make personal choices, the Jews—and, by implication, all others who subject themselves in the same way to any law—destroyed the freedom of responsibility which is the essence of human dignity. By their attitude towards the Law, they reduced themselves to the sub-human condition of Death. This is why Paul can say the "the power of Sin is the Law" (1 Cor 15:56).

Sin also exercised its influence in the domain of interpersonal relations both on the social and the individual level. Various blocks inherited antagonistic attitudes which forced them apart, and within those blocks individuals were subject to a conditioning which made anything more than a functional collectivism impossible. The consequent isolation made individuals even more vulnerable to the inauthentic orientation of society and, as a result, they became the centers of their own private worlds constituted by the visible and the tangible. Because they felt that they could control and dominate 'things' their 'covetousness' was given free rein. This permitted 'things' to gain the upper hand and thus to intensify the alienation of the authentic self. Paradoxically, however, this also brought material creation into bondage (Rom 8:21) because the order of nature was distorted (cf. Lev 26:33-35). The vanity and corruption of material creation is the consequence of humanity's Death.

The Apostle's concept of inauthenticity, therefore, is highly unified, and the above outline has the effect of pinpointing Sin as the most fundamental element. Once humanity is freed from Sin, its liberation from Death and the Law, and the liberation of creation, follow naturally. This focuses our attention on the key question: How is freedom from Sin effected? And so we now turn to Paul's vision of authentic existence.

PART 3
COMMUNITY

VIII
THE GIFT OF CHOICE

In the transition from inauthenticity to authenticity, does humanity find itself or is it found by another? Existentialists will reply that humanity finds itself, but when they are pushed to specify how this actually happens their answers are anything but satisfying.

Despite the variety of perspectives, all see dying as the ultimate reality, and it is from death that they derive their concepts of authenticity. For Heidegger death is the pre-eminent possibility that all must realize. We become authentic by living in the anticipation of death and by making it the unifying factor in our existence. It is death which gives life meaning, and its acceptance frees us from concern with 'things' and from the tyranny of the 'crowd'. Sartre, however, points out that this approach is self-destructive. It frees from inauthenticity only by devaluing all existence. This, for him, became the clue and he proclaims, "It is absurd that we are born; it is absurd that we die". He, therefore, sees authenticity as the acceptance of the absurd meaninglessness of existence.

Common sense rebels against such so-called 'solutions'. The existentialists deserve credit for shattering the illusory complacency of inauthenticity. When taken seriously they make it impossible for those who are 'dead' to believe that they are 'alive'. But for illusion they can only substitute despair. If the present is meaningless and the future nothingness there can be no hope, and there is no reason to struggle out of inauthenticity. In providing a semblance of meaning an illusion at least has value, and it will not be abandoned until an alternative positive value is proposed. To a philosopher the acceptance of despair may seem an heroic gesture that separates one from the herd, but to ordinary common sense it appears as nothing more than silly dramatics. In the last analysis the existentialists are forced to confess their impotence to deal with the situation. The implication of their 'solutions' is that the human condition is irremediable.

Paul would agree, but only up to a point, because his acceptance of the Creator-creature relationship permitted him to make a distinction that they could not envisage. He saw the human situation as irremediable from within but not from without. Hence, he consistently emphasizes that authenticity is made possible only through divine intervention, e.g. "You who were dead . . . God has made alive" (Col 2:13).

A New Creative Act

The statement that 'God has made alive', and parallel assertions such as 'God justifies' (Rom 8:33), must be analyzed more closely, because they cannot be literally true. 'Life', as we have seen, is the Pauline term for authenticity. The human creature, however, is possibility determined by decision. It is a form of being that creates itself by means of its choices. To say that 'God bestows righteousness' implies that God overrides the fundamental possibility that he built into human nature. Were this in fact the case the Creator would contradict himself and bring into existence an entirely different type of being. Authenticity, therefore, cannot be conferred. It can only be chosen. The human creature, if it is to be true to its own nature, must decide for authenticity.

In the state of 'death', as we have seen, humankind cannot choose. Its freedom is nullified by enslavement to Sin. The overwhelming and unavoidable pressure of the false value-system of society sweeps all into an inauthentic behaviour pattern. Authenticity remains an ontological possibility, but on the level of reality it cannot actually be chosen. Hence, God's part in the transition from 'death' to 'life' consists in restoring authenticity to the status of a real option. In the last analysis salvation consists in the gift of choice.

God's first step in this process consists in the sending of his Son, "God has done what the law weakened by the flesh could not do: sending his own Son in the likeness of sinful flesh and for sin, he condemned sin in the flesh" (Rom 8:3). Despite his real integration into the historical situation ('in the likeness of sinful flesh') Christ did not merely reflect what the rest of humanity was. He manifested what humankind could become. The mere fact of his existence as the embodiment of authentic humanity demonstrated that the mode of existence that the world considered normal was not the only one possible. Prior to the advent of Christ only inauthentic existence was visible and, if we abstract from Christ and from those who followed him authentically as the existentialists do, then what we see is humanity in its inauthentic mode. It is hardly surprising, therefore, that the existentialists should be forced to despair. Their abstraction from the presence of the other Christs in the world can be construed as an objection, but the saints are so few that on this count it is hard to fault the existentialist perspective.

This point, however, is not our concern at present. For Paul, the authentic humanity of Christ was the revelation that the mode of being determined by Sin was not the only option. Those who had eyes to see could now perceive that within the human situation there existed, not only the ego-centric isolation to which they had become habituated, but a creative reaching out to the other. His presence gave humanity a new standard by which to judge itself, thus creating the opportunity to see inauthenticity for what it really was. It also forced humanity to recognize that the bonds of Sin were not unbreakable, that the tyranny of contemporary attitudes and values could be shaken off. If one man was not subject to the domination of Sin all could be free. Paul does not speculate as to how Christ escaped enslavement to Sin despite his immersion in the human situation. It was simply a fact which he took as the basis of his theological system, and were he pushed on the point I suspect that he could only suggest a providential disposition.

We are now in a position to appreciate the importance of Paul's insistence that salvation takes place within history. This comes to the fore in the letter to the Colossians. Paul was conscious of this crucial element from the beginning, and in his earlier letters it is taken completely for granted. At Colossae, on the contrary, Paul had reason to fear that this supremely important aspect was being lost sight of. Our knowledge of the so-called Colossian 'heresy' is sketchy, but it is generally agreed that there was a tendency among the Colossians to attribute a role in their salvation to purely spiritual beings, i.e. angels. Hence, he has to insist, "As therefore you received Christ *as Jesus the Lord,* so live in him, having been rooted and being built up in him, and being confirmed in the faith as you were taught" (Col 2:6). The Christ who saves is not a heavenly being who operates through the spirit powers. Under God the saviour is the Jesus who became Lord (cf. Rom 14:9). It has been pointed out that Paul uses 'Jesus' to evoke the historicity of Christ. This interpretation is confirmed by the oldest commentary on Col 2:6, "You did not learn Christ in that way, assuming that you heard (about) him and were taught in him (in the way in which) he is truth, (namely) in Jesus" (Eph 4:21). Jesus is the truth of the saving Christ because it is the perfection of his humanity that is significant. In a variation on this theme Paul writes, "Those whom God foreknew he also predestined to be conformed to the image of his Son, in order that he might be the first-born among many brethren" (Rom 8:29).

The presence of Christ in the world created an alternative. Inauthenticity was now confronted with authenticity. The existence of an alternative, however, is only a precondition for choice. One cannot be said to choose if there are no alternatives. The actual making of a choice is a different matter, and Paul's hardheaded realism forced him to recognise that the mere fact of the existence of Christ did not make it really possible for humankind to decide for him. The reality of Sin was not destroyed by the presence of Christ, and the pressure it exercised continued to orientate humanity to inauthenticity. The rulers of this age were only 'doomed to pass away' (1 Cor 2:6). Something was required to counterbalance this influence, and since power is matched only by power, Paul affirms that Christ is 'the power of God' (1 Cor 1:24). His person did not only propose, it enabled, because it embodied 'the love of God' (Rom 8:35, 39). The creative love of God becomes effective in the loving of Christ. The power that brought the world into being is displayed in Christ to enable humanity to achieve authenticity and thus be what the Creator intended. This is the grace which makes the decision of faith possible (Eph 2:8).

The Existential Call

Paul's situation was parallel to ours in that he had to deal with those who had never known Christ in the flesh. Nonetheless, Christ remained the model of authentic humanity, and he demanded explicit recognition of Jesus as Lord as the first step in the acquisition of authenticity, "If you confess with your lips that Jesus is Lord and believe in your heart that God raised him from the dead, you shall be saved" (Rom 10:9). If Jesus was to be known and his power experienced, this could come about in only one way:

Everyone who calls upon the name of the Lord will be saved.

> But how are they to call on him in whom they have not believed?
> And how are they to believe him whom they have not heard?
> And how are they to hear without a preacher? (Rom 10:14).

The second rhetorical question is highly condensed and, as in 1 Thess 2:13, two distinct ideas are interwoven. The logic of the argument demands, 'How are they to believe in him *of whom* they have not heard?', and this has exercised a determinant influence on all current translations. That Paul had this dimension in mind there can be little doubt because he elsewhere proclaims, "we are ambassadors on behalf of Christ" (2 Cor 5:20). What Paul actually wrote, however, is quite different, because the rules of Greek grammar permit only the translation 'how are they to believe him *whom* they have not heard? Since it is a question of the Lord, this rendering necessarily implies that those who hear listen to the one in whom they are called to believe, namely, Christ. In the preaching which leads to authenticity it is Christ who speaks.

What Paul means by this is clearly articulated in 2 Cor 4:10-11:

> We always bear in our body the dying of Jesus in order that the life of Jesus may be manifested in our body. For continually while still alive, we are being handed over to death in order that the life of Jesus may be manifested in our mortal flesh.

At first reading the paradoxical tone of this statement is disconcerting, but it is so typical of Paul. The seeming paradox is rooted in the fact that he uses 'life' in two distinct senses. By 'while still alive' he means his ordinary physical existence which is threatened by persecution. Yet that ordinary existence of Paul is capable of manifesting 'the life of Jesus'. It has been noted that the term 'Jesus' is Paul's way of formally underlining the historicity of him who is now the Risen Lord, and 'life' is here used in the pregnant sense of authentic existence. The authentic humanity that Jesus embodied is now displayed in the person of Paul. This is so because he carries in his body, i.e. the physical self, the 'dying of Jesus'.

This phrase is often taken to mean that the Apostle's life, like that of his Lord, was a perpetual martyrdom. The basis for this interpretation is the assertion in the next verse that Paul and his co-workers are continuously in danger of death. The two statements, however, are not identical. One deals with the factual aspect of Paul's situation, whereas the other represents an attempt to bring out its significance. It is not sufficient to claim, as some exegetes do, that the frequent deliverances from difficulty, danger, and death are evidence that Christ is still alive and has divine power. From a purely secular point of view such escapes would prove only that Paul was lucky. From a more religious perspective they would prove nothing more than that he was under divine protection. They prove nothing concerning Christ, particularly in view of the theocentricity of Paul's teaching. Paul, on the contrary, explicitly evokes 'the dying of Jesus'. The very rare term 'dying' (*nekrosis*) suggests life as culminating in death. We have seen, however, that the death of Jesus was much more than the termination of his earthly existence. It was revelatory of the quality of his entire life. The absolute character of the self-giving highlighted in his death demonstrated the creatively loving altruism which is the essence of authentic humanity. Because of his commitment to Christ — "I live now not I but Christ lives in me" (Gal 2:20; contrast Rom 7:20) — which was actualized in his dedication to others in the face of all difficulties and dangers (cf. 2 Cor 11:23-30), Paul felt that he could claim to manifest the same quality of existence. His very being, stamped with 'the dying of Jesus' revealed 'the life of Jesus'. Hence he spoke "in Christ" (2 Cor 2:17).

It seems clear that for Paul effective or power-laden preaching about Christ is possible when the preachers reflect in their personality the quality of authentic humanity about which they speak. And it could hardly be otherwise once we recall that the sending of Jesus Christ inaugurated a new era in the Creator-creature relationship. Christ did not merely proclaim as did the prophets of the Old Testament. He *was* the will of God for humanity (1 Thess 5:18), the power and wisdom of God (1 Cor 1:24), and above all, the love of God (Rom 8:39). The word of God was no longer merely verbal; it was enfleshed. To revert to a purely verbal proclamation devoid of any existential reinforcement would be to deny the newness introduced by Christ. To be effective the preachers must *be* as Christ was. By exhibiting the authentic humanity that was Christ's, they demonstrate the continued viability of an alternative to inauthenticity and at the same time empower others to choose it. "If I speak in the tongues of men and of angels, but have not love, I am a noisy gong or clanging cymbal" (1 Cor 13:1).

It needs to be emphasized that this re-presentation of Christ is not limited to those who are officially commission-ed to preach. It is an integral part of the responsibility of all those who have accepted Christ. In his very first letter Paul draws attention to this point:

> You became imitators of us and of the Lord . . . so that you became an example to all the believers in Macedonia and in Achaia. For not only has the word of the Lord sounded forth from you in Macedonia and Achaia, but your faith in God has gone forth everywhere, so that we need not say anything (1 Thess 1:6-8).

Even if we concede an element of rhetorical exaggeration, the last phrase is indicative of the impact of the Thessalo-nian community. What is significant, however, is that this impact was twofold. It was both verbal ('the word of the Lord') and existential ('your faith in God'). In consequence, they constituted an 'example' to other believers. The Greek term here translated by 'example' (typos) is better rendered by 'pattern'. The Thessalonians exhibited a pattern of behaviour in which words and deed proclaimed the same reality. In this they showed themselves to be imitators, not only of Paul, but of Christ in whom word and being were totally in harmony.

In 1 Thess 1:6-8 Paul is formally concerned only with the influence of one Christian community on others, but it would be a mistake to limit the import of his words to this situation alone. The authenticity of the Thessalonians would also have had an impact on their pagan environment. This was certainly true in the case of the Philippians:

> Do all things without grumbling or disputation, that you may be blameless and sincere, children of God without blemish in the midst of a crooked and perverse generation, among whom you shine as lights in the world, holding forth the word of life (Phil 2:14-16).

Here the contrast between authenticity and inauthenticity is expressed in terms of light. By being 'sincere', i.e., all of one piece, without any foreign admixture, the believers at Philippi demonstrate their difference from the rest of the world. No verbal element comes into the picture. It is simply a question of the quality of their lives and this alone is a 'holding forth of the word of life'. Their being what they are is a demonstration of the real possibility of the new mode of existence which differs radically from what was accepted as normal. Their gospel is not a theory but a fact, which is why Paul terms it a word of 'life'. The Law spoke of authenticity but, since it was only a 'thing', it lacked the power to turn a theoretical possibility into a real one. Only the living can communicate life; it cannot be generated by words alone. The creative love which informed the existence of the Philippians was an invitation which created the possibility of response. This is the fruitfulness of authenticity (Col 1:10; Eph 2:10).

Imitation

Nowhere, perhaps, does the existential dimension come so clearly to the fore as in the exhortation "Become imitators of me, as I am of Christ" (1 Cor 11:1; cf., 4:16-17). This extraordinary statement is not unique. The same theme appears when he writes to the Thessalonians (1 Thess 1:6), to the Galatians (4:12), and to the Philippians (4:9). The only ecclesial epistles in which it does not appear are Romans and Colossians. This fact in itself is highly significant, because these latter two communities were the only two who did not know Paul personally. He could not propose imitation to them, because imitation demands physical presence. Equally, he had to propose imitation to the communities in which he had preached, because there was no other way to justify his assertion that a new form of human existence had entered the world with Christ. Words alone might outline an attractive possibility, but too many promises had remained unfulfilled, too many utopias had withered in the searing blast of realism. A theoretical possibility could be talked about. A real possibility had to be *seen*. To justify his claim concerning the *present* reality of the creative love of God he could not content himself with referring to an individual of the *past*. Those with whom he had to deal had never encountered Jesus in the flesh. In all honesty, therefore, he could not recommend that they imitate Him. Even if his hearers were prepared to accept that the humanity of Christ was different from that which they ordinarily encountered, they might reasonably claim that this was a unique and unrepeatable case. In order to be convincing Paul had to say, 'In me you see him'. If his audience could not perceive the difference between Paul and them, and if they could not experience the attraction of wholeness reaching out to them nothing was likely to happen.

Paul was sufficiently realistic, however, to recognize no witness is given unless it is received. He thus exhorts the Galatians, "Become as I am, because I became as you" (4:12). Neither his preaching nor his personality were thrown at those whom he had to convince. He inserted himself into their situation in a way that parallels the insertion of Christ into the human situation. How far he went is fully described in the famous passage where he enunciates his principle of adaptation:

> To the Jews I became as a Jew in order to win Jews. To those under the Law I became as one under the Law —though not being myself under the Law—that I might win those under the Law. To those outside the Law I became as one outside the Law — not being without the law toward God but under the law of Christ — that I might win those outside the Law. To the weak I became weak that I might win the weak. I have become all things to all men that I might by all means save some (1 Cor 9:19-22).

A superficial reading of this passage gives the impression of ruthless opportunism. That such an accusation was in fact levelled against him there can be little doubt (cf. Gal 5:11; 2 Cor 1:17), and the impassioned character of his defense indicates that he was sensitive to this charge precisely because there was in it an element of truth, though falsified by exaggeration. The truth was that Paul did vary in his approach to communities and individuals, but not to the extent — or with the motives — imputed to him by his opponents. He knew that there is no absolute witness valid for all times and in all places. If his re-presentation of Christ were not completely integrated with the needs and capabilities of a concrete individual or group, it could not be a vital and effective summons to authenticity. Hence, he had to know and understand and not from without but from within. Here we find the counterbalance to the Apostle's extremely bleak picture of the world, because it is clear that his attitude was not one of contempt. He did not permit his hope to cloud his vision. He saw and described reality as it was, but he knew his fellows to be the victims of a tragic error. That error could be rectified. Christ gave his life for that cause. Why should not he sacrifice his self-respect? Consistency would be a cheap and easy victory. The struggle to walk the narrow edge that separates flexibility from compromise was a more worthwhile battle. He accepted the challenge with all the risks that it implied, because then his love was at full tension, and its power transformed but did not impose.

Suggested Readings

J. Macquarrie, *Existentialism,* New York: World Publishing, 1972, ch. 11 (Authenticity).

_____, *An Existential Theology,* London: SCM, 1965, ch. 6 (Authenticity).

J. Murphy-O'Connor, *Paul on Preaching,* New York: Sheed & Ward, 1964.

D.M. Stanley, " 'Become Imitators of Me': The Pauline Conception of Apostolic Tradition," *Biblica* 40 (1959) 859-877.

W.P. de Boer, *The Imitation of Paul,* Kampen: Kok, 1962.

H. Chadwick, "'All Things to All Men' (1 Cor 9:22)," *New Testament Studies* 1 (1954-55) 261-275.

IX
LIBERATION

Authenticity is rooted in freedom which, in consequence, is presented by Paul as the goal of Christ-like proclamation, "you were called to freedom" (Gal 5:13). The Apostle, however, immediately goes on to exhort the Galatians, "Do not use your freedom as an opportunity for the flesh" (5:13). This text warns us that freedom has two facets. Most fundamentally it implies a lack of restraint or compulsion, and this in turn implies the opportunity for action. Thus, while recognizing that the two are always intimately associated, we must distinguish between 'freedom *from*' and 'freedom *to*'.

Few themes are closer to the heart of existentialism than freedom. The word occurs with almost monotonous regularity, but when we try to grasp the underlying concept it continuously slips away. We are given partial glimpses but the totality eludes us. The reason for this is that the existentialists focus primarily on 'freedom *to*', i.e. on the level of action which is founded on decision. They take for granted 'freedom *from*', and it is precisely here that they become evasive because their own analysis of the human condition contradicts this assumption. We have already seen how much they insist on the subjection of the individual to the 'herd' or the 'crowd'. Such domination negates 'freedom *from*' on the ontic level, because the individual is in fact subjected to restraint and compulsion. In reality, therefore, there is no basis for 'freedom *to*'. This confusion was made possible by the existentialists' understanding of the relationship between the ontic and the ontological. Ontological freedom is given with human nature. One cannot conceive a human being without this possibility. The existentialists slide from the ontological to the ontic by assuming that what is true in theory must be true in fact.

Paul was too close to reality to make this mistake. He took ontological freedom for granted. His concern was with ontic freedom, and he proclaimed to believers, "You who were once slaves of Sin...have been set free from Sin" (Rom 6:17-18). The questions then is: how is the believer freed from Sin?

The 'How' of Freedom

There is a vast literature dedicated to the exposition of Paul's concept of freedom, but to read it with the above question in mind is a most disconcerting experience because an adequate response is never forthcoming. In the vast majority of cases the question is never even asked. A few authors are exempt from this criticism, but their answers can hardly be considered satisfactory. Thus for example, in his book *Theology and Ethics in Paul* (Nashville, 1968) V. P. Furnish writes:

> The believer is no longer under sin's power (the law), but under the power of God (grace). He has a new Master whose power is sovereign without being tyrannical, for in the service of God, in bondage to his Lord, he is free to receive the promised inheritance of life. (p. 180).

All this means is that believers are no longer enslaved to Sin because they have placed themselves in bondage to Christ. The paradoxical tone makes the formulation attractive and gives the impression of profundity, but instead of focusing on 'freedom *from*' which is the crucial issue, Furnish passes immediately to the idea of service which belongs to the domain of 'freedom *to*'. He thus remains on the purely descriptive level, and leaves unanswered the question of *how* the power of Christ acts on the believer. Bultmann is open to the same objection. With great accuracy and precision he affirms that freedom from Sin "is not a magical guarantee against the *possibility* of sin... but release from the *compulsion* of sin" (*Theology of the New Testament* I, p. 332), but then he continues:

> The power of the Spirit is manifested in the fact that it gives the believer freedom, opens up the future, the eternal, life. For freedom is nothing else than being open for the genuine future, letting one's self be determined by the future. (p. 334)

The possibility of being determined by the future (whatever this might mean) is certainly a quality of 'freedom *to*'. 'Freedom *from*' is conceived as a gift of the Spirit, and this is certainly correct, but the problem of how this freedom is given is bypassed.

Other authors draw attention to the fact that Paul relates freedom from Sin very closely to baptism:

> Do you not know that all of us who have been baptized into Christ Jesus were baptized into death? We were buried therefore with him by baptism into death, so that as Christ was raised from the dead by the glory of the Father, we too might walk in newness of life . . . . We know that our old self was crucified with him so that the body of sin might be destroyed, and we might no longer be enslaved to Sin. For he who has died is freed from Sin (Rom 6:3-7).

They fail, however, to appreciate the real meaning of this text by interpreting it in terms of an internal power communicated to the believer. This leads them into incredible convolutions when they are pressed to explain what actually happens in this case. A beautiful example of the sort of thing that has to be said is provided by R. Schnackenburg in the second volume of his *L'existence chrétienne selon le Nouveau Testament* (Bruges, 1971):

> There is no question of a physical change; the dispositions and powers of the natural man remain. It is rather that the baptized receives the Spirit of God as a new power and capacity to banish all evil and all obscurity.... There is no question of a new attitude, but a new power is given us by God, the ever-active Spirit, omnipotent in works and supremely alive.
>
> As modern men we are likely to be invaded by a wave of scepticism. Does God really communicate his Spirit? Is man created anew in baptism? Do we feel anything of the power of the Spirit given us? It would be impossible to prove it to an unbeliever, and even we who are gifted with faith do not always 'feel' the Spirit of God. But if we nurture our life of faith, if we recall in prayer what God has done for us . . . . (pp. 252-3).

The last part of this citation makes it appear that Schnackenburg is counselling auto-suggestion. If we keep telling ourselves that a power is operative within us we shall end up by generating the conviction that such a power is in fact at work. It thus appears that it is we who bring into existence this power — a view that cannot be reconciled with Paul's perspective.

In order to bring out what is implicit in Schnackenburg's position, let us take a concrete example. In our world it is difficult if not impossible to succeed in business without cutting corners. If dishonesty does not enter into the process of production and sale, there is a tendency to cheat on taxes. This attitude is so widespread that it is taken completely for granted. Here, then, we have a good example of what is meant by the compulsion of Sin. Such dishonesty is condoned by society and everyone happily conforms. Christians who are imbued with the spirit of the gospel immediately become aware of this pressure once they try to resist it. To be under pressure, however, is to be unfree, because 'freedom *from*' implies lack of compulsion or restraint. Yet they are told every Sunday that simply because they have been baptized they are free, and when they venture to express doubts they are merely informed that they must strengthen their faith in prayer. Is it any wonder that some become sceptical and find theology to be meaningless double-talk?

The Sinless Community

Paul's point in relating 'freedom *from*' to baptism becomes clear when we recognize that baptism is a rite of initiation. It is the solemn entrance into the community of believers. It is by focusing on this aspect that we can begin to understand how the Apostle conceived freedom from Sin.

Paul inherited from his Jewish background the idea that the eschatological community of the Messiah would be entirely free from sin. This theme first appears in the assertion of Trito-Isaiah that "all my people will be just" (60:21). What this means is clarified by Ezechiel, "I will put my spirit within you, and cause you to walk in my statutes and be careful to observe my ordinances . . . I will deliver you from all your uncleannesses" (36:27-29). The theme is taken up in the sapiential literature (e.g. "those who work with my help will not sin", Sir 24:22), but the greatest concentration of testimonies is found in the apocryphal literature which flourished at the time of Paul. Not only do we have the continuous insistence of the Essenes on the sanctity of their community (especially CD 20:2-8 and 1QS 4:20-23), but we encounter such explicit statements as:

> Then there shall be bestowed on the elect wisdom, and
> they shall all live and never again sin either through

ungodliness or through pride....And they shall not again transgress, nor shall they sin all the days of their life (*1 Henoch* 5:8-9).

In his [the Messiah's] priesthood the gentiles shall be multiplied in knowledge upon the earth, and enlightened through the grace of the Lord. And in his priesthood shall sin come to an end (*Test. Levi* 18:9).

The most striking evocation of this theme comes from a Christian author:

No one who abides in him [Christ] sins; no one who sins has either seen him or known him....No one born of God commits sin, for God's nature abides in him, and he cannot sin because he is born of God (1 Jn 3:6-9).

The influence of the theme on Paul is clearly insinuated in his presentation of the community of believers as a spiritual temple (1 Cor 3:16-17; 2 Cor 6:16), and comes to explicit voice in the exhortation, "Cleanse out the old leaven that you may be a new lump (of dough) as you are unleavened" (1 Cor 5:7). The metaphor is explained in the next verse where "the leaven of malice and evil" is contrasted with "the unleavened bread of sincerity and truth". The ideal is that the community should be completely unleavened by wickedness.

From Paul's perspective, therefore, the Christian community is an environment in which no one sins, in which all are authentic and no one is inauthentic. Sin, as we have seen, is the corroding force of a corrupt environment. As long as individuals 'belong to the world' they cannot escape the orientation of the society in which they belong. Sin was not destroyed by the death of Christ. Its power is still active in the world. Fundamentally, therefore, freedom from Sin must be a form of protection, a barrier erected around individuals to prevent the influence of Sin from reaching them. This is precisely what the Christian community provides. Those who 'belong to Christ' (1 Cor 3:23; 15:23; 2 Cor 10:7; Gal 3:29; 5:24) are 'no longer enslaved to Sin' (Rom 6:6) because they live in an environment which has an authentic orientation. The basic idea is very simple. The pressure exercised by Sin does not touch them because they do not live in the company of sinners. Only this interpretation does justice to the realism displayed in Paul's citation of the Greek proverb, "Bad company ruins good morals" (1 Cor 15:33).

Paul's point can be brought home by a very simple parable. A very poor person lived in a highly polluted industrial city. The toxic gases which permeated the entire atmosphere gave him a respiratory disease, and with every breath he drew his condition grew worse. He went to a doctor who informed him that he would certainly die unless he began to breath pure air. The man's poverty was so great that he could not afford to move out of the city, and so obedience to this wise and well-meant directive proved impossible. One day, however, a social worker came to tell him that a generous benefactor had arranged for him to go and live in the mountains. There, in the crisp pure air, he quickly recovered his health and became whole again.

The sick man is humankind, and the industrial city is the world. The polluted atmosphere is the false value-system of society. The doctor is the Law but also the Sunday preacher. The directive was good, but it did nothing more than inform humanity of the dangers of its situation under Sin, and its practical consequence was only to make humanity even more conscious of its impotence to change its situation. The social worker is Paul, and the generous benefactor is God "who has delivered us from the dominion of darkness and transferred us to the kingdom of his beloved Son, in whom we have redemption, the forgiveness of sins" (Col 1:13-14).

In this text we see clearly the contrast between two environments, one is characterized by darkness and 'death', the other by light and 'life'. In one individuals are contaminated by the 'dead', but in the other they are inspired by the 'living'. The transfer from the former to the latter is liberation. Individuals, therefore, enjoy 'freedom *from*' only to the extent that they belong to an authentic community. In this environment they are under no compulsion to be other than their true selves. No longer subject to bad example, they are inspired and encouraged by the examples of authenticity that they see all around them. They are free to be as the Creator intended them to be.

Manifestly, such freedom is not something that they possess as individuals, but something in which they share as members of a wider whole. The freedom of the individual is consequent on the authenticity of the community. The realism of Paul's concept, which is founded on a keen awareness of the conditions which obtain in the world, stigmatizes the sterility of all attempts to present Christian freedom as an internal power proper to the individual. In an authentic community the individual can *experience* freedom. He is consciously aware that he is no longer subject to the pressures that once dragged him down. The reality of this freedom, however, depends entirely on the vitality of the community which is the incarnational channel by which grace touches him. Here we rejoin Bultmann's extremely perceptive insight, "Everything indicates that by the term Spirit Paul means the eschatological existence into which the believer is placed by having appropriated the salvation deed that occurred in Christ" (*Theology of the New Testament* I, p. 335). The power of the Spirit which produces freedom is the creativity of love displayed by other members of the community. The authenticity of their being is the force which holds Sin at bay. It will be remembered to what extent Paul emphasises individualism as a sign of inauthenticity.

Children and the Community

This understanding of what freedom from Sin means for Paul throws new light on one of the most controverted passages of his epistles. The wide variety of opinions as to the exact meaning of 1 Cor 7:12-16 is due to the fact that commentators persist in trying to interpret it individualistically. What we have already seen clearly indicates that this is a false approach. Paul's understanding of salvation is rooted in his insight into the nature and function of the Christian community, and this must be taken as the presupposition of everything he says with regard to believers. If we assume that he was thinking in terms of the community in writing 1 Cor 7:12-16 many of the problems that have so bothered exegetes are seen to be false problems. The passage runs as follows:

> (12) To the rest I say, not the Lord, that if any brother has a wife who is an unbeliever, and she consents to live with him, he should not divorce her. (13) If any woman has a husband who is an unbeliever, and he consents to live with her, she should not divorce him. (14) For the unbelieving husband is sanctified by his wife, and the unbelieving wife is sanctified by her husband. Otherwise your children would be unclean, but as it is they are holy. (15) But if the unbelieving partner desires to separate, let it be so. In such a case the brother or sister is not bound. For God has called us to peace. (16) Wife, how do you know whether you will save your husband? Husband, how do you know whether you will save your wife?

It is clear that it is a question here of a case proposed to Paul for judgement by the Corinthian community (cf. 1 Cor 7:1). There appears to have been a movement in the community to break up marriages in which only one partner was a Christian. Why this should have been so is clear in the light of what Paul had taught regarding freedom. The believers created a barrier against the influence of the world by the authenticity of their common life. An unbeliever was by definition inauthentic. He or she represented the world of Sin that they had left behind. By permitting such a person to remain in close contact with the community, therefore, the believers were putting their own freedom at risk.

There was no saying of Christ which could aid Paul in finding a solution, and so he had to go ahead on his own. His first step was to make a distinction based on the quality of the relationship between the two partners. If the unbelieving partner refused to live with the convert, he agreed that the marriage should be dissolved (v. 15). Otherwise there would be a continual situation of strife, and the influence of Sin would be effectively present within the community. If, on the other hand, the believer consented to live with the convert, he refused dissolution of the marriage (vv. 12-13). His reasons for this decision constitute the kernel of the issue.

As we might have expected, Paul's basic concern is with the conversion of the unbelieving partner, "Think of it: as a wife/husband you may be the salvation of your husband/ wife" (v. 16 NEB). The believer who exhibits the wholeness of authentic humanity is an existential call to salvation. Paul's thought at this point is finely expressed by another New Testament writer who had to deal with precisely the same problem:

> Likewise you wives, be submissive to your husbands, so that some, though they do not obey the word, may be won without a word by the behaviour of their wives, when they see your reverent and chaste behaviour (1 Pt 3:1-2).

Given the minimum good-will demonstrated by the consent to live with the convert, Paul saw the unbelieving partner as drawn within the sphere of influence of the community through the contact provided by the believer. He refused to see the unbeliever as a danger to the community. Rather, he presents him or her as having been changed by the community, "The unbelieving husband/ wife is sanctified by his wife/ her husband" (v. 14).

What is meant by 'sanctified' here? The immediate context provides but one clue. The state of 'sanctification' stands somewhere between the state of 'uncleanness' and the state of 'salvation'. This in itself is curious because elsewhere in Paul 'sanctification' is identical with 'salvation'. The letter from which the text under discussion comes is addressed "To the church of God which is at Corinth, to those sanctified in Christ Jesus, to those who are saints in virtue of a call" (1 Cor 1:2), and later on he says of them, "you were washed, you were sanctified, you were justified" (1 Cor 6:11) which is an obvious allusion to baptism. The only other text in which the same verb appears speaks of Paul's apostolic ministry to present the gentiles to God as "sanctified by the Holy Spirit" (Rom 15:16).

Paul's use of the corresponding substantive is perhaps more helpful in an effort to determine his meaning here. 'Sanctification' is God's will for humanity (1 Thess 4:3), and this state implies a pattern of behaviour which is contrasted with that of those who are 'dead'. Thus, in 1 Thess 4:7 'sanctification' is opposed to 'uncleanness' which designates the behavioural attitudes of the pagans (vv. 4-5), and this idea is paralleled by Rom 6:19, "Just as you once yielded your members to uncleanness and to greater and greater iniquity, so now yield your members to righteousness for sanctification". Paul then continues, "What return did you get from the things of which your are now ashamed? The end of these things is death. But now that you have been set free from Sin and have become slaves of God, the return you get is sanctification and its end, eternal life " (Rom 6:21-22).

These passages permit us to say that 'sanctification' connotes the pattern of behaviour appropriate to authenticity which is made possible by freedom from Sin. The unbelieving partner, therefore, is sanctified by being influenced by the existential attitudes of the believing community at Corinth to which his or her partner belongs. The evidence of such santification is the way he or she behaves. All that is lacking is the express commitment to the truth revealed in Christ which 2 Thess 2:13 presents as the concommitant of 'sanctification'. When the two elements are present 'sanctification' becomes 'salvation'.

Paul's teaching in this passage clearly demonstrates to

what extent his thought moved on the level of reality. Theory was important, but it was behaviour which manifested separation from the standards of the 'world'. One point, however, remains to be elucidated. Paul's statements regarding the sanctification of the unbelieving partner are expressed in the past tense. Yet it seems unlikely that he had any personal experience of what was actually happening. He spoke with the certitude of hope. Hence, we must ask what justified this expectation, and he himself gives the answer, "Otherwise, your children would be unclean, but as it is they are holy" (1 Cor 7:14).

This verse has given rise to intense discussion. Is Paul referring to the children of the community in general or only to those of mixed marriages? Were the children baptized or unbaptized? It would be impossible to say that there is any consensus on the answers to these questions. What is essential to Paul's argument is that there be a real parallel between the situation of the children and that of the unbelieving partner. This has led some to say that the children, in consequence, must have been unbaptized. This, to me, seems likely, but we do not know at what age baptism was administered in the first century AD. We move to more solid ground when we turn to the aspect of acceptance of Christ. Children by definition are incapable of the mature adult commitment to Christ which is of the essence of faith. Thus, the question of whose children they were becomes irrelevant. All the children in the Corinthian community, therefore, were in a situation parallel to that of the unbelieving partner insofar as neither had made the decision which is the basis of authenticity. Nonetheless, the children were 'holy' and not 'unclean'.

Only one meaning is possible here. Paul is appealing to the common experience that children imbibe the attitudes of their parents. Growing up in an atmosphere of authenticity which caught them up into the lives of those who were 'in the Spirit' the children were in fact 'led by the Spirit' (Rom 8:14) in the concrete existential sense so dear to Paul. Having been born into freedom, i.e. into an environment into which the influence of Sin did not penetrate, they had never been subject to the value-system of the 'world'. In other words, they had never been enslaved to Sin and had never been touched by the 'uncleanness' which is the behaviour pattern determined by Sin. In consequence, they were 'alive'. They had never been 'dead' because, even prior to the age of adult decision, they had participated in the freedom of those who had chosen authenticity. Here, then we see a very concrete example of what is meant by the statement, "Where the Spirit of the Lord is, there is freedom" (2 Cor 3:17).

The Fragility of Freedom

Paul was sufficiently a realist to recognize that perfect freedom is an ideal situation. It is something towards which the Christian community must strive, but which may fail to be perfectly realized in the present. This was borne in on him by the experience of his own communities which were composed of adult converts. The fervour of an authentic community protects the believer from being further influenced by the social forces which Paul terms Sin, but the Apostle was forced to admit that even within a Christian community residual traces of the inauthentic mode of being may remain. This dimension of his thought comes to clearest expression in Gal 5:13-26.

What the Galatians were going through constrained Paul to concede that "the desires of the flesh are against the Spirit, and the desires of the Spirit are against the flesh, for these are opposed to each other to prevent you from doing what you would" (v. 17). 'Flesh' and 'Spirit' in this context connote the two modes of existence which Paul elsewhere characterizes as 'death' and 'life' respectively, and which we have interpreted as meaning inauthenticity and authenticity. Here he is formally concerned with the effect that these modes of being have on individuals. 'Flesh' evokes the attitudes that they absorbed during the long period when they 'belonged to the world' and were under the influence of

Sin. Such attitudes are repudiated in the act of conversion
by which they committed themselves to a different pattern
of behaviour. It is a fact of experience, however, that deep-
seated habits are not eradicated by a single contrary decision. Hence, despite their new mode of being with its thrust
towards authenticity, there remained a 'desire' for the
'works of the flesh' which are summarized in the vice-list of
vv. 19-21. This may result in their 'using freedom as an
opportunity for the flesh'. A later chapter will provide a
more appropriate occasion to determine what precisely this
means. The extent to which this 'desire' for inauthenticity is
counterbalanced by the authentic orientation of the Christian community ('the desires of the Spirit') will depend on
the degree of real commitment to Christ, and above all on
the success of the members in reducing that commitment to
practice. In Paul's own words, "If we are led by the Spirit, let
us also walk by the Spirit" (v. 25). Christians are 'called to
freedom' (v. 13), but if their conquest of the habitual attitudes derived from their past is a victory only in principle
then their freedom will also exist only in principle. The
reality of their freedom is conditional on the reality of that
victory, because "For freedom Christ has set us free. Stand
fast therefore, and do not again submit to a yoke of slavery"
(Gal 5:1). The true use of freedom — and in fact its ultimate
constituent — is to be "thorough love servants of one
another" (v. 13).

Because of the communal character of Christian freedom,
the freedom of one member of the community depends on
the creative love displayed by the others. This is the power
which holds the influence of Sin at bay. Hence, the failure of
one had significant implications for the very existence of
other members. "None of us lives to himself, and none of us
dies to himself" (Rom 14:7). The sin of one had a social
dimension; it was a sin against the community.

The Corinthians forced Paul to formally underline this
point. In order to demonstrate the freedom that Paul had
preached with such conviction one member went so far as to
set up house with his step-mother. This was "immorality of a

kind which does not exist even among pagans"(1 Cor 5:1). This uniqueness, the Corinthians felt, redounded to the glory of the community (vv. 2, 6). It was a concrete manifestation of their independence with respect to all those who were still in bondage to attitudes and conventions from which the Corinthians had been freed. Paul's reaction described the situation precisely, "Do you not know that a little leaven ferments the whole lump of dough? Cleanse out the old leaven that you may be a new lump of dough, as you (in theory) are unleavened" (1 Cor 5:6-7). The false decision taken by the offender had infected the whole group. Through him the poison of Sin had crept into a sphere designed to be immune to its influence. Paul returns to the same theme in 2 Cor 2:5, "If any one has caused pain, he has caused it, not to me, but in some measure — not to put it too severely — to you all". A different case is in view, but Paul's attitude is identical. All have lost something through the laxity of one.

In this latter instance the community apparently did take action, and the situation was restored. The Corinthians had learnt the lesson of the first episode, and it is worth while noting how Paul handled the situation because it is extremely instructive:

> As for me, absent in body but present in spirit, I as one who is present have already judged him who has done this thing in the name of the Lord Jesus. When you are assembled, I being with you in spirit, and are empowered by our Lord Jesus, such a person should be handed over to Satan for the destruction of the flesh in order that the spirit may be saved in the day of the Lord (1 Cor 5:3-5).

The most notable feature of this passage is Paul's emphasis on his spiritual presence. This is explicable only on the assumption that the community was responsible for ensuring its own freedom by eradicating elements that betrayed the presence of Sin, and the validity of this assumption is confirmed by the rhetorical question, "Did you not rather go into mourning (and show the sincerity of your grief by taking the necessary action) in order that he who had committed this deed might be removed from among you?" (v. 2). Since the community had not fulfilled its responsibility, Paul, as the founder, felt obliged to intervene. But, as we have seen (cf. above p. 117), he was aware that the imposition of authoritative precepts breeds irresponsibility because it inhibits the growth which comes only through free decisions. He had to guide without dominating. By insisting on his spiritual presence he gave himself a voice in the deliberations of the community, but he contents himself with pointing out what he considers *they* should do. The sinner should be expelled. As the fulfilment of the eschatological promises the community was supposed to be sinless. To permit the continued presence of pertinacious sinner would be to make the communty a living lie, because it could no longer afford to its members completely efficacious protection from the pressures of the 'world'. Had the Corinthians cherished their freedom sufficiently they would have been spurred to take action to protect it. Their failure on this obvious point explains the irritation betrayed by the awkward Greek of this passage.

Most significant of all, however, is Paul's understanding of what excommunication implies. It is a handing over "to Satan for the destruction of the flesh, in order that the spirit may be saved in the day of the Lord" (1 Cor 5:5). A number of exegetes find here an allusion to physical suffering and even death, but had Paul been thinking along these lines he would have expressed himself in terms similar to those found in 1 Cor 11:30. In itself the language is no stronger than that employed in Rom 6:6-7. Moreover, the contrast between 'flesh' and 'spirit' is most naturally interpreted existentially, and sound methodology demands that other avenues should be explored only if this approach should prove abortive.

By being expelled from the community the sinner is no longer protected by it. He is exposed without defense to the value-system of the 'world' and so subjected to pressures hostile to his authentic development. Here Paul uses 'Satan' to connote the same reality that he elsewhere designates as Sin. We should expect such exposure to reinforce the impulses of the 'flesh' because, as we have seen, it is only in the freedom guaranteed by the community that the 'spirit' has an opportunity to dominate the residual desires of the 'flesh'. Paul, on the contrary, claims that excommunication will lead to 'the destruction of the flesh'. This apparent contradiction, however, only serves to deepen our understanding of the way Paul conceived the Christian community. From his perspective the situation of the excommunicate was quite different from that of the unbeliever. The latter has no possibility of real choice, and so the 'spirit' cannot dominate. The excommunicate, on the contrary, had been exposed to the benefits of belonging to a community of the free whose values are the antithesis of those held in honour by the 'world'. Within the community he was assisted by the creative love of the other members. In the 'world' he would be but one isolated unit among many because this love would be withdrawn from him (1 Cor 5:11). Since creative love is an experienced reality its deprivation would be a form of physical suffering which Paul hoped would bring the sinner to his senses. He expected the excommunicate to become acutely conscious of the sudden difference in his personal situation and, in consequence, to reconsider his behaviour. To this extent, therefore, the grace of Christ incarnate in the community would continue to exercise an influence on him, making it possible for the 'spirit' to be saved. Paul does not speak of a return to the community but nothing in the context excludes this possibility.

The difference between the community and society could hardly be emphasized more graphically than by what Paul says regarding the remedial effect of expulsion. It shows that the expression of the difference in terms of light and darkness (Phil 2:15; Col 1:13) is no exaggeration. This forces us to ask the question: does the local church of today stand out from its environment in the same way? In answering this question it must be kept in mind that we are concerned, not with the theoretical stance of the local church, but with its existential stance. It is perfectly obvious that the ideology of the Christian community is different from that of the world, but this is not the issue. The question concerns the behaviour pattern of the Christian community. It deals with the local church *as it actually is,* as a visible, tangible, reality.

The importance of the question is this. If there is no perceptible difference between the local Christian community and its environment, the reality of the believers' freedom (in the Pauline sense) is brought into serious doubt. If there is any hesitation as to where precisely the community begins and the 'world' ends the solidity of the barrier which should protect the believer from the influence of Sin becomes highly suspect. I find evidence for such hesitation in the contemporary attitude towards excommunication. In practice this sanction has been abandoned. This could be interpreted as witnessing to a growth of charity within the church, and many do in fact take satisfaction and pride in the fact that the sinner is cherished rather than punished. The harshness of the past has been set aside. This benign view, however, has little to do with reality. The sanction of excommunication is no longer applied because it was seen to be ineffective. It no longer produced the existential shock which should lead to reconversion. Thus, while in theory affirming its difference from the 'world', the church in practice attests the fact that the supposedly authentic community is not significantly different from the inauthentic society in which it exists.

My point here is not to argue for greater use of the sanction of excommunication. That would be meaningless. My only concern is to raise the extremely serious question of the reality of Christian freedom in the church of today. All the evidence points to its non-existence. The value-system by which Christians really live is that of the 'world'. Within the church and outside we find the same lack of concern for the poor and underprivileged, the same desire for material possessions, the same hostilities and bitterness. There are, of course, exceptions but these are statistically insignificant. If we adopt the generic perspective of Paul, we are forced to concede that Sin reigns everywhere and, if Sin means enslavement, where then is freedom? Christians cannot take it for granted that they are free. The magnificent assertions of Paul have been reduced to the status of promises because his vision of the true nature of Christian community has been lost sight of. It is to this point, therefore, that we must now turn.

Suggested Readings

R. Bultmann, *Theology of the New Testament,* London: SCM, 1965, 38-40 (Freedom).

J. Macquarrie, *Existentialism,* New York: World Publishing, 1972, ch. 9 (Freedom).

I. de la Potterie-S. Lynonnet, *The Christian lives by the Spirit,* Alba: Staten Island, 1971, ch. 7 (Sinless Community.

J. Murphy-O'Connor, "Faith Without Works in 1 Cor 7:14," *Revue Biblique 84 (1977) 349-361.*

F. Mussner, *Theologie der Freiheit nach Paulus,* Freiburg: Herder, 1976 (cf. my review in *Revue Biblique 83 (1976) 618-623).*

G. Forkmann, *The Limits of Religious Community. Expulsion from the Religious Community within the Qumran Sect, within Rabbinic Judaism, and within Primitive Christianity,* Lund: Gleerup, 1972.

X
THE LIVING CHRIST

The most succinct expression of Paul's understanding of the nature of the Christian community is given in a passage from the epistle to the Galatians:

> In Christ Jesus you are all sons of God, through faith, because as many of you as were baptized into Christ have put on Christ. There is neither Jew nor Greek, neither slave nor free, there is neither male nor female, for you are all one man in Christ Jesus. And if you belong to Christ, then you are Abraham's offspring, heirs according to promise (3:26-29).

Paul begins by evoking the decision of faith which turns those hostile to God into his children. This decision, however, is not merely an internal orientation, but an attitude which is externalized in the form of a specific social commitment by submission to the rite of baptism. The believers are reconciled with God through faith *because* they have been baptized. Faith and baptism are two moments of a single act; neither is complete without the other. It would be a total misunderstanding of Paul to think that faith simply gave the capacity to enter into a new social relationship because this would imply that a person could have faith without this social dimension. Faith, for Paul, *is* the choice of a mode of being that is essentially social. Faith is a new way of being with others.

This was an extremely difficult concept for Paul's converts to grasp because they had come from a mode of being where their relationship with others was characterized above all by division. In Part 2 we saw the details of the Apostle's understanding of inauthentic existence which is evoked here by the list of opposed pairs, Jew against Greek, slave against free, male against female. In the new mode of being these divisions no longer exist, and it is in order to get this point across that Paul employs a variety of different expressions to evoke the communal nature of authentic existence: 'in Christ', 'putting on Christ', 'belonging to Christ', and most dramatically 'you are all *one man* in Christ Jesus'. No words could express more graphically the radical difference between the inauthentic and the authentic modes of being. If division is constitutive of the former, unity is constitutive of the latter. Note that it is a question of 'unity'. 'You are all one man' means something quite different to 'you are in fellowship'. Unless this point is clearly understood Paul's concept of community will be distorted. Hence, we shall first examine Paul's insight into the organic unity of the community of believers, and then investigate the relationship of this community to Christ.

Organic Unity

The glorification of the individual in existentialism is symptomatic of an outlook on humanity which has characterized western thought since the Renaissance. Children are encouraged to be independent and self-reliant, just as their parents consider it a virtue to be beholden to no one. The song entitled "I did it my way", which Frank Sinatra made famous, was bought by millions because it touched a deep chord. It articulated what the vast majority believe, namely, that the lack of ties and responsibilities is the key to freedom. The contemporary hero is the one who has the courage to go it alone.

This bias towards the individual is made perfectly understandable by the oppressive structures of contemporary society. There are so many rules and regulations, so many economic pressures that all feel constrained and tied down. To assert one's individuality is to break free and thereby justify the deep-seated conviction that each individual is unique.

We are all, therefore, conditioned to think individualistically, and this attitude is reinforced by the church. Theologians insist on the primacy of the individual conscience. It is widely believed that my sins are between me and God, and that I can save myself without saving others. Each one is free to construct his or her personal theology.

How much this attitude is opposed to that of Paul should be evident from what has been said in Part 2. He saw individualism as characteristic of inauthenticity, and the extent to which individualism has permeated the church only serves to confirm what was said in the last chapter regarding the non-existence of Christian freedom. There is no real barrier to Sin, and the values of the groping 'dead' are complacently accepted by the supposedly 'alive'. In order to understand what Paul is getting at, we have to make a very conscious effort to divest ourselves of this mentality. His perspective is so radically different that we need to be continuously on our guard against transposing his thought into categories acceptable to our individualistic preconditioning.

By way of introduction to the Pauline texts let us reflect for a moment on the implications of the Apostle's understanding of authenticity as founded in the notion that humankind was created in the image of God. We have seen above that the formal point of resemblance between the Creator and his human creatures lies in the creativity of the latter. This creativity is displayed in an empowering love which makes it possible for the other to be as the Creator intended. The exercise of such creativity *is* authentic existence. But such creativity necessarily involves at least one other person; it cannot be exercised in an individualistic vacuum. Hence, without the other a human creature cannot exist authentically. In order to be as God intended us to be we need to love and be loved, to empower and to be empowered. The other, in consequence, enters into the very definition of the authentic human being. One cannot be authentic and be alone. We exist as God intends only when we are related to others in the vital reciprocity of creativity. Our new being, which Paul terms 'life', is *constituted* by this interchange of power. "If I have not love, I am nothing" (1 Cor 13:2), i.e. I do not exist.

Once this perspective has been grasped it becomes startlingly clear why Paul never speaks of 'new men' but only of 'the new man'. We have noticed one instance of this already in Gal 3:28, "You are all one man in Christ Jesus". The other appears in a letter written many years later:

> You have put off the old man with its practices, and have put on the new man who is being renewed in knowledge after the image of his Creator, where there cannot be Greek and Jew, circumcised and uncircumcised, barbarian, Scythian, slave or freeman, but Christ is all in all (Col 3:9-11).

The stress on the centrality of Christ, the image of 'putting on', and the list of opposed pairs link this passage very closely with Gal 3:26-29, thus showing that this complex of ideas was a deeply rooted and consistent element in Paul's thought. In preaching on this text it is customary to interpret the allusion to 'the new man' in terms of an individual turning over a new leaf by adopting a new set of moral attitudes. This is a perfect illustration of the effect of our preconditioning to think individualistically. Because it comes most naturally to us, we assume that Paul must have thought in the same way. Nothing could be further from the truth, because the spatial particle 'where' prohibits us from interpreting 'the new man' individualistically. The 'new man' can only be a grouping *where* there is no room for religious or social differences. The unity that is constitutive of authenticity is the type of organic unity which characterizes a living human being. Authenticity excludes autonomy.

The importance of this aspect for Paul is evidenced by the consistency with which he uses organic images to explain our relationship to Christ who is the source of all authenticity. These are in striking contrast to the static images he uses to bring out the relation of the believers to God. With respect to God and the Spirit, believers are a 'building' and a 'field' (1 Cor 3:9) or a 'temple' (1 Cor 3:16; 6:19; 2 Cor 6:16). It is otherwise with respect to Christ. Believers are 'grafted into' him (Rom 6:5) or are 'rooted' in him (Col 2:7). These images are identical with the allegory of the vine in Jn 15:1-10. The dominant image, however, is that of the living human body. Believers are members of the body of Christ (1 Cor 10:17; 12:12-27; Rom 12:4-5; Col 1:18; 24; 2:18-19; 3:14-15; Eph 1:22-23; 2:13-16; 4:4, 11-16).

In elaborating this theme Paul twice evokes the parallel with the physical Body (1 Cor 12:12; Rom 12:5). How is the parallel to be understood? What did he see as the formal point of contact between the physical body and the community as the Body of Christ? Because of our orientation towards individualism we are immediately tempted to think in terms of coordination and cooperation. Just as the various parts of the physical body operate in a harmonious relationship, so too should the members of the community. If this was what Paul intended it is very difficult to see any difference between the Body of Christ and any other society because the unity is conceived only in functional terms. The actual state of the church unfortunately is highly conducive to an interpretation along these lines. The divisions between the various Chrisian communions and the bitter tensions within each heighten our awareness of multiplicity to the point where at worst we give only notional assent to unity and at best conceive it on a purely functional level.

This only goes to show how far we are from the thought of Paul, because he was so conscious of the unity of the community that he alludes to the multiplicity of its members only in subordinate clauses. "We, who are many, are one body because the bread is one, for we all partake of the one bread" (1 Cor 10:17); "We, who are many, are one body in Christ" (Rom 12:5). If, for us, the multiplicity is obvious and the unity problematic, the reverse was true of Paul. The reason for this is that he saw the Body of Christ not as a functional unity but as a unity on the level of being. It was unified by a shared life derived from a single vital principle, as he unambiguously states in his exhortation to the Colossians to hold fast to the Head "from whom the whole body, nourished and knit together through its joints and ligaments, grows with a growth that is from Christ" (2:19; cf. Eph 4:11-16). What the physical body suggested to Paul was the the idea of *coexistence* in the strict sense of that much abused term because this conveyed perfectly his understanding of authenticity.

The limbs of a human body all share a common existence because they are related as integral parts of a single whole. Their very reality as limbs is conditional on their being parts of the body. An amputated limb may look like an arm or leg, but in fact it is something radically different, because the mode of existence appropriate to an arm or leg demands vital participation in the shared life of the body. In its very essence an arm is not a whole but a part. When it is given the status of a whole, as by amputation, it is no longer what it was destined to be. It has the appearance of an arm but it can achieve nothing of what an arm was created to achieve. The animation of life has given place to the stillness of death.

The parallel between an amputated arm and an inauthentic human being hardly needs emphasis. In both the appearance belies the reality. An amputated arm cannot do anything, and an inauthentic person, as we saw, is incapable of realizing the possibility of decision-making which is the distinctive potentiality given with human nature. An amputated arm is dead, and Paul considers those outside the Body of Christ as 'dead' (2 Cor 2:16), 'severed from Christ' (Gal 5:4). Both exhibit only a travesty of life.

All that we have seen of Paul's understanding of 'life' and 'death' indicates that, when he speaks of the Christian community as a body, he intends to be understood very literally. Authentic existence is the existence of a part within a whole. The reciprocal creativity of love creates a 'life' in which the members share. They do not possess. They participate. They need each other in the same way that the arm needs the body. Without each other they cannot be themselves. This is the whole point of Paul's assertion that the body needs many members (1 Cor 12:14), and the meaning of his apparently cryptic statement that "we are one body in Christ and *members of one another*" (Rom 12:5). These striking words, which are repeated in Eph 4:25, formally underline the interdependence of the members of the Body. The wholeness of authenticity demands that we belong to one another.

Christian Individuality

Paul's stress on organic unity as constitutive of authentic existence must serve as the framework within which Christians understand their individuality. This is a crucial problem which has received no attention, because it is assumed that the concept of individuality prevalent in the 'world' is valid also for Christians. An individual is commonly conceived as an entity having an independent and separate existence. This definition is perfectly true on the biological level of physical existence. My physical existence is separate from and independent of that of anyone else. Given this obvious fact it seems logical to speak of an authentic or an inauthentic individual. No problem arises with regard to the formulation 'inauthentic individual' because, for Paul, such separatedness is precisely what characterizes inauthenticity. The situation is completely otherwise with regard to the formulation 'authentic individual' because, as we have just seen, authenticity is conditional on being a dependent, completely integrated *part*. The commonplace definition is no more applicable to a member of the Body of Christ than it is to an arm or leg. Strictly speaking it is applicable only to 'the new man' because he alone has the status of a complete entity. The true subject of authentic existence is the community to which the members belong, and that which belongs to something else as a part is not normally said to be an individual.

In great part our blindness with regard to this problem is due to a tendency to understand the Christian community in terms of secular society. From this perspective the local church appears as a collection of individuals which has a great deal in common with the local dramatic society. Most believers would be very hard pressed to define the difference between the two, and the majority would certainly lean to a definition expressed in functional terms. The church exists to do one thing, while the dramatic society exists to do something else. What has been said up to this point should indicate that the difference is in fact infinitely more radical. The dramatic society is brought into being by individuals who band themselves together for this purpose. In consequence, the individuals constitute the society. In the thought of Paul, precisely the reverse is true of the church. The Christian community preexists the members who belong to it, and it is the community which makes them what they are by empowering them to move from 'death' to 'life'. Thus, whereas individuals bring a dramatic society into being, the Christian community brings its members into being, the new being of authenticity.

The problem at issue, then, concerns the individuation of this new being, and the precise point is sharply focused in Paul's statement "It is no longer I who live, but Christ lives in me, and the life I now live in the flesh I live by faith"(Gal 2:20). Here we have the negation of the individual "I" which is the logical consequence of the organic unity of the Body to which Paul belongs, and in the very next breath that same "I" appears as subject. The tension is obvious. Paul recognizes that it is Christ who is the true subject, but at the same time the physical framework which is the underpinning of authentic existence leads him to see himself as an individual.

The tension is significantly diminished if we make a distinction between reality and the perception of that reality. An arm does not have a separate existence. It coexists with the other components of the body. Nonetheless it can be considered separately. Similarly, in the Body of Christ the members do not have separate existences, but can still be considered separately. This would seem to be the only way to make sense of Paul's very obscure formulation in 1 Cor 12:27 which can be paraphrased, "You are the Body of Christ and, considered separately, members of it". The context shows that Paul is thinking in terms of the different contribution that each member makes to the whole (1 Cor 12:7). There is a diversity within the Body, but that diversity is rooted in unity and exists to promote unity (1 Cor 14:26). The variety of spiritual gifts of which Paul often speaks in a context which emphasizes the organic unity of the Body (1 Cor 12:4-31; Rom 12:3-8; Eph 4:1-16) are but facets of love (1 Cor 13), that creative power which animates the 'new man'.

The uniqueness of the gift accorded by God to each person implies that they can be considered separately from the others. They can be treated *as if* they were separate individuals. This exposes them to the unavoidable danger of thinking of themselves *as* individuals and, in consequence, of substituting affirmation for service. Should this happen reality as perceived is confused with reality as it actually is. In Paul's framework no Christian can say 'I think, therefore I am' because this implies an individuation that is divisive. What the Christian can say is 'I exist to serve you', because here we encounter an individuation that is at once submerged in the unity of creative love. The self is sacrificed because one's whole being is directed towards the other. The Christian is individuated only as a distinctive capacity for self-giving in imitation of Christ who revealed the authentic mode of human existence by 'emptying himself" (Phil 2:7).

The New Man Is Christ

To say that Paul saw the unity of the community as primary and envisaged individuals as being changed by absorption into that unity might seem to be at best a meaningless paradox and at worst an unwarranted denigration of the role of Christ. Does it not attribute to the community a function that properly belongs to the saving Christ? Paul would answer in the negative because, for him, the community is Christ.

This appears most clearly in the statement which introduces his exposition of the Body of Christ in 1 Cor 12:12, "For just as the body is one and has many members, and all the members of the body, though many, are one body, *so also Christ*". In speaking of 'Christ' rather than of the 'Body of Christ' it cannot be claimed that Paul made an accidental slip whose importance should not be exaggerated because precisely the same idea appears earlier in the same epistle, "Do you not know that our bodies are members of Christ?" (1 Cor 6:15). The question form of this verse is highly significant because it is generally understood to denote a doctrine with which Paul felt his converts should be familiar. The application of the name 'Christ' to the community must, in consequence, be considered to have formed part of Paul's habitual vocabulary.

This directs our attention to the famous formula 'in Christ' which appears 155 times in the Pauline epistles. Here, however, we have to be careful because the formula does not always have the same value. In some cases Paul certainly has the individual person Jesus Christ in view. In this series of texts the 'in' connotes either instrumentality (e.g. "through the redemption which is in Christ Jesus whom God put forward as an expiation" Rom 3:24; cf. 1 Cor 15:22; 2 Cor 5:19; 1 Thess 2:14) or the object of the act (e.g. "faith in Christ Jesus", Gal 3:26; cf. Rom 15:17; Phil 3:3). Paul is also capable of using the formula in a very weak sense, as when he says "I speak the truth in Christ" (Rom 8:9; cf. 1 Cor 4:10). There is, however, a whole series of texts where 'in Christ' is most naturally understood as referring to the community:

> Thus do you consider yourselves also as dead to Sin, but alive to God in Christ Jesus (Rom 6:11).

> There is therefore now no condemnation for those in Christ Jesus. For the law of the spirit of life in Christ Jesus has set us free from the law of Sin and Death (Rom 8:1-2).

> Greet Prisca and Aquila my fellow-workers in Christ Jesus (Rom 16:3).

> They were in Christ before me (Rom 16:7).

> Those sanctified in Christ Jesus (1 Cor 1:2; cf. Phil:1:1; Col 1:2; Eph 1:1).

> From Him you are in Christ Jesus (1 Cor 1:30).

> (For the Jews) the veil remains unlifted because only in Christ is it taken away (2 Cor 3:14).

> If anyone is in Christ he is a new creation (2 Cor 5:17).

> In Christ Jesus neither circumcision nor uncircumcision is of any avail, but faith working through love (Gal 5:6).

This list is intended to be representative rather than exhaustive, and it is immediately evident how many of the themes previously discussed are evoked. In some cases there may be a doubt as to whether the 'in' is instrumental or local. Thus, for example, 1 Cor 1:30 could be translated as "From him you are through Christ Jesus". This rendering throws the emphasis on 'you are' and thereby highlights the aspect of new 'being' which comes to the fore in 2 Cor 5:17. But one must immediately ask how this comes about, and the answer forces us back to the community for it is there that this new being becomes possible. The same is true of 2 Cor 3:14, but the immediate context (v. 16) shows that the veil is lifted for individuals only by conversion which necessarily implies membership in the community. Rom 16:7, and other texts such as 1 Cor 3:1; 2 Cor 12:2; 1 Thess 4:16, might appear at first sight to be better translated by 'Christian', but a Christian is one who belongs to a specific type of community.

Only recognition of the fact that Paul on occasion terms the community 'Christ' enables us to make sense of the expression 'to be baptized into Christ' (Rom 6:3; Gal 3:27). It simply means to be admitted into the community through submission to the sacramental rite of initiation (cf. 1 Cor 12:13). The power of the Risen Christ is operative through this communal act enabling us to die to Sin and rise to 'newness of life' (Rom 6:4). This new life is defined in Gal 3:27 as "you have put on Christ" (cf. Rom 13:14). In itself this phrase could mean a number of things, but what Paul has in mind is clarified by the parallel expression "You have put on the new man" (Col 3:10) because, as we have seen, the 'new man' can only be the community. Christ is the new man who is the community. We must always ask, however, what this means in practice, and Paul does not fail us, because in Colossians he immediately goes on to specify what is involved by exhorting:

> Put on therefore as God's chosen ones, holy and beloved, compassion, kindness, humility, meekness, and patience, forbearing one another and, if one has a complaint against another, forgiving one another; as the Lord has forgiven you, so must you also forgive. And above all these put on love, which binds everything together in perfect harmony. And let the peace of Christ rule in your hearts, to which indeed you were called in the one body (Col 3:12-15).

In the concrete the being of the Body of the New Man is constituted by an array of *social* virtues (cf. Gal 5:22-23; 1 Cor 13:4-7) which are but facets of love. It is the creative force which binds the diversely gifted members into a complete unity. To put on 'Christ' is to put on an other-directed love, just as to be 'rooted in Christ' (Col 2:6) is to be 'rooted in love' (Eph 3:17).

It would be absurd to imagine that by predicating 'Christ' of the community Paul intended to identify the community with the historical individual Jesus Christ. In Col 1:18 he makes explicit the distinction between the Head and the Body which is implicit in previous letters. If an explanation in static terms is thereby excluded, we are forced to consider an explanation in terms of function. In this perspective the name 'Christ' could be predicated of the community if it is possible to conceive Christ and the community as performing the same identical function. Once the problem has been posed in this way it becomes easy to see how Paul's mind worked.

The community mediates Christ to the world. The word that he spoke is not heard in our contemporary world unless it is proclaimed by the community. The power that flowed forth from him in order to enable response is no longer effective unless manifested by the community. As God once acted through Christ, so he now acts (2 Cor 5:19-20) through those who are 'conformed to the image of his Son' (Rom 8:29; cf. 2 Cor 3:18) and whose behaviour-pattern is in imitation of his (1 Thess 1:6-8; 1 Cor 11:1). What Christ did in and for the world of his day through his physical presence, the community does in and for its world. The imperative which demanded that authenticity be *manifested* within the framework of history remains valid. In order to continue to exercise his salvific function the Risen Christ must be effectively represented within the context of real existence by an authenticity which is modelled on his. Only those who have put on Christ by heeding the exhortation "Let all you do be done in love" (1 Cor 16:14) can demonstrate the continuing *reality* of 'the love of God in Christ Jesus our Lord' (Rom 8:39), for it is they alone who 'hold forth the word of life' (Phil 2:16).

This Is My Body

The existential dimension of the intimate relationship between the Head who is the Risen Christ and the Body which is Christ in the world emerges clearly from Paul's treatment of the Eucharist:

> For I received from the Lord what I also delivered to you, that the Lord Jesus on the night when he was betrayed took bread, and when he had given thanks, he broke it and said, 'This is my body which is for you. Do this in remembrance of me.' In the same way also the cup, after supper, saying, 'This cup is the new covenant in my blood. Do this, as often as you drink it, in remembrance of me.' For as often as you eat this bread and drink the cup, you proclaim the death of the Lord until he comes (1 Cor 11:23-26).

The first verse of this citation contains the technical terms 'to receive' and 'to deliver' which place Paul as an intermediary in a chain of tradition. The same verbs appear apropos of the kerygmatic creed in 1 Cor 15:3, but only here does Paul explicitly designate the one from whom he received the tradition, "I received *from the Lord*". The formula in question, however, betrays characteristic signs of liturgical usage in a Greek-speaking community. In what sense, then, can Paul say that he received the Words of Institution from the Lord? For some scholars Paul simply intended to evoke Jesus as the remote origin of a tradition that he had actually received from other men. Other exegetes understand the phrase as a claim that the Words of Institution were communicated to him directly in a vision of the Risen Christ. Both of these views present obvious difficulties. If the first respects the characteristics of the institutional formula, it does violence to the words of Paul. The second, while doing justice to the Apostle's statement, ignores the liturgical colouring of the formula. A much more satisfactory solution is suggested by what we saw in the preceding section.

Christ is not only the founder of the community of believers, but in a real sense he is the community because it is through the community that the saving reality of Christ is made effective in the world. What Paul has received from the community, therefore, he has received from Christ. In itself this is a valuable clue to the perspective in which Paul here views the Eucharist.

The most significant clue, however, is the fact that Paul has added the second command to perform the rite 'in remembrance' of Jesus. He intended, therefore, to emphasize this aspect, and this raises the question of what Paul understood by 'remembrance'. Fortunately, he answers the question himself in v. 26, "For as often as you eat this bread and drink this cup you proclaim the death of the Lord until he comes". The opinion that Paul saw the broken loaf and the outpoured wine as a symbolic separation of body and blood and thus a declaration of the death of Jesus is without foundation. Hence, a number of scholars insist, at first sight justifiably, that the verb 'to proclaim' necessarily involves a verbal element and in consequence claim that the verse must be understood as an allusion to the retelling of the Passion, or at least that section concerning the Last Supper, during the celebration of the Eucharist. Nothing seems more natural than that the Passion should have been evoked on such an occasion, but were this what Paul had in mind he would surely have expressed himself otherwise. The impression given by his formulation is that the proclamation takes place through the action of eating and drinking. The action is a statement and what is 'said' is the death of Christ. The proclamation is existential (cf. 1 Thess 1:6-8; Phil 2:14-16) and, in consequence, the 'remembering' must be something more than an intellectual glance towards the past.

What Paul has in mind comes into clearer focus when we recall his understanding of the death of Christ as a lesson demonstrating how authentic humankind should live, "he died for all that those who live might live no longer for themselves" (2 Cor 5:15). Genuine remembrance is articulated in imitation. The purpose of Paul's effort to evoke remembrance of his ways in Christ among the Corinthians was that they should do likewise (1 Cor 4:16-17). If they did imitate him they would also imitate Christ (1 Cor 11:1). In remembering Christ they acknowledge the demand implicit in the death which made their new mode of being possible. By their comportment they proclaim that possibility to others. What they are is highlighted in the unity of the sacramental act, and Christ becomes a reality in the world. They incarnate the saving love expressed in his death, and will continue to exercise this function until it is rendered unnecessary by his return, 'until he comes'. This evocation of the physical presence of Christ in the eschaton reinforces the existential interpretation of the proclamation of his death. Love gave substance to the Words of Institution and only loving can continue to do so.

Thus far we have been discussing what might be termed Paul's theoretical approach to the Eucharist, i.e., what would happen if the Eucharist were celebrated in an ideal community. The real situation at Corinth was very different. The Corinthians were far from perfect, not in the sense that they had not yet attained the ideal, but in the sense that their over-confidence had led them to misunderstand the way in which the Eucharist achieves its effect. They imagined themselves to be in a definitive state of authenticity whereas in reality they were only part of a process that could be aborted. This is why Paul prefaces his exposition of the Eucharist in 1 Cor 10 by drawing a parallel between the situation of the Corinthians and that of the Israelites in the desert. Authenticity is not a privilege conferred once and for all. It is a continuing effort. The relevance of Paul's reaction to our contemporary situation where many so-called communities have no organic life can hardly be over-emphasized.

The situation at Corinth is described in explicit detail. "Firstly when you assemble for a church meeting, I hear that there are divisions among you" (1 Cor 11:18). The absence of any 'secondly' in the continuation of the text suggests that 'firstly' was intended by Paul to underline what first struck him about the Corinthian situation. That the fact of divisions should have gripped his attention is perfectly comprehensible in the light of his understanding of authenticity and inauthenticity. The divisions of which it is a question here are not the parties mentioned in 1 Cor 1:12 and 3:4 but sub-groups created by selfishness. "For in eating, each one goes ahead with his own meal, and one is hungry and another is drunk. What! Do you not have houses to eat and drink in? Or do you despise the house of God and humiliate the have-nots?" (1 Cor 11:21-22).

From this attitude Paul draws the conclusion, "When, therefore, you assemble together it is not to eat the Lord's supper" (1 Cor 11:20). In this literal translation the verse gives the impression that Paul is referring to the intention of the Corinthians. They came together, not with a view to eating the Lord's supper, but with some other purpose in mind. This interpretation is untenable because what Paul criticizes is the way the Lord's supper is celebrated. Hence, the only viable interpretation is that found in the RSV paraphrase, "When you meet together it is not the Lord's supper that you eat". No matter what the Corinthians think they are doing, they are not in fact eating the Lord's supper because their attitude towards one another precludes it. The shared being that is their new mode of existence in Christ should come to expression in the practical concern which sees that no one is in want. The selfishness of the Corinthians is the antithesis of what should be and so makes the celebration of the Eucharist impossible.

Since the transformation of bread and wine into the body and blood of Christ is what differentiates the Lord's supper from an ordinary meal, the impossibility must derive from the fact that the Words of Institution have no validity when spoken in a situation characterized by egocentric divisions. This is entirely congruent with the Apostle's existential identification of the community of believers with Christ. In theory the community is Christ, but Paul is not concerned with this speculative aspect. His function as a pastor was to ensure that the community was *in fact* Christ, truly animated by his life, fully penetrated by his spirit. As such the community could act with the power of Christ, and could speak with the authority of Christ. In an inauthentic community as Corinth was, Christ was not present. The Words of Institution were his but the voice that spoke them was not. The transforming authority was lacking and in consequence nothing happened. The Words of Institution did not effect what they signified.

It is impossible to prove apodictically that this was Paul's view, but nothing he says contradicts this interpretation which is the only one that harmonizes with his existential approach. As translated by the RSV 1 Cor 11:27 might appear to constitute an objection, "Whoever, therefore eats the bread or drinks the cup of the Lord in an unworthy manner will be guilty of profaning the body and blood of the Lord". The implication of this rendering is that the unworthy participant in the Eucharist commits a sacrilege by consuming the body and blood of Christ which are there under the sacramental species in virtue of the words alone and without reference to the attitude of the community. This interpretation, however, depends on the participle 'profaning' which does not appear in the Greek text which says simply "will be guilty of the body and blood of the Lord". This suggests a quite different explanation because 'to be guilty of the blood of someone' is most naturally understood as meaning to be responsible for the death of that person (cf. Dt 19:10). The true intention of the verse, therefore, is to range the unworthy participant among those responsible for the killing of Jesus (cf. Heb 6:6; 10:29).

Ideally the Eucharist should be a life-giving proclamation of Christ's death (1 Cor 11:26), but the attitude of the participants can make it an occasion of murder (1 Cor 11:27). Inauthenticity reached its apogee in crucifying Christ (1 Cor 2:8), and the attitude of those who destroy the unity of Christ-community by their selfishness merits the same condemnation. They are classed among those who killed Jesus because they negate the reality of Christ in the world. Instead of holding forth life they bring death. It would be difficult to find a more graphic presentation of the responsibility assumed by those who participate in the Eucharist. Paul's preoccupation with the existential attitude of the participants is further underlined by his stress on the necessity of self-examination, and the criterion to be used is formally articulated, "Anyone who eats and drinks without discerning the body eats and drinks judgement upon himself" (1 Cor 11:29).

Some take 'the body' here to mean the physical body of Christ under the sacramental species, as if the fault of the Corinthians was to have confused the Eucharist with ordinary food. There is no hint of this in the context. The concern of Paul bears on divisions within the community, and this alone would suggest that 'the body' should be understood as referring to the community as Christ's Body — a theme that had already been introduced and precisely in a context concerning the Eucharist (1 Cor 10:17). The allusion to 'judgement' confirms this interpretation because in v. 33 we read, "So then, my brethren, when you come together to eat wait for one another . . . lest you come together to judgement". Those who do not care for their fellow members do not discern the Body.

The Corinthians had given notional assent to the concept of the community as the Body of Christ, but their behaviour revealed all too clearly that they had no real grasp of the demands that it imposed. Their tolerance of jealousy and strife within the community (1 Cor 3:1-4) indicated that they had failed to appreciate just how realistically Paul intended his stress on organic unity to be understood. It is fortunate that they made this error because otherwise we would have been deprived of the increase in clarity which comes from seeing theory reduced to practice. The challenge of Paul's treatment of the Eucharist is inescapable. Unless the members of the community *actually* love one another Christ is not present in the Eucharist, and he is not present in the world. Unless they are united organically as parts within a living whole, they have not love and are nothing (1 Cor

13:2). In consequence, they can achieve nothing, not even in the liturgical prayer of the assembly.

Women In Christ

In today's church it would be highly unusual for any community to tolerate the blatant discrimination in terms of food and drink that negated the Eucharist at Corinth. There are, however, other forms of discrimination which manifest the same lack of love, and it is only love that transforms the assembly into the community that is Christ. The most widespread discrimination in the contemporary church is evident in the official attitude towards the active participation of women in the liturgy, an attitude that is endorsed by many men. None would subscribe to the vicious caricature outlined on p. 130, but the community has to examine itself as to the damage done by the perpetuation of the divisions which, for Paul, characterized unredeemed humanity (Gal 3:28). It may be the explanation of why the Eucharist produces so few fruits! Since the Apostle is often quoted in support of such discrimination, it is important to determine what his attitude towards women really was, and this brings us to that section of 1 Cor 11 immediately preceding his discussion of the Eucharist.

1 Cor 11:2-16 is normally given a title which gives the impression that Paul is here concerned only with women in the community, e.g. 'Headress of Women' (New American Bible) or 'Women's Behaviour at Services' (Jerusalem Bible). The point of his argument is presumed to be that women must wear a veil because they are inferior and subordinate to men. An honest reading of the passage reveals this to be false. Paul makes just as many statements about men, and the word 'veil' does not appear at all in the Greek text. Our first concern, therefore, must be to determine what the problem at Corinth was. Only then can we begin to understand what Paul was trying to do about it.

He criticises any man who officiates "with something

hanging down from his head" (v. 4a). This is most naturally understood as referring to long hair, an inference that is confirmed by the later statement that "if a man wears his hair long it is a dishonor to him" (v. 14). It is easy to accumulate texts from 1st cent. A.D. Greek and Roman authors to show that long hair was associated with homosexuality. They grew their hair long in order to dress it elaborately. Philo, for example, condemns "the provocative way they curl and dress their hair" (*Spec. Leg.* 3:36). The slightest exaggeration was interpreted as a sign of effeminacy; it proclaimed an ambiguous sexuality.

On the contrary, it was natural for women to have long hair (v. 15a), but Paul insists that it was given to her as 'a wrapper' (v. 15b). Roman coins and medals make the meaning of this unusual term clear, for they show women whose plaited hair was wound round the top of the head to give the appearance of a little cap. This is the 'covering' of which Paul speaks in v. 6a. In consequence, a woman who officiates 'uncovered' (v. 5b) is simply one whose hair is not done in the customary fashion. To this extent it is unfeminine. No ancient text suggests that undone hair on a woman carried the same connotation of deviancy as long hair in the case of the man. He was 'unmasculine' in a very specific sense; she is 'unfeminine' only in a very generic sense. But the association of the two induced Paul to assert, with rather heavy irony, that if the woman refuses to be 'feminine' then she might as well go the whole way and appear 'mannish' (v. 6).

What appears to have happened is that some Corinthians took Paul literally when he proclaimed that in Christ there is "no more male and female" (Gal 3:28), and the rest of the community did not object. Paul found the infantilism (cf. 1 Cor 3:1; 14:20) of this response intolerable because it projected a completely false image of the nature of the Christian community. The distinction between the sexes was being blurred in a way that could only nullify the witness value of the community. Hence, he had to argue that the distinction between the sexes was important and must be respected.

This is his sole concern in 1 Cor 11:2-16. His argument, however, is not as clear as one would wish, because he experienced the embarrassment that many feel when dealing with homosexuality, but the key points are easily detected once one knows what the problem was. In the first place, it is obvious that he does not intend to prove that woman is subordinate to man; that would in no way serve his purpose. In fact, he explicitly repudiates this interpretation of woman's role based on Gen 2:18-23 and which was current in Judaism. According to the Jewish historian Josephus, "The woman, says the Law, is in all things inferior to the man. Let her accordingly be submissive, not for her humiliation but that she may be directed, for authority has been given by God to the man" (*Against Appion* 2:201). If man was the source of woman's being (v. 3b), woman is now the source of man's being, and this was just as much God's will (v. 12). Thus, "In the Lord, i.e. Christ, woman is not otherwise than man, nor man otherwise than woman" (v. 11); in terms of roles within the church both stand on the same footing. In this perspective the point of vv. 7-9 must be that, if God had intended no distinction between the sexes he would have created them in the same way. However, since Gen 2:18-23 reveals a difference in the mode of creation, then the distinction was willed by God and must, in consequence, be respected.

Only this approach permits us to grasp the meaning of the enigmatic v. 10, "The woman ought to have authority on her head because of the angels." Paul's presupposition in this whole discussion is that women can exercise a leadership role in the liturgical assembly (v. 4). She, therefore, has an authority that was denied to her in the Jewish interpretation of the Law. The angels who acted as mediators in the giving of the Law (Gal 3:19) observed what was going on in the world (1 Cor 4:9) and reported on breaches of the Law (*Jubilees* 4:6; cf. *1 Enoch* 99:3). As members of God's court they had been made aware of the change in the status of women, but they might be perturbed if they saw this new authority was exercised by a being of indeterminate sex. It was given to woman precisely as woman and in its exercise she must proclaim her womanhood by the way she does her hair; it is in this respect that her hair-do symbolizes here authority to pray and prophesy. It should be noted that the equality of women in terms of church authority was so evident to Paul and the Corinthians that it could serve as the *basis* of an argument for the distinction of the sexes! What Paul means by 'prophecy' is clear from 1 Cor 14. "The one prophesying speaks to men with a view to edification, encouragement, and consolation (v. 3). It is "a sign for believers" (v. 22), so that "all may learn and be encouraged" (v. 31). It is, therefore, a ministry of the word and, given the way the term was used in Paul's time, it concerned the exposition of the Scriptures. It would be impossible to justify a distinction between prophecy in this sense and our contemporary liturgical homily. In other words, Paul is asserting that women have a God-given authority to preach in the liturgical assembly. Much less evidence is available regarding the nature of 'prayer' but the social context established by what has been said about 'prophecy' clearly indicates that the reference is to the inspired prayer which crystalized the faith of the community and to which public assent was given by the Amen of the assembly (1 Cor 14:16; 2 Cor 1:20). Some of the New Testament hymns (Phil 2:6-11; Col 1:15-20; 1 Tim 3:16) may be typical of such prayer (cf. Col 3:16).

In practice, therefore, Paul was entirely faithful to the theory enunciated in Gal 3:28. Just because he had problems with the way some did their hair, he could not deny woman's rights. On the contrary, he explicitly defends them. This gives a new and much more profound dimension to the equality of women implicit in their contribution to the establishment of the Pauline communities. No distinction is made between Euodia or Syntyche and Clement as Paul's 'fellow-workers' (Phil 4:2-3; cf. 1:5), and there is no justification for postulating different roles for Gaius (Rom 16:23) and Nympha (Col 4:15) in the direction of their respective house-churches.

Unfortunately, Paul's wise insight into the practical import of the love commandment (1 Cor 13:1-7) did not prevail. After he disappeared from the scene reactionary tendencies quickly asserted themselves. Both 1 Cor 14:34-35 and 1 Tim 2:11-15 — neither of which was written by Paul — reduce the role of women to the passive one they enjoyed under the Law. This surrender to the demands of a culture whose standards are condemned by the gospel has had serious consequences for the unity of the Body of Christ; there is reason to doubt the reality of the love which binds all together in perfect harmony (Col 3:14). Where does this leave the church in terms of 1 Cor 13:2?

Suggested Readings

E. Best, *One Body in Christ,* London: SPCK, 1955.

R.H. Gundry, *Soma in Biblical Theology with Emphasis on Pauline Anthropology,* Cambridge: CUP, 1976.

E. Schweizer, *The Church as Body of Christ,* London: SPCK, 1965.

B. M. Ahern, "The Christian's Union with the Body of Christ in Corinthians, Galatians, and Romans," *Catholic Biblical Quarterly* 23 (1961) 199-209.

G. Panikulam, *Koinonia in the New Testament,* Rome: Biblical Institute, 1979.

V. P. Furnish, *The Love-Commandment in the New Testament,* Nashville: Abingdon, 1972.

R. Banks, *Paul's Idea of Community,* Exeter: Paternoster, 1980.

E.A. Judge, *The Social Pattern of Christian Groups in the First Century,* London: Tyndale, 1960.

M.N. Tod, "Clubs and Societies in the Greek World," in *Sidelights on Greek History,* London: OUP, 1932, 71-96.

F.V. Filson, "The Significance of Early Church Houses," *Journal of Biblical Literature* 58 (1939) 105-112.

J.M. Peterson, "House-Churches in Rome," *Vigiliae Christianae* 23 (1969) 264-272.

A.J. Malherbe, "House Churches and Their Problems," in his *Social Aspects of Early Christianity,* Baton Rouge: Louisiana State University Press, 1977.

J. Koenig, *Charismata: God's Gifts for God's People,* Philadelphia: Westminster, 1978.

J.D.G. Dunn, *Jesus and the Spirit,* London: SCM, 1975.

E. Käsemann, "The Cry for Liberty in the Worship of the Church," in his *Perspectives on Paul,* London: SCM, 1971, 122-137.

J. Murphy-O'Connor, "Eucharist and Community in First Corinthians," *Worship* 50 (1976) 370-385; 51 (1977) 56-69.

————, "Sex and Logic in 1 Corinthians 11:2-16," *Catholic Biblical Quarterly* 42 (1980) 482-500.

XI
THE MIND OF CHRIST

From Paul's point of view, as we have seen, authenticity
begins with the choice of a highly specific mode of being.
The believers by faith commit themselves to a form of
existence that is essentially social. They thereby assume
responsibility for the very being of others in the community
and also for the transformation of the world. The exercise of
this responsibility necessarily involves other decisions. This
brings us into the area of moral judgements which is the
most critical issue in Paul's understanding of the nature of
the Christian community. How can a multiplicity of decisions corresponding to the number of members be related to
the organic unity of the Body? We are concerned here with
the use of freedom on the part of those who experience
'freedom from'.

No Binding Precepts

There is one obvious way of ensuring that the practice of
the members reflects the unity of the Body to which they
belong, namely, tight regulation of their acts by means of
binding legislation. This solution was unacceptable to Paul
for the reasons that have been outlined in ch. 6. For Christians to give full obedience to a new law would place them in

the position of the Jews whose exaggerated respect for the Mosaic law condemned them to inauthenticity. All that legislation can achieve is uniformity of action. It is incapable of bringing about the gift of self which is the very essence of unity. Paul's teaching does not merely contain the seeds of antinomianism, as some have maintained, it is fundamentally and radically antinomian. This point has been most clearly and accurately stated by John Knox:

> But, it may be asked, is Paul's rejection of the law as binding on the believer so radical as this? Is not the 'law' he rejects simply an external code, a list of thou shalts and thou shalt nots, in particular the code of Judaism? Whatever may seem to be implied in some of his practical teaching, I feel sure that in his 'theory' of the Christian life Paul went much further than this. Although undoubtedly he is frequently referring to the Jewish law, one cannot deny the presence —often, if not always — of a more radical, more inclusive, reference . . . Law, as such, is no longer valid for the Christian. (*The Ethic of Jesus in the Teaching of the Church,* London, 1962, pp. 98-99).

This view is highly disconcerting for anyone brought up in a traditional Christian environment where the Commandments played a major role, and it is not surprising that there should have been reactions to it. In an article entitled "Obligation in the Ethic of Paul" which appeared in the Festschrift offered to John Knox (Cambridge, 1967, pp. 392-393), C.F.D. Moule attempts to show that Paul used the term law with two distinct connotations which he terms 'revelatory' and 'legalistic', and he maintains that the Apostle was not concerned with the Law in itself but with two attitudes towards law. One is the recognition of law as the revelation of God's will and purpose, and the other is the attempt to use the law to establish one's own righteousness. The Christian, he argues, must submit to the demands of law as the revelation of God's will while rejecting any temptation to place it at the service of selfish ambition.

This distinction is meaningless in existential terms. When viewed as excerpts of the divine will moral directives can only be understood as absolutely binding, and this makes a legalistic attitude inevitable. There is no choice but to submit, and the believer's whole attention will focus on satisfying specific obligations. It is precisely when law is understood as revelatory that we get the situation that Paul condemns so radically in Rom 2:17-20 (cf. p. 116 above).

This generic argument is confirmed by a survey of those passages in which Paul mentions the will of God in an ethical context. The specific object of the will of God is the authentic being (1 Thess 4:3) to which humankind is summoned by the 'call' (1 Thess 4:7). Within the global context established by the obedience of faith (Rom 1:5) the believers are expected to work out the specific demands of the will of God for themselves (Col 1:9; 4:12), and this comes about as the fruit of an internal transformation (Rom 12:2) which is but an aspect of the gift of self (2 Cor 8:3-5). Moral imperatives are twice juxtaposed to references to the divine will (1 Thess 4:3; Rom 12:2), but nowhere is there the slightest hint that the two are to be identified. Correspondingly, Paul never speaks of obedience to a specific law or precept. In the epistles obedience is always a synonym for faith (Rom 6:16; 10:17; 15:18; 16:26; 2 Cor 10:5; 2 Thess 1:8) i.e., acceptance of the mode of existence demonstrated by Christ (Rom 5:19; Phil 2:8).

Paul's refusal to blindly acquiesce in any authoritative directive was a principle by which he actually lived. His practice makes certain what we have deduced to be his theoretical position. Given the central position that Christ has in Paul's theology, one can assume that if any directive carried binding authority it would be a command of the Lord. This highlights the importance of the way in which the Apostle reacted to the two commands of the Lord that he quotes. The first concerns the attitude of preachers. "The Lord commanded those who proclaim the gospel to get their living by the gospel" (1 Cor 9:14). In other words, the ministers of the gospel were to devote their entire attention to their task and were not to waste time earning their own living, Paul refused to recognize this command as an 'obligation' and reclassified it as a 'right' (1 Cor 9:12, 18) which he took pride in not using (1 Cor 9:15). He made a practice of earning his own living, thus flatly disobeying the dominical precept. He felt that to receive financial support would obscure the fact that he preached out of sheer conviction (1 Cor 9:16). Here, from another point of view, we again encounter the existential aspect of the apostolate to which Paul attached such importance. The second directive concerned divorce. This was forbidden in the form of a negative precept which permits of no exceptions (1 Cor 7:10-11), but once Paul saw a case which justified making an exception he permitted divorce (1 Cor 7:15).

In the two instances where Paul was confronted with dominical precepts he did not treat them as having binding force but submitted them to critical evaluation. When he found it appropriate he accepted them (cf. Phil 4:14-20; 1 Cor 7:11a), and when he found them inappropriate he simply set them aside. He was consistently faithful to the advice he gave the Thessalonians, "Test *everything*" (1 Thess 5:21).

The Function Of Moral Directives

If Paul refused to consider the directives of the Law and of Jesus as precepts it is hardly logical to imagine that he intended his own directives to impose a binding obligation. Hence, we need to discover what value he attached to them. Furthermore, since many of his converts were formed in an attitude towards law which the Apostle repudiated as characteristic of inauthenticity, we need to determine why he took the risk of giving such directives.

The simplest way to answer these questions is to look at the typical list of directives that Paul gave in his earliest letter:

(1) Finally, brethren, we beseech and exhort you in the Lord Jesus, that as you learned from us how you ought to love and to please God, just as you are doing, you do so more and more. (2) For you know what counsels we gave you through the Lord Jesus. (3) For this is the will of God, your sanctification: that you abstain from immorality; (4) that each one of you know how to possess his own body in holiness and honour, (5) not in the passion of desire like the pagans who know not God; (6) that no one overreach and defraud his brother in the matter, because the Lord is an avenger in all these things, as we solemnly forewarned you. (7) For God has not called us for uncleanness but in sanctification. (8) Therefore whoever disregards this disregards not man but God, who gives his Holy Spirit to you. (9) But concerning love of the brethren you have no need to have anyone write to you, for you yourselves have been taught by God to love one another, (10) and indeed you do love all the brethren throughout Macedonia. But we exhort you, brethren, to do so more and more; (11) to aspire to live quietly, to mind your own affairs, and to work with your hands as we counseled you; (12) so that you may command the respect of outsiders and have need of nothing (1 Thess 4:1-12).

This list contains both negative and positive directives which must be examined in some detail in order to ensure that their implications are correctly understood:

v. 3: It is difficult to determine the precise meaning of 'immorality' (*porneia*). In ordinary Greek usage it meant commerical and/or cultic prostitution. In biblical usage the span of meaning is much wider for it includes incest, adultery, homosexuality, bestiality, idolatry, and in general anything that was forbidden by the Law. 'Immorality', therefore, is a generic term describing a self-centered existence which disregards the rights of the Creator or of others, or which uses others as instruments for its own gratification It is not surprising, in consequence, that it is a constant element (together with its correlative 'uncleanness', v. 7) in the vice-lists that Paul uses to catalogue the characteristics of inauthentic existence.

vv. 4-5: Here we find an explicit contrast between the existence of believers and that of non-believers. The latter are dominated by 'the passion of desire'. 'Desire' here renders the Greek term that we have elsewhere translated by 'covetousness' (cf. p. 109 above). It can have a sexual connotation, but of itself it is not limited to this area of behaviour. In Paul's lexicon it evokes the fundamentally selfish desires which are fostered by the pressures of Sin to which the inauthentic are enslaved. Through their incorporation into the community the believers are freed of this pressure, but in order to give reality to this freedom they have to acquire mastery over the instincts of their bodies. On account of their long domination by forces outside themselves, they have to learn the '*self*-control' (Gal 5:23) which is the antithesis of self-gratification.

v. 6: It is impossible to determine with any certitude what exactly 'in the matter' means. What is clear, however, is that it involves an injury done to a fellow-member of the community. This is excluded because it is incompatible with the empowering love that each one owes the other.

v. 9: 'Brotherly love' is the constituent factor of authentic existence, and regarding this essential feature of their lives Paul says that the Thessalonians have been 'taught by God'. Various interpretations of this phrase have been proposed. Some see a reference to the inspired discourses of Christian prophets in the liturgical assemblies, while others find an allusion to the preaching of the kerygma or a knowledge of the words of Jesus. Had Paul any of these possibilities in mind he would surely have expressed himself differently. The term 'taught by God' occurs only here in the Pauline writings, and the closest analogy is to be found in 1 Cor 2:13 where Paul claims that he speaks "in words taught by the Spirit". His meaning there is clarified by the previous verse, "We have received not the spirit of the world, but the Spirit which is from God that we might understand the gifts bestowed on us by God". Just as one type of knowledge is given with inauthentic existence ('the world'), so another is given with authentic existence ('the Spirit'). Fallen humanity instinctively adopts the structures of that mode of being. The new being in Christ is due to God's initiative and in consequence the instinctive knowledge given with it must be attributed to him. To anyone who has accepted Christ the primordial importance of loving is inescapable. Authentic existence is inconceivable without the recognition of the other as a 'brother'. Paul's concern is to bring to full consciousness what is already there and in particular to highlight the practical dimension.

vv. 10-11: Both the structure of the phrase and the form of this paragraph reveal that Paul is not talking about something distinct from brotherly love. It is a question of drawing out some of its virtualities. Since 1 Thess 3:10 probably belongs to another letter, I find no compelling reason to relate these admonitions to a specific situation at Thessalonica. Conversion can be a heady and distracting experience, and Paul's intention is to counteract a natural tendency to exaggeration by counsels of prudence and moderation. Religious enthusiasm deriving from conversion is fundamentally selfish because the experience is unique to the individual. As such it is opposed to the shared existence which is supposed to be the believer's mode of being. To be quiet, to mind one's own business, and to work are not necessarily expressions of brotherly love. Paul's concern is to get new converts into the frame of mind where love for each other could manifest itself.

Two important conclusions emerge from this analysis of 1 Thess 4:3-12. First, no attempt is made to cover all the possibilities. All that is provided is a series of very generic pointers. Second, all the injunctions are related to Paul's understanding of the two modes of being open to humanity. He warns against behaviour which betrays the egotism of covetousness, and against the nosiness and idleness which are notoriously disruptive of community life. He encourages the self-control which is indispensable in interpersonal relations, and advocates attitudes which permit genuine concern for others. In other words, his directives are essentially *educative*. They are designed to orient those who have moved from the egocentric mode of existence of the 'world' to the other-directed mode of being in 'Christ'. The change was so radical that the converts needed guidance in working out a pattern of behaviour appropriate to their new state.

The text also makes it clear that these directives were given by Paul as part of his oral preaching (1 Thess 4:1-2), and this remains true if, as seems probable, 1 Thess 2:11-12 was the original introduction to the list. That this was his habitual practice is attested by 2 Thess 3:10 and Gal 5:21. These texts highlight the absurdity of the claim that Paul issued moral directives only when trouble developed in his communities or only when he was confronted with the problems posed by the delay of the Parousia. Nowhere is his sense of the imminence of the eschaton more evident than in his letter to Thessalonica. His common sense indicated that new converts would be at sea for a while in their efforts to give practical expression to the ideal they had accepted, and his concern displayed itself in a series of generic guidelines which he hoped would enable them to find their feet as soon as possible. This was imperative even if Christ was to return after an interval of only weeks or months.

The situation thus produced was very delicate. The guidelines could not function as Paul intended unless they were taken seriously, and this is why he repeats them, even though he is assured that the Thessalonians are not doing otherwise (1 Thess 4:1, 10). Yet, if they were taken too seriously and given the status of binding precepts, growth in authenticity would be completely frustrated. The risk, however, has to be taken because realistic concern could dictate no other course.

Precisely because Paul's position was so subtle it was wide open to misunderstanding, and the two possible reactions are exemplified by the Galatians and the Corinthians. The former experienced the sense of insecurity that Paul expected, but it gripped them with an intensity that he had not anticipated. His directives illuminated certain areas of behaviour, but left much to their own judgement. Since their mentality was that of those who aspire to qualify rather than to excel, they wanted to be completely sure and so elevated his guidelines to the status of binding obligations. Nothing else can explain the welcome they accorded to the Judaizers who arrived with the 613 precepts of the Law. This array of commandments filled in all the dark areas which Paul had deliberately left blank in order that they might exercise their own initiative in determining the behaviour befitting a member of Christ. Hence, the tremendous insistence on 'freedom' that we find in Galatians. Paul is categorical in his insistence that they accept the responsibility of freedom because otherwise his labours on their behalf will have been in vain (Gal 4:11). Hence, in this letter his major concern is to show that the believers now exist in a different way, and that submission to binding laws is a thing of the past. His efforts are directed towards correcting a fundamental attitude which compromised all that has been achieved.

The Corinthian Error

The situation at Corinth was diametrically opposed to that which obtained in Galatia. The insecurity of the Galatians was totally absent among the Corinthians. With exuberant over-confidence they eagerly grasped at the responsibility of making decisions for themselves. Since this was fundamentally what Paul wanted, his tone in the Corinthian correspondence is quite different to that in the letter to the Galatians. In the latter we encounter the brusque exasperation occasioned by an error on a basic issue. It enshrines the simple message: You are now different. You are no longer enslaved to Sin and the Law. Hence you must act in freedom. The Corinthians, on the other hand, were right in theory but wrong in practice and, in consequence, Paul's approach is much more reasoned. He goes to great pains to show them in detail why certain decisions were incompatible with the shared existence to which they had committed themselves.

The basis of the Corinthian approach was their acceptance of Paul's teaching that they had been freed from Sin. This freedom is absolute. In an authentic community the believers are no longer in bondage to a false value-system. They are under no restraint which holds them back from fidelity to their true selves. The Corinthians, however, transferred this absolute character to 'freedom *to*' (cf. p. 154 above) and believed themselves to be free to do exactly what they liked, as their slogan "All things are lawful to me" (1 Cor 6:12; 10:23) proclaimed. They applied this principle in at least two domains, the use of their sexual power and the use of their reason in moral matters. Because two fundamental drives are involved Paul argues these cases very fully in order to show the Corinthians that 'freedom *to*' is not unlimited, and that if it is pushed too far the result is the loss of 'freedom *from*'. He clearly conveys that freedom is rooted in unity, and that once unity is broken freedom vanishes.

In the first case the Corinthians made a wrong choice in deciding that it was permissible for a Christian to sleep with a prostitute (1 Cor 6:12-20). It would be much easier to follow Paul's discussion if we knew exactly what arguments the Corinthians used to support this conclusion. As it is we have to deduce their position from what he says, and this inevitably introduces an element of incertitude. It would appear, however, that the Corinthians made a sharp distinction between the body and the spirit, and maintained that as long as their spirits were united to the Lord their bodies could follow their natural inclinations. Hence, just as the body could satisfy its need for food and drink casually, it could equally satisfy its desire for sexual relations (v. 13). In their view, carnal union with a prostitute stood in an entirely neutral relationship to spiritual union with the Lord.

In response Paul argues that the proposed dichotomy between body and spirit is untenable. The body is an integral part of the human person, and this is proved by the fact that it will be raised from the dead (v. 14). More significantly the bodies of Christians constitute the physical dimension of Christ's presence in the world (v. 15). It is through the activity of the body that the commitment of the spirit acquires reality and effectiveness (v. 20b). Though body and spirit differ they belong together in the service of Christ. The function of the body is precisely to serve as the concrete manifestation of the creative love to which the spiritual commitment of faith binds the person. Hence, the physical union effected by intercourse is designed to express the empowering love which binds the two persons into authentic unity (v. 16b). Coitus with a prostitute, then, is wrong because this commitment to the other as a person is excluded (v. 15). The very being of the Christian is to give, but in casual fornication he only takes. The other person is used, and thereby given the status of a 'thing', for selfish gratification.

By thus committing themselves to a form of behaviour which corresponds to the egocentricity of the world (cf. 1 Cor 6:9-10) the Corinthians are in proximate danger of once again becoming enslaved to Sin. Hence, Paul attaches two riders to the Corinthian slogan, "Not all things are for the best" and "I will not be enslaved by anything" (1 Cor 6:12). Certain actions are not for the best because of their very nature they imply a return to inauthenticity. As members of Christ the Corinthians must existentially affirm the truth "You are not our own" (1 Cor 6:19b) if they are to safeguard their freedom. An exclusively intellectual commitment to unity is meaningless.

This latter point comes into even clearer focus in the second case because in this instance the Corinthians made a theoretically correct decision (1 Cor 8:1-13; 10:23-30). The point at issue was: Could Christians buy and eat meat which had once formed part of pagan sacrifices? Some members of the community answered in the affirmative, basing themselves on such speculative truths as 'An idol has no real existence', 'There is no God but one' (1 Cor 8:4), and 'The earth is the Lord's and everything in it' (1 Cor 10:26). Paul finds no fault with them for their initiative in making a rather

delicate moral judgement. They had accepted the responsibility of their freedom. Nor does he find himself in disagreement with their solution. Food is morally neutral (1 Cor 8:8)
and so Christians can consume whatever they find in the
meat market (1 Cor 10:25) or whatever is offered to them in
the homes of unbelievers (1 Cor 10:27). This is true, however, only in theory, and the nature of the Christian community demands that one other factor be taken into account
before such theory can be legitimately translated into
practice:

> Take care lest your use of your freedom become a stum-
> bling block to the weak. For if any one sees you, a man of
> knowledge, at table in an idol's temple, might he not be
> encouraged, if his conscience is weak to eat food offered
> to idols? And so by your knowledge this weak man is
> destroyed, the brother for whom Christ died (1 Cor 8:9-
> 11).

The situation that Paul envisages is clearly indicated.
There may be some in the community who because of their
previous conditioning are not convinced by the theoretical
arguments, but who are drawn into eating such meat
because they cannot resist the authority of the stronger
minded members. They are subjected to a pressure to do
something they feel to be wrong, to act in violation of their
own convictions. From Paul's point of view the fact that the
perspective of the weak is objectively erroneous is totally
irrelevant. Their right, because of the nature of the community, is to be empowered, not to be destroyed. Hence, the
primary factor in a Christian moral decision must be the
probable effect *on others* of the action envisaged. An action
that is theoretically appropriate to the Christian's new being
can be wrong in practice if it causes hurt to others.

Paul was fully aware of the ability of self-love to give itself
a veneer of respectability by means of speculative principles.
"Knowledge puffs up but love builds up" (1 Cor 8:1). Speculative reasoning can engender a feeling of pride and self-

confidence which gives believers a sense of independence. If its importance is exaggerated it is totally destructive of the unity of the community. Those who feel that they can stand alone on principle indicate that they do not really need others, and thus they deny the very basis of their authentic existence in Christ. An authentic moral decision is one which intensifies the unity of the community. "Let no one seek his own good but the good of the other" (1 Cor 10:24). A choice cannot be good for a Christian unless it is also good for the others in the community to which he belongs. The touchstone of moral truth is the edification of the community (1 Cor 10:23).

Renewal of the Mind

We are now in a position where we can begin to perceive that, although Paul refuses the validity of any binding law for a Christian community, his moral teaching is not a pure situation ethic. Current presentations of situation ethics (e.g. J. Fletcher) conceive the moral subject as an individual confronted with a unique situation. To the extent that he saw the demand of God manifested through the needs of others in a concrete situation, Paul was a situationist, but he refused to admit that the individual could be an adequate moral subject. The logic of his understanding of the nature of Christian community could not permit him to do otherwise. The very being of believers was that of parts within a whole. As members of the Body they only participated in the life of an organic unity. The could not, in consequence, be totally independent in their moral judgements. If the unity of the community was to be a fact and not a dream the moral judgement of the Christian could only be a participation in, and reflection of, the moral judgement of the community. For Paul, therefore, the community was the true moral subject. This appears with particular clarity in two passages.

The most formal and explicit occurs in Colossians:

> You have put on the new man who is being renewed in
> knowledge after the image of his creator (3:10).

The last phrase clearly indicates that Paul has the Genesis
narrative in mind, and in particular the words of the serpent
to Eve, "God knows that when you eat of it, you will be like
God, knowing good and evil" (Gen 3:5). Humanity was
created in the image of God but fell through seeking moral
knowledge in a manner contrary to the will of God. As a
result its moral sense was stultified. For the Jews this defect
was remedied somewhat by the gift of the Law, so that its
effects were fully evident only in the gentiles, as the oldest
commentary on this verse affirms, "You must no longer live
as the gentiles do, in the futility of their minds. They are
darkened in their understanding, alienated from the life of
God because of the ignorance that is in them" (Eph 4:17-18).
Recreated in Christ (2 Cor 5:17; Gal 6:15), who is the image
of God (Col 1:15), the new man recovers his capacity for
moral judgement. As we have seen, however, this new man
is not the individual believer, but the Christian community
(cf. p. 183 above).

The contrast between the 'old man' and the 'new man',
and the emphasis on the progressive quality of moral knowledge ('is *being* renewed'), link Col 3:10 very closely with the
second text:

> Do not permit yourselves to be conformed to this Age,
> but permit yourselves to be transformed by the renewing
> of the mind, so that you may judge the will of God, the
> good and acceptable and perfect (Rom 12:2).

The contrast here is between 'this Age', which is a Pauline
synonym for the 'world', and the Body of Christ (cf. Rom
12:5). What Paul has in mind emerges very clearly if we take
into account Rom 1:18-32, a passage which exhibits striking
parallels in both vocabulary and concern with Rom 12:1-2.
As a consequence of their rejection of the demand of God
implicit in their creaturehood, the pagans "became futile in

their reasonings and their undiscerning heart was darkened"
(Rom 1:21). The same idea appears a little later, but this
time expressed in a semitic mode which abstracts from the
distinction between primary and secondary causes, "God
gave them up to a debased mind to do unfitting things"
(Rom 1:28). The parallel between 'heart' and 'mind' indicates that Paul is thinking of the rational faculty, not in
isolation, but precisely insofar as it gives an orientation to
the entire personality. In this type of context, therefore,
both are best translated by 'mentality' in view of the subtle
fusion of the collective and the individual. 'Heart' is a collective in v. 21 but the individual comes to the fore with the use
of the plural in v. 24, "God gave them up to the desires of
their hearts". Similarly 'mind' is a collective in v. 28, but the
plural 'reasoning' appears in v. 21. This is perfectly comprehensible in the light of what we have seen regarding the
relation of inauthentic creatures to the 'world' (cf. ch. 4
above). They are dominated by its corporate orientation
which they reinforce by their conformity. The 'debased
mind', therefore, is the 'mentality' of the world which all
unconsciously assimilate and reveal in their individual 'reasonings' (cf. Eph 4:17-19).

If the 'debased mind' is the mentality which dominates the
inauthentic mode of being, the 'being renewed mind' (Rom
12:2; Eph 4:23) is the mentality of its antithesis, namely, the
community which is the Body of Christ. In Paul's own
words it is "the mind of Christ" (1 Cor 2:16). The use of the
collective is made imperative by the organic unity of the
community. The 'mind of Christ' is a perspective proper to
the New Man of whom individuals are only members.

What this means can be defined a little more precisely if
we turn for a moment to the only other passage in which
Paul evokes the idea of 'transformation':

> And we all with unveiled face, reflecting as in a mirror the
> glory of the Lord, are being transformed into the same
> image from glory to glory (2 Cor 3:18).

As in Rom 12:2 the passive 'being transformed' shows that the believers are not the primary agents of their own transformation. God acts in and through the saving community. By its openness to Christ, the community is transformed into his image. Note the same combination as in Rom 12:2 of plural verbs and the key substantive ('mind' — 'image') in the singular. As the community deepens its commitment to the ideal, the existential attitude of Christ (cf. Phil 2:5) becomes progressively more manifest, primarily in the community and as a derivative in the individuals who constitute it. To the extent that the community exemplifies the authentic humanity manifested by Christ, it judges from the standpoint of Christ. It is in this sense that it can be said to possess 'the mind of Christ'. This possession, however, is not a static once-for-all achievement, but an on-going process which harmonizes with the growth of the Body (Col 2:19; Eph 4:13).

Only in this perspective does it become possible to understand how Paul can define 'the will of God', which is the object of the corporate mind's activity as 'the good and acceptable and perfect' (Rom 12:2). Commentators commonly assume that the unexpressed point of reference is God both because 'acceptable to God' appears in the previous verse and because 'acceptable' elsewhere in Paul is always used in conjunction with 'to God' (Rom 14:18; Phil 4:18) or 'to the Lord' (2 Cor 5:9; Col 3:20). Surely this argument must work the other way. If Paul habitually inserts the point of reference, its omission here must be deliberate and therefore significant. The three substantivized adjectives 'good, acceptable, perfect' stand in apposition to 'the will of God', and so are directly related to the 'judging' or more accurately 'testing' of the mind. What Paul means, then, is that whatever the corporate mind tests and finds to be 'good, acceptable and perfect' is in fact the will of God. This has been perceptively noted by C.H. Dodd in his commentary on this verse:

> The will of God for man is not some mysterious and
> irrational form of holiness . . . It consists of that kind of
> life which the renewed mind of the Christian man can see
> to be good in itself, satisfying, and complete.

He is not entirely accurate, however, in suggesting that
this mind is the possession of the individual believer
because, as Paul insists, "we are one Body in Christ and
individually members of one another" (Rom 12:5). The
moral estimate of the community is uppermost in the Apostle's intention, and this acts as a check on the judgements of
individual believers who possess the 'mind of Christ' only to
the extent that their being is truly rooted 'in Christ'. They
are directed by 'the Spirit of Christ' only insofar as they
'belong to him' (Rom 8:9).

The perspective that we have been developing is one of
those ideas which, while very clear in theory, seem to evapo-
rate when one tries to reduce them to a practical level. It is
very clear that Paul does not have in mind an explicit moral
consensus to which all must subscribe because that would be
equivalent to another law. How he would conceive it posi-
tively is another matter, and here he gives us only one clue:

> It is my prayer that your love may abound more and more
> in knowledge and all discernment so that you may judge
> the things that really matter (Phil 1:9-10).

The formulation of this prayer is immediately evocative of
Rom 2:17-18 to which it is diametrically opposed (cf. p. 116
above). The essential difference lies in the source of moral
knowledge. For the Jew it was derived from the Law, but for
the Christian it is derived from love. Here we touch the
kernel of Paul's thought for the insight which enables the
believers to discern the demand of God in a concrete situation flows from the same empowering love which creates the
organic unity of the community. Only love can dissipate the

threat to unity posed by 'freedom *to*'. A moral decision that is truly inspired by the self-giving love which animated Christ (2 Cor 5:15) affirms and strengthens the very being of the community, and so the believer's dependence in being is actualized in freedom. "Bear one another's burdens, and so fulfill the law of Christ" (Gal 6:2) whose single precept is that of love.

The Model of an Authentic Decision

Much of what we have been considering is perfectly summed up in the one instance where we are permitted to see Paul working out a personal moral problem. Writing from prison in Ephesus he says:

> It is my eager expectation and hope that I shall not be at all ashamed, but that with full courage now as always Christ will be honoured in my body, whether by life or by death. For to me to live is Christ and to die is gain. If it is to be life in the flesh, that means fruitful labour for me. Yet which I shall choose I cannot tell. I am hard pressed between the two. My desire is to depart and be with Christ, for that is far better. But to remain in the flesh is more necessary on your account. Convinced of this, I know that I shall remain and continue with you all, for your progress and joy in the faith (Phil 1:20-25).

What matters to Paul is that his physical existence should be a manifestation of the compassion and love of Christ, that Christ should be made tangible in his person. This manifestation can take place either through his apostolic life or through the manner of his death. Paul does not know what the decision of his captors will be, and so he wonders whether he should desire to live or to die. He finds it hard to make a decision because there are arguments on both sides. Since his whole existence is focused on Christ, and since he perceives death as the way to a more intimate union with

Christ, he finds that to die is 'far better'. Nothing in the context suggests a repugnance for the burden of life. From the mode of being that Paul now enjoys Christ has passed to another life that the Apostle wishes to share. In theory it was as simple as that, and so Paul concludes, "My desire to depart and be with Christ'.

Theoretical perfection, however, can never be the primary criterion in the moral judgement of a Christian, nor can personal preference, no matter how closely it may be related to the abstract ideal. Hence, Paul ultimately decides in favour of living because 'it is more necessary on your account . . . for your progress and joy in the faith'. Life in Christ is a shared existence, and the sole criterion of an authentic decision is: will what I contemplate concretize and actualize that sharing? The needs of others, therefore, must always take precedence over personal satisfaction however speculatively justifiable the latter may be. In the present instance Paul finds himself poised between the ideal in its abstract perfection and the ideal in its embryonic realization, between Christ in himself and Christ in the community. His situation is analogous to that of the Corinthians who were confronted with a choice between the truth of principles and the truth of reality. But where they erroneously opted for the simplicity of the abstract, Paul decides for the complexity of the real, and so participates fully in the 'mind of Christ' whose standard is provided by the self-sacrifice of the Cross, whose depth is derived from the accumulation of lived community experience, and whose clarity is refined by continued sharing in love.

Suggested Readings

B. Holmberg, *Paul and Power. The Structure of Authority in the Primitive Church as reflected in the Pauline Epistles,* Lund: Gleerup, 1978.

J.H. Schütz, *Paul and the Anatomy of Apostolic Authority,* Cambridge: CUP, 1975.

D.M. Hay, "Paul's Indifference to Authority," *Journal of Biblical Literature* 88 (1969) 36-44.

D.G. Dungan, *The Sayings of Jesus in the Churches of Paul,* Philadelphia: Fortress, 1971.

J. Murphy-O'Connor, *L'existence chrétienne selon saint Paul,* Paris: Cerf, 1974, chs. 4-6.

_____, "Corinthian Slogans in 1 Cor 6:12-20,"*Catholic Biblical Quarterly* 40 (1978) 391-396.

_____, "Freedom or the Ghetto (1 Cor 8:1-13; 10:23-11:1)," *Revue Biblique* 85 (1978) 543-574.

_____, "The Divorced Woman in 1 Cor 7:10-11," *Journal of Biblical Literature* 100 (1981) 601-606.

E. McDonagh, "The Structure and Basis of the Moral Experience," *Irish Theological Quarterly* 38 (1971) 3-20.

_____, "The Moral Subject," *Irish Theological Quarterly* 39 (1972) 3-22.

G. Therrien, *Le discernement dans les écrits pauliniens,* Paris: Gabalda, 1973.

V.P. Furnish, *Theology and Ethics in Paul,* Nashville: Abingdon, 1968.

AFTERWORD

This book first appeared in 1977, but without the subtitle, which led to its being reviewed in the women's page of an Irish newspaper as a treatise on marriage! The bewilderment of the reviewer, who thought that I must have been speaking allegorically, is still a treasured memory. That error was rectified in the second edition, which was published in 1982. I also made a number of other changes, particularly the expansion of part 1, because of course I had continued to learn about Saint Paul.

In the intervening quarter century my interest in Paul's life and letters has not abated in the slightest. The fruits of my research first saw the light in numerous articles, which were subsequently synthesized into two books, the very technical *Paul: A Critical Life* (Oxford: Oxford University Press, 1996) and the more popular *Paul: His Story* (Oxford: Oxford University Press, 2004). Such detailed investigations inevitably delved into aspects of Paul's thought, which were not envisaged when I wrote *Becoming Human Together.* I was delighted to discover, however, that the conclusions I reached tended to reinforce the hypotheses I had put forward in that book.

The purpose of this Afterword is to indicate briefly how I now see the issues. There will be some corrections, but amplifications will greatly predominate. It will follow the order of the chapters and subheadings of *Becoming Human Together*.

I. PAUL AND JESUS

In Phlm 9 Paul describes himself as "elderly," which would mean that he was around the age of sixty, given the way his contemporaries understood that term. If Philemon was written in the summer of A.D. 53, then Paul would have been born in or around 6 B.C. In other words, he was almost an exact contemporary of Jesus.

The Pharisaic Tradition

Paul would have come to Jerusalem at the age of twenty or so, having finished a four-year course in rhetoric in Tarsus. Thus he would have lived in Jerusalem as a Pharisee from about A.D. 15 until his conversion in A.D. 33. He was old enough to have been a member of the Sanhedrin in the years following the resurrection of Jesus, but I have now become much more sceptical regarding the historical value of the information given by Luke in Acts 9:1–19 and 26:9–11.

Neither the high priest nor the council of chief priests had the authority to send Paul to Damascus on the mission described in Acts 9. The area they controlled was limited to the eleven toparchies around Jerusalem and the city itself. They could not empower anyone to make arrests even in Galilee.

More importantly, Paul offers his persecution of Christians as proof of his erstwhile "zeal" for the Law (Phil 3:6; Gal 1:13). To have evidential value, this activity must have been a personal initiative. It cannot have been an imposed duty. Thus we must conclude that it was part of Luke's literary strategy to highlight the dramatic, miraculous character of Paul's conversion by presenting him as an official prosecutor of Christians. Thus his membership in the Sanhedrin is highly problematic.

This is not to say, however, that Paul was not a Pharisee. We have his own word for that, both explicit (Phil 3:6) and implicit (Gal 1:14). I would now be much more precise regarding what the Pharisees knew of Jesus, because I have come to accept the substantial authenticity of the *Testimonium Flavianum*. This is a note about Jesus composed by Josephus, who was himself a first-century Pharisee, but which was later expanded by a Christian (italics in the text).

> Now there was about this time Jesus, a wise man, *if it be lawful to call him a man*, for he was a doer of exceptional/unbelievable works, a teacher of those with an appetite for pleasurable novelties (*such men who receive the truth with pleasure*). He drew over to him many of the Jews, *and many of the Gentiles. He was the Christ.* And when Pilate, at the suggestion of the principal men amongst us, had condemned him to the cross, those that loved him at first did not forsake him; *for he appeared to them alive again on the third day, as the divine prophets had foretold these and ten thousand other wonderful things concerning him.* And the tribe of Christians, so named for him, are not extinct at this day. (*Antiquities of the Jews* 18.63–64)

If we remove the italicized words, what is left is a report so banal and ambiguous that no Christian could have written it. Any follower of Jesus would have been much more positive about his Master. This said, it is important to keep in mind also that an undisputed text from elsewhere in the work of Josephus shows that he knew that Jesus' disciples thought of him as "the Christ" = Anointed One = Messiah (*Antiquities of the Jews* 18.200).

When I wrote *Becoming Human Together* I did not give adequate importance to Paul's persecution of Christians. It seemed to be axiomatic that the first believers had to suffer. It took some time for it to dawn on me that none of the persecutions described in Acts were initiated by Pharisees. On the contrary, it was the most eminent Pharisee, Gamaliel I, who demanded tolerance for Christians (Acts 5:38–39). Nicodemus, also a Pharisee (John 3:1) argued that Jesus should be given a fair hearing before being condemned (John 7:51). This made Paul's hostility to Christians unique. It was not the normal activity of the group to which he belonged. Hence, his motivation has to be explained.

I first thought his motive was purely personal, redirected anger against the death of his wife and children. On reflection I realized that that hypothesis was too speculative to be adequate. I gradually came to the view that Paul's objection was simply to the fact that Christians considered Jesus to be the Messiah. He saw the implications with a clarity that believers in Jerusalem did not share. They believed that they could live in two worlds, the world of the Law and the world of the Messiah. They saw no contradiction between their lives as normal Jews who frequented the temple and their proclamation of Jesus as the Messiah (Acts 2:46; 5:42). For Paul, however, it was extremely sloppy thinking to imagine that they could have it both ways. It was not a "both-and" situation but an "either-or" situation. Either the Christians were right or the Pharisees were right. But if the Christians were right, the Pharisees were wrong, and this what Paul could not tolerate.

The cause of the tension was the traditional relationship between the Law and the Messiah. The present was the time of the Law. Sometime in the future the Messiah would appear, and the Law would no longer be necessary because there would be no sinners in the eschatological community (see the references on pp. 158–59 above). Obedience to the Law would give way to allegiance to the Messiah as the touchstone of salvation. Inevitably there were those Jews who could not envisage existence without the Law. Thus they invented the idea of a "new covenant" that would be written on the heart (see Jer 31:31–34). But they had to recognize that it was completely different from the covenant of Moses. Paul had no time for such subterfuge. Anyone who claimed that Jesus was the Messiah in fact rejected the Law, whether he or she made this explicit or not. From Paul's perspective, therefore, Christians were a threat to the whole Pharisaic enterprise. And there was no chance that they could be right.

We must assume that Paul subscribed to the Pharisaic vision of the Messiah as it is revealed in *Psalms of Solomon* 17 and 18. These two psalms look forward to the advent of a king, who will be the son of David and the Anointed Lord or Anointed of the Lord. He will rid the nation of its enemies and restore Jerusalem, making it holy as of old. His weapon will be his word. As a righteous king, taught by God and pure from sin, he will be judge and shepherd. By destroying sinners and driving out Gentiles, he will gather together a holy people in whom unrighteousness will have no place. The messianic community will be sinless.

When measured against this template, Jesus could not possibly be the Messiah. He had not purified Jerusalem. He had done nothing about the Roman presence and pagan influences. He had not even gathered round him a large following. His followers, in consequence, must have been deceived. Paul took it as his personal responsibility to bring them back to the truth.

This explanation of why Paul persecuted Christians has one important corollary. It shows that, prior to his conversion, Paul's mind was fixed in an "either-or" mode: either the Law or the Messiah. Once he was convinced by his experience on the Damascus road that Jesus was the Messiah, his commitment to the Law vanished immediately. It was not something from which he had to struggled to divest himself slowly. The release was immediate. He had demanded that Christians surrender one for the other, so when the moment came he was psychologically conditioned to know that acceptance of Christ meant rejection of the Law. By accepting Jesus as the Messiah he said, in effect, that the Law was irrelevant; it no longer had a place in the divine scheme of salvation. Christ was the end of the Law (Rom 10:4). Thus Gentiles could be saved without any reference to the Law. This was the good news that he rushed off to proclaim in Arabia (Gal 1:17), that is, Nabataean territory in which at that moment he could be sure there were no Jews.

Paul's Conversion Experience

It is possible to delve a little more deeply into Paul's conversion experience, if we attend to his own descriptions. The most important is "I was apprehended by Christ Jesus" (Phil 3:12). The image that comes to mind is that of a policeman clamping his hand on the shoulder of a malefactor and swinging him around completely. Paul's life was radically altered by his encounter with Christ. The mastery of his destiny had been taken over by someone else. The most natural way to understand his call to belief was as an act of lordship. Hence, Paul's first postconversion conviction regarding the true identity of Jesus must have been that he was "Lord." Once this idea had entered his head, he had to acknowledge that Jesus was "the Christ." He was not just any Lord but the Messiah for whom the Jewish people hoped. This immediately implied that Jesus was "the Son of God," because the two notions were intimately associated in Judaism.

These key insights, therefore, were born of Paul's experience of power in his conversion. Contrary to what many believe, Paul did not inherit these fundamental titles of Jesus from converted Jews in Damascus or Jerusalem. In a sense, they came with the conversion experience as filtered through his theological formation. He no doubt found these titles in use in these communities. This did not teach him anything that he did not know already. The effect was to convince him that other followers of Jesus had undergone the same experience. They spoke the same language because they had interpreted their experience of divine power in the same way.

The Christian Tradition

My emphasis on Paul's quotations from the sayings of Jesus did not give sufficient importance to his many allusions to such sayings. It would have been appropriate for him to provide explicit indications of his source only if he was speaking to outsiders. Believers, with whom he had laid the groundwork in his oral preaching during his founding visit, could be expected to recognize references to the teaching of Jesus. When recognition met trust, a bond was created that contributed to the building-up of the community. It was "insider" language that flattered the hearers and drew them together in shared pride. It was to be expected, therefore, that Paul would allude to the sayings of Jesus rather than quote them.

The estimates of how many times Paul alludes to the teaching of Jesus range from a thousand or so to very few. In my opinion, those in the following list carry a very high degree of probability:

Rom 1:16 = Mk 8:38; Rom 2:1 = Mt 7:1–2; Rom 12:14

= Mt 5:44; Rom 12:17 = 1 Thess 5:15; Rom 12:18 = Mk 9:50; Rom 13:7 = Mk 12:17; Rom 13:9 = Mk 12:31; Rom 14:13 = Mk 9:42; Rom 14:14 = Mk 7:15; Rom 14:17 = 1 Cor 4:20 = Gospels passim; 1 Cor 2:7 = Mt 13:35; 1 Cor 13:2 = Mt 17:20; 1 Thess 4:8 = Lk 10:16; 1 Thess 5:2–6 = Mt 24:43; 1 Thess 5:13 = Mk 9:50; 1 Thess 5:16 = Lk 6:23; Col 3:5 = Mt 5:29; Col 3:13 = Mt 7:12; Col 4:2 = Mk 14:38; Col 4:6b = Mt 5:13; Col 4:6b = Mt 10:19.

In addition to the Missionary Discourse (Lk 10 = 1 Cor 9), which I have mentioned above, it has also been pointed out by Dale Allison that two blocks of gospel material seem to have been particularly well known to Paul:

1) The central portion of the Sermon on the Plain in Luke:

Lk 6:27–36	=	Rom 12:17, 21; 1 Thess 5:13
Lk 6:28	=	Rom 12:14
Lk 6:35	=	Col 4:6
Lk 6:37	=	Rom 14:10

2) A Community Rule in Mark:

Mk 9:42	=	Rom 14:13; 1 Cor 8:13
Mk 9:43–48	=	Col 3:5
Mk 9:50	=	1 Thess 5:13; Col 4:6

In *Becoming Human Together* I completely ignored an aspect of Paul's knowledge of the historical Jesus, namely, his comportment, that I now believe should be given much more prominence. The allusions are entirely incidental but nonetheless most revelatory:

"The steadfastness of Christ" (2 Thess 3:5)
"The fidelity of Christ" (Gal 2:16; 3:22; Phil 3:9; Rom 3:22, 26)
"He was not Yes and No, but in him it was an enduring Yes" (2 Cor 1:19)

"The affection/tenderness of Christ" (Phil 1:8)
"The gentleness and kindness of Christ" (2 Cor 10:1)

Two salient characteristics emerge from this list, which we are entitled to assume were the aspects of the personality of the historical Jesus that Paul found most striking. The first three texts emphasize Jesus' total dedication to his mission. Such single-mindedness can often breed a self-centered coldness, but in the case of Jesus his manner was characterised by "gentleness and kindness." In his dealings with others he displayed "tenderness." The Greek term translated by this last word is *splagchnon* (literally "bowels"; the seat of the emotion of love). The cognate verb *splagchnizomai* "to have pity, feel sympathy" is used virtually exclusively of Jesus in the gospels to express his reaction to those in any kind of need (see Mk 1:41; 6:34; 8:2; Mt 9:36; 14:14; 15:32; 20:34; Lk 7:13).

In these texts we catch a glimpse of how Paul felt about Jesus, and only this makes it possible to understand what he meant when he said "Imitate me as I imitate Christ" (1 Cor 11:1).

II. CHRIST THE CRITERION

The Divine Intention

The point of my discussion of 2 Cor 4:4–6 could be brought out more clearly by a more detailed treatment of Christ as "the glory of God." The Pauline concept of glory has multiple aspects, but we need to consider only those texts where "glory of God" is predicated of humanity. Even here there must be a limitation because only one of three series of passages is relevant to our purpose, namely, those texts that speak of the *present* glory of Christ.

In this respect Paul reflects the Jewish tradition enshrined in the *Apocalypse of Moses*, which overlaps to a great extent with the *Life of Adam and Eve*. It seems probable that the tradition they enshrine was in existence in the first century A.D. Once Eve had eaten the fruit she said,

> In that very hour my eyes were opened, and straightaway I
> knew that I was bare of the righteousness with which I had been
> clothed, and I wept and said to him [the serpent], "Why have
> you done this to me that you have deprived me of the glory with
> which I was clothed?" As soon as Adam had eaten, his eyes were
> also opened and he said, "O wicked woman! What have I done
> to you that you have deprived me of the glory of God?" (*Life of
> Adam and Eve* 20:1–2; 21:5–6)

Yet this "glory" would be restored in the eschaton, because God
later said to Adam, "Your grief I will turn to joy, and I shall trans-
form you to your former glory" (*Apocalypse of Moses* 39:2).

Clearly here "glory" is "righteousness," and the "glory of God"
is simply the capacity to give glory to God. Sinners are unrighteous,
and so lack this capacity. The fact that Christ manifests the "glory
of God" simply affirms that he is the New Adam who represents
the pristine state of humanity when God first created it.

Authentic Humanity

This section contains the most original insight of the book,
namely, that Christ would not have died had he not chosen to do so.
Thus, for Paul, the death of Christ revealed the decision that made
him unique as a human being. The background against which Paul
made this assessment was the Jewish conviction that death was not
integral to human nature but punishment for sin. As evidence for
this claim I quoted only Wis 2:23, which some have dismissed as
an insignificant anomaly. There are many more texts, which I now
present in chronological order as far as possible:

Genesis
And the woman said to the serpent, "We may eat of the fruit of
all the trees of the garden, but God said: You shall not eat of the
fruit of the tree which is in the midst of the garden, neither shall
you touch it, lest you die." (3:2–3; cf. 3:19)

Isaiah
I formed you not for destruction, to make (you) perish. (LXX 54:16)

Wisdom
Do not invite death by the error of your life, nor bring on destruction by the works of your hands, because God did not make death and he does not delight in the death of the living, for he created all things that they might exist. (1:12–14)

God created man in a state of incorruptibility; in the image of his own eternity he made him, but through the devil's envy death entered the world. (2:23–24)

Sirach
From a woman sin had its beginning, and because of her we all die. (25:24)

1 Enoch
Human beings were created to be like angels, permanently to maintain pure and righteous lives. Death, which destroys everything, would have not touched them, had it not been through their knowledge by which they shall perish; death is now eating us by means of this power. (69:11)

Philo
God did not use any intermediary to urge Him or exhort Him to give others a share of incorruptibility. While man's mind was pure and received no impression of any evil deed or word, he had secure enjoyment of that which led him to piety which is indisputable and true immortality. But after he began to turn to wickedness and to hurl himself down thereto, desiring mortal life, he failed to obtain immortality. (*Questions and Answers on Genesis* 1.55)

2 Enoch
And I said, "After sin there is nothing for it but death." And I assigned a shade for him, and I imposed sleep upon him, and he fell asleep. And while he was sleeping, I took from him a rib. And I created for him a wife, so that death might come to him by his wife. (30:16–17)

4 Ezra

You laid on Adam one commandment of yours but he transgressed it, and immediately you appointed death for him and for his descendants. (3:7; cf. 3:21–22)

O Adam what have you done? For though it was you who sinned, the fall was not yours alone, but ours also who are your descendants. For what good is it to us, if an immortal time has been promised to us, but we have done deeds that bring death. (7:118–119)

2 Baruch

What did it profit Adam that he lived 930 years and transgressed that which he was commanded? Therefore the multitude of time that he lived did not profit him, but it brought death and cut off the years of those who were born from him. (17:2–3)

Even if every one had been happy continually since the day death was decreed against those who trespassed, but was destroyed in the end, everything would have been in vain. (19:8)

When Adam sinned and death was decreed against those who should be born, then the multitude of those who should be born was numbered, and for that number a place was prepared where the living might dwell and the dead be guarded. (23:4; cf. 2 En 49:2 and b. Hag 15a)

Although Adam sinned first and has brought death upon all who were not in his own time, yet each of them who has been born from him has prepared for himself the coming torment. And further, each of them has chosen for himself the coming glory. (54:15–16)

When he transgressed, untimely death came into being. (56:6; cf. 46:1)

Nobody will again die untimely. (73:3; cf. 21:23)

Apocalypse of Moses

Adam said to Eve, "Eve, what hast thou wrought in us? Thou hast brought upon us great wrath, which is death, lording it over all our race." (14:2)

Genesis Rabbah

Rabbi Tifdai said in rabbi Aha's name: The Holy One, blessed be He, said, "If I create him of the celestial elements he will live for ever and not die, and if I create him of the terrestrial elements, he will die and not live (in a future life). Therefore, I will create him of the upper and lower elements; if he sins he will die, while if he does not sin he will live." (8:11 on Gen 1:27)

Exodus Rabbah

Behold I send an angel before thee (xxiii 20). Thus it is written, *I said: Ye are godlike beings* (Ps lxxxii 6). Had Israel waited for Moses and not perpetrated that act [the golden calf], there would have been no exile, neither would the Angel of Death have had any power over them. ... When Israel exclaimed: *"All that the Lord had spoken will we do, and harken"* (Exod xxiv 7), the Holy One, blessed be He, said: "If I gave but one commandment to Adam, that he might fulfil it, and I made him equal to the ministering angels—for it says, *Behold, the man was as one of us* (Gen iii 2)—how much more so should those who practise and fulfil all the 613 commandments—not to mention their general principles, details and minutiae—not be deserving of eternal life?" This is the meaning of *And from Mattanah* [the Gift, a name for the Law] *to Nahaliel* - nahalu (Num xxi 19); for they had *inherited* (through the Torah, given as a gift), from God eternal life. As soon, however, as they said, *"This is thy god, O Israel"* (Ex xxxii 4), death came upon them. God said: "You have followed the course of Adam who did not withstand his trials for more than three hours, and at nine hours death was decreed upon him. '*I said: Ye are godlike beings,*' but since you have followed the footsteps of Adam, *Nevertheless ye shall die like men.*" What is the meaning of *And fall like one of the princes?* R. Judah said: Either as Adam or as Eve [the footnote explains: "Before they sinned, they were like angels"]. (Exodus Rabbah 32:1)

Leviticus Rabbah

Rabbi Judah explains: If a man should tell you that if Adam had not sinned and eaten from that tree, he would have lived and endured for ever, tell him that there has already been the case of Elijah who did not sin, and lives and endures for ever. *And that which is to be hath already been* (Eccl 3:15). If a man should tell you that the Holy One, blessed be He, will in the future bring us a resurrection of the dead, tell him: "It has already occurred through Elijah, Elisha, and through Ezekiel." (24:7)

Deuteronomy Rabbah
Lord of the world, in the scriptures 36 commandments are punished by death, if a man disobeys one of them, he is guilty of death. Have I disobeyed one of them? Why do you impose death on me? He answered: You die on account of the sin of the first man; he introduced death into the world. (9)

The temporal range of these texts is noteworthy. The idea that death is punishment for sin is not a momentary aberration but remained solidly rooted in Jewish tradition from the creation narrative to the rabbis. One can safely assume that it was common knowledge and would have formed part of the teaching that Paul absorbed during the fifteen years or so that he spent as a Pharisee in Jerusalem.

Just as Paul alone saw that it was either the Law or the Messiah, so he was the only one to perceive that a dead Messiah represented a major problem. First, the Messiah was by definition sinless (even though this is explicitly stated only in *Pss. Sol.* 17:36) and thus should not have died. Second, the bliss expected in the kingdom of the Messiah would have been considerably diminished, if the just expected the Messiah to die one day. It was taken for granted that he would live eternally.

There are two possible objections to this view. The first is drawn from the book of Daniel, where we find, "the anointed one will be cut off" (9:26). The date of this document in the second century B.C. means that it could well have been available to Paul. The force of the objection is strengthened by the suggestion of Jerome that Jews understood this text to refer to the death of the Messiah. This interpretation, however, is not confirmed by any known Jewish source that might have been known to Paul. On the contrary, specialists on the book of Daniel unanimously see here a reference to the murder of the high priest Onias III in 171 B.C. (2 Macc 4:23–28). A non-messianic use of "anointed one" is well-documented at Qumran (Fitzmyer, *The One Who Is to Come,* 102).

The second objection is to be found in the Second Book of Esdras, which is also known as the Apocalypse of Ezra or 4 Ezra:

My son the Messiah shall be revealed together with those who
are with him, and shall rejoice the survivors four hundred years.
And it shall be, after these years, that my son the Messiah shall
die, and all in whom there is human breath. Then shall the world
be turned into the primaeval silence, like at the first beginnings;
so that no man is left. And it shall be after seven days that the
Age which is not yet awake shall be roused, and that which is
corruptible shall perish. And the earth shall restore those that
sleep in her, and the dust those that are at rest therein. (7:28–32;
trans. Box)

According to this scenario, the Messiah and the surviving righteous shall all die after a reign of four hundred years, and the world
shall return to the original state of chaos for seven days. Then the
Messiah will arise with the rest of the just and will live and reign as
God's vice-regent forever.

Fortunately, an exegesis of this extraordinary vision of the end
time, in which the existence of the Messiah is interrupted tempo-
rarily, is not necessary, because Paul could not have known this
document. It was written after his death. The contents unambiguously indicate that its composition must fall between the destruction
of Jerusalem in A.D. 70 and the death of Domitian in 96, and
experts put it in the latter part of that period (Stone, *ABD* 2:612).

To quote Mowinckel, "The thought of the Messiah as an eternal
being in an eternal kingdom was ... the dominant conception in the
time of Jesus" (*He That Cometh*, 327). This is confirmed by the
silence of Fitzmyer in his authoritative *The One Who Is to Come*;
the death of the Messiah is never mentioned.

To return to Paul's contemporaries. They confessed Jesus as the
Messiah but at the same time insisted that he had died for their sins
(1 Cor 15:3). Confronted with this dilemma, Paul could only reason
thus: if someone on whom death had no claim in fact died, *he must
have chosen to die.* Thus inevitably he presents the death of Christ
as an act of self-sacrifice.

The Pauline Letters

"The [one] having given himself for our sins." (Gal 1:4)

"The Son of God who loved me that is gave himself for me." (Gal 2:20)

"He emptied himself." (Phil 2:7)

"He humbled himself, becoming obedient unto death." (Phil 2:8)

The Deutero-Pauline Letters

"Christ loved us and gave himself for us." (Eph 5:2)

"Christ loved the church and gave himself for her." (Eph 5:25)

"The man Christ Jesus, who gave himself as a ransom for all." (1 Tim 2:6)

"He who gave himself for us to redeem us." (Titus 2:14)

"He who through the eternal Spirit he offered himself without blemish to God." (Heb 9:14)

The distribution of statements concerning the death of Jesus that use the reflexive pronoun "himself" is highly significant. They all appear in the Pauline letters or in those attributed to his school, and nowhere else in the New Testament. The only other text to come anywhere close is, "The Son of Man came not to be served but to serve and to give his life as a ransom for many" (Mk 10:45 = Mt 20:28). Here "himself" is missing, but "gave his life" is a perfectly adequate synonym. It is, of course, possible that Paul borrowed from the Jesus tradition, which he knew well (see above), but if so, Paul moved the theme to the very core of his theology. It is equally possible, and in my view more probable, that it was an original insight developed by Paul, which eventually found its way into Mark. Be that as it may, one cannot escape the fact that Paul consistently emphasizes the activity of Jesus in his own death. It was not something that he passively accepted but something that he chose freely.

Naturally, having reached this point, Paul had to ask himself why Jesus made the choice he did. This question was all the more urgent in that Paul had to justify the modality of Jesus' death. If he died an agonizing death by crucifixion, he must have chosen that particularly horrible way to die. Why? Paul was given a clue by the kerygma he had inherited, "Christ died for our sins" (1 Cor 15:3; cf. 1 Thess 5:9). If, according to the traditional belief, the death of Christ resulted in benefits for humanity, then the simplest answer to Paul's question was that Christ had intended those benefits. His motive, therefore, in choosing to be crucified was to do good to others. Some such reasoning as this must underlie Paul's interpretation of Christ's decision as an act of love (Gal 2:20). It was also an act of obedience (Phil 2:8) because it occurred in the context of Christ's mission from the Father (1 Cor 15:20–28). The two answers, of course, are not contradictory. Only supreme love could inspire such extreme obedience.

Only now does it become possible to understand why Paul lays such emphasis on the fact that Christ died by crucifixion. The traditional teaching that surfaces from time to time in his letters (e.g., 1 Thess 1:9–10; Gal 1:3–4; 1 Cor 15:3–5; Rom 1:3–4; 4:24–25; 10:9) mentions the death of Christ but nowhere specifies its modality. It never says *how it happened*. This, of course, is perfectly understandable. It was difficult enough to preach a Saviour who apparently had achieved nothing. Why make things worse by insisting that he was a crucified criminal?

Paul, on the contrary, mentions "cross" nine times and uses the verb "to crucify" ten times. He breaks the beautiful structure of the two liturgical hymns that he cites (Phil 2:6–11; Col 1:15–20) by inserting a reference to crucifixion, namely, "death on a cross" (Phil 2:8) and "making peace by the blood of his cross" (Col 1:20).

The importance that Paul gave the crucifixion is graphically illustrated by one of the few hints he gives as to how he founded communities. "You foolish Galatians. Who has put the evil eye on you? It was before your eyes that Jesus Christ was publicly exhibited as crucified" (Gal 3:1). Paul's preaching of the way Christ died was so graphic and "real" that it transformed his hearers into spectators. He made it happen before their eyes.

According to the masters of rhetoric, only those who had the sympathetic imagination (1) to re-create the event for themselves (2) to the point where they experienced the appropriate emotions could achieve the verbal vividness that Paul claims here (Quintilian, *Institutio Oratoria* 6.2.34). Paul had been profoundly touched by the motive of Jesus in opting for crucifixion. It was the concrete proof of the immensity of his love for humanity. The thought became so much part of him that he could say, "I have been crucified with Christ; it is no longer I who live, but Christ who lives in me" (Gal 2:20). The Christ who lives in Paul is not "the Lord of Glory" (1 Cor 2:8) but the crucified Jesus who died for us. Hence Paul cannot do otherwise, "Always carrying in the body the dying of Jesus in order that the life of Jesus may be manifested in our body. For while we live we are always being given up to death on Jesus' account in order that the life of Jesus may be manifested in our mortal flesh" (2 Cor 4:10–11).

III. JESUS CHRIST AND GOD

The Crux of Romans 9:5

Another text in which scholars have found explicit mention of the divinity of Christ is in the first line of the Philippian hymn (Phil 2:6). This view used to be so dominant that it influenced major translations of this verse, such as "He whose state was divine" (JB) and "He who had always been God by nature" (Phillips). The Greek words are *morphē theou* "form of god," which obviously is far less explicit than the meaning thrust upon it. Perhaps "form" could be expanded to include the very "nature" of God, but this meaning is excluded by the next line, which as we have seen above (p. 46), should be translated, "he did not use to his own advantage his right to be treated *as if he were a god.*" The italicized phrase unambiguously indicate that "form of god" cannot be a reference to the divinity of Christ. The turn of phrase is common in Greek literature to indicate that certain individuals were granted "divine honours" (e.g., Homer, *Odyssey* 15.520). It goes without saying that this did not make them gods. It was simply a way of describing the treatment accorded to them for a period. They remained humans. Thus "form of God" is functionally equivalent to "image of God" (hence my translation on p. 46 above), which is the definition of humanity in Gen 1:26–27. Rather than speaking about the divinity of Christ, Phil 2:6 presents him as Adam before the Fall.

We can go a step further when we recall that "form of God" cannot be understood without taking into account "form of a slave" in the fourth line of the first strophe of the Philippian hymn (2:7b). The underlying connection between the two is the idea of "glory." For Hebrew thought the visible "form of God" was his glory. We have already seen above (p. 000) that the pristine state of Adam and Eve was characterized by possession of the "glory of God," which they then lost through their sin. By definition, "glory" cannot be associated with a slave. Hence "form of a slave" is intended to evoke the condition of fallen humanity. Suffering and death had no claim on Christ as the sinless New Adam, but he freely chose to be so integrated into fallen humanity that he became subject to suffering and death. As the hymn says, "he emptied himself" (Phil 2:7a = Isa 53:12).

Preexistence

In my discussion of the "Christ-God" relationship I dealt with the question of the preexistence of Christ explicitly only apropos of 1 Cor 10:4 in the section headed "Wisdom" and implicitly in what I said about Phil 2:6–7 both immediately above and on page 46. In neither case did I find any reference to the type of preexistence that might seem to imply the divinity of Christ. One further text, however, should have been brought into the debate. In appearing to present Christ as the agent of God in creation, and therefore preexistent to all created reality, 1 Cor 8:6 needs to be examined closely.

The translations of this verse vary considerably because the Greek has no verbs. Some commentators content themselves with the minimum by inserting only the static verb "to be, to exist" (e.g., NRSV). For other scholars the prepositions "from," "to," and "through" strongly suggest that verbs of motion would be more appropriate, and this is certainly correct. Thus the verse should be rendered:

> For us (there is)
>> one God, the Father, from whom (come) all things and
>> toward whom we (go), and
>> one Lord, Jesus Christ, by whom (come) all things and
>> by whom we (go).

God is presented as the first and final cause, while Christ is the instrumental cause. When I first wrote about this verse I argued that it referred only to redemption. I then believed that "all things" in both lines evoked only the soteriological benefits accorded by baptism, whose power is acclaimed. I found no cosmological dimension. There was no allusion to the first creation and, in consequence, no reference to the preexistence of Christ.

I have now been persuaded that this "either-or" approach does not do justice to what Paul could reasonably have expected his readers to understand. Every Jew knew the first verse of the Bible, "In the beginning God created heaven and earth" (Gen 1:1), and recognized that the power of this act continued to govern every aspect of their being. Reflection on the goodness and organization thus displayed in ongoing creation stimulated two lines of thought within Hellenistic Judaism.

First, God was thought of as a benevolent Father. The earliest attestation of this insight is perhaps "Have we not all one Father? Has not one God created us?" (Mal 2:10). The best witness to this development is undoubtedly Philo. The essence of Jewish belief was that "there was but one God, their Father and Creator of the universe" (*Leg.* 115). God is "the Creator and Father of the universe" (*Spec. Leg.* 2.6) or even more simply "the Father of the universe" (*Ebr.* 81). The climax of Philo's argument against idolatry is that "all created things are brothers to one another, inasmuch as they are created, since the Father of them all is one, the Creator of the universe" (*Decal.* 64).

The second line of thought is more complex. Just as Philo took the divine commands of Genesis seriously and ascribed an instrumental role in creation to the "Word" (*logos*), others were more impressed by the marvellous interrelated complexity of the universe and attributed instrumentality to Wisdom: "The Lord by Wisdom founded the earth" (Prov 3:19); "The Lord created me at the beginning of his work.... When he established the heavens I was there" (Prov 8:22–30); "On the sixth day I commanded my Wisdom to create humanity" (2 Enoch 30:8). This theme is very rare in Philo. He once refers to "wisdom by means of which the universe was completed" (*Det.* 54). The "Word," however, was his preference for the supreme intermediary. He thus summarizes the four causes of creation "God is the cause of it [the universe], *by whom* it was made,. The materials are the four elements, *of which* it is composed. The instrument is the Word of God, *by means of which* it was made. And the *object* of the edifice you will find to be the display of the goodness of the Creator" (*Cher.* 127).

Although the Christian community at Corinth was predominantly of pagan origin, there were a number of Jewish converts, whom one would expect to be familiar with the wisdom literature of the Hellenistic synagogue. More specifically, the intellectual and leisured section of the community, presumably ex-pagans, had been greatly impressed by the teaching of Apollos (1 Cor 3:6), an Alexandrian Jew who, given his qualifications (Acts 18:24–28), must have been taught by Philo. Thus the baptismal acclamation quoted by Paul in 1 Cor 8:6 would have set up familiar resonances in the minds of believing Corinthians of Jewish origin. Mention of first, final, and instrumental causes would immediately have caused them to think in terms of creation.

Once an allusion to creation has been established, the essential question concerns the relationship between the cosmological dimension and the soteriological dimension in 1 Cor 8:6, which no one denies. It is understandable that some commentators should tend to give primacy to the cosmological aspect. Not only is it the more striking and unusual, but it appears to offer a new insight into the person of Christ, in that it attributes to him preexistence and a role in creation.

This first impression, however, is completely unreliable. It is contradicted by everything else that Paul tells us about Christ. For Paul Christ is accorded the title "Lord" as a reward (Phil 2:11); it is not his by nature. Furthermore, the power of lordship is given to Christ for a specific purpose, and when it is accomplished, that power will be surrendered to God (1 Cor 15:20–28). Finally, the sonship of Christ is not his by nature, but is consequent on the resurrection (Rom 1:3–4; 14:9; 1 Thess 1:10) and is the fruit of obedience (2 Cor 1:19–20). When read in the light of these texts, 1 Cor 8:6 cannot be understood as a statement of the divinity of Christ.

Conceptually the "Word" or "Wisdom" as the instruments of creation must predate all created beings. 1 Cor 8:6 implicitly at least identifies Christ with the "Word" or "Wisdom." This cannot mean that Christ is pushed backwards in time to become in effect a second eternal God. This would have been completely alien not only to Paul's thought but to that of any Jew who subscribed to Wisdom speculation. Wisdom was never a threat to monotheism. This forces us to recognize that the true thought process is the reverse. The preexistent "Word" or "Wisdom" is in fact drawn forward into the present by being predicated of Christ. He is presented as the embodiment of an idea, which had not been fully developed within Judaism. It would eventually play a role in leading the church to the conviction of the divinity of Christ, but this insight did not come *from* 1 Cor 8:6. It is rather a perfect instance of Catholics finding their faith in Scripture. The words of 1 Cor 8:6 are adequate to express the divinity of Christ, but this was not their original meaning.

Paul's concern with the present rather than the past is underlined by the shift from "all things" to "we" in both members of 1 Cor 8:6. In theory, "all things" can reach all the way back into the immensity of the past, but in practice "we" focuses "all things" on the present. The power displayed in the creation of all things interests Paul only insofar that it now has an impact on the members of the community. Creation is evoked, not in or for itself, but because of the inconceivable power therein displayed. Believers are to understand that power of the same magnitude is at work in their redemption.

The same intimate association of creation and redemption as we find in 1 Cor 8:6 is a faithful echo of the teaching of Deutero-Isaiah, as in "Thus says the Lord, your Redeemer, who forms you in the womb: I am the Lord who makes all things" (Isa 44:24; cf. 42:5; 45:9–13; 51:12–16). The verbs here should be translated by the present tense because the prophet envisages the *first* creation as an ongoing work in the *present* redemption of Israel. The ancients were interested in the creation of the physical world only as an explanation for the appearance of the human race or a particular people. As regards the Jews, creation is clearly subordinate to their redemption. Yahweh is Israel's creator because of what he does redemptively for and in Israel. The finality of creation is redemption. The power that brought their world into being is the same power that saves them. This is not the place to go into further detail; it is sufficient to note that the perspective of Deutero-Isaiah provides an illuminating precedent for the smoothness of the shift from cosmology to soteriology in 1 Cor 8:6. Even though two dimensions may be distinguished, creative redemption is the single movement demanded by the verbs of motion.

IV. THE DIVISION WITHIN HUMANITY

"Life" and "Death"

Paul's use of "life" and "death" in the three distinct senses of (A) physical, (B) existential, and (C) eternal will appear less extraordinary when we recall how familiar the different senses would have been to his contemporaries. For example, the great Jewish philosopher, Philo of Alexandria (?15–10 B.C.–A.D. 50?) wrote:

> For instruction I went to a wise woman, whose name is Consideration, and I was released from my difficulty, for she taught me that some persons who are living (A) are dead (B), and that some who are dead (A) are still alive (C). She pronounced that the wicked, even if they arrive at the latest period of old age, are only dead (B) inasmuch as they are deprived of life (B) according to virtue. The good, however, even if they are separated from

all union with the body, live (C) for ever, inasmuch as they have received an immortal portion. (*De Fuga* 55; trans. Yonge)

Moreover, she confirmed this opinion of hers by the Sacred Scriptures, one of which ran in this form: "You who cleave unto the Lord your God are all alive to this day" [Deut 4:4]. For she saw that those who sought refuge with God and became his suppliants were the only living (B) persons, and that all others were dead (B). (*De Fuga* 56; trans. Yonge)

She also confirmed her statement by another passage in Scripture, which runs as follows "Behold I have set before your face life and death, good and evil" [Deut 30:15]. Therefore, O all-wise man, good and virtue mean life (B), and evil and wickedness mean death (B). (*De Fuga* 58; trans. Yonge)

I have inserted the bracketed capital letters into this translation in order to bring out which sense Philo intended in each case. The only sense that he does not explain is the most familiar one of physical life and death. Philo's division of humanity into those who are "alive" and those who are "dead" in *De Fuga* 56 differs from Paul's only in the criterion that they employ. For Philo it is obedience to the Law, whereas for Paul it is faith in Jesus Christ working through love.

One particular Pauline passage mirrors Philo's play on the different senses of "life" and "death":

We are the aroma of Christ to God among those who are being saved and among those who are perishing, to one [the latter] a fragrance from death (B) to death (C), to the other [the former] a fragrance from life (B) to life (C). (2 Cor 2:15–16)

The consciously rhetorical character of this phrase is underlined by the chiastic structure. The present participles "those being saved" and "those who are perishing" (see also 1 Cor 1:18) divide humanity into those whose respective patterns of behaviour display existential "life" or "death." Thus the movement can only be toward eternal "life" or "death."

V. SIN AND THE WORLD

My thoughts on the material in the introduction to this section
have been clarified by the insistence of E. P. Sanders that Paul's
theology is best understood on the assumption that he argued from
solution to problem, not the other way around (*Paul and Palestinian Judaism*, V, §2). In other words, Paul did not first analyse the
human situation and then devise the type of saviour that the situation required, as my text might appear to suggest. Sanders is right
but only up to a point.

I suggested rather vaguely that Paul should have been aware of
the pessimism that permeated his world. In particular I argued that
the Jewish expectation of a Messiah witnessed to the conviction
that no change in the condition of humanity could come about as
the result of intrahistorical human effort.

I would now insist more strongly on this latter point on the basis
of the *Psalms of Solomon*, whose first century B.C. date and probable Pharisaic origins are commonly accepted. The task facing the
Messiah was considerable:

> Behold O Lord, and raise up unto them their king, the son of
> David.... Gird him with strength, that he may shatter unrighteous
> rulers, and that he may purge Jerusalem from nations that tram-
> ple her down to destruction. Wisely, righteously he shall thrust
> out sinners from the inheritance.... He shall destroy the godless
> nations by the word of his mouth.... And he shall gather together
> a holy people, whom he shall lead in righteousness, and he shall
> judge the tribes of the people that has been sanctified by the Lord
> his God. And he shall not suffer unrighteousness to lodge any
> more in their midst. Nor shall there dwell with them any man
> that knows wickedness.... Neither sojourner nor alien shall live
> with them any more.... He shall purge Jerusalem making it holy
> as of old. (*Pss. Sol.* 17:24–33)

Were Paul the most enthusiastic Pharisee in the world, I cannot
imagine that his optimism could envisage a day *under current conditions* when all Israel would perfectly obey the Law and when

all the nations would accept its beneficent influence. It would be asking too much of human nature. Such perfection could only be the work of the Messiah, the last agent of God in history.

This is not to say, however, that Paul had the slightest doubt about the God-given nature of the Law or about his own ability to comply with its demands. One has only to read Gal 1:14 and Phil 3:5–6 to recognize the complacency with which Paul surveyed his accomplishments as a Pharisee. There is not the slightest hint of any fear of failure or of any worry that obedience would not keep him in the saving covenant.

It is precisely at this point that Sanders's observation acquires its full force. Only when Paul had become convinced that Christ had come to save *even those who observed the Law perfectly* did he realize that the Law did not propose a way of life that was salvific. Salvation is by faith in Jesus Christ, and the Law is not Christ.

Humanity as "Dead"

See the addition above under the subsection *"Life" and "Death"* in IV. THE DIVISION WITHIN HUMANITY.

Sin and the World

In his article "Sin, Sinners (NT)" for the *Anchor Bible Dictionary*, E. P. Sanders rightly devotes a special section entitled "Sin as an Enslaving Power" to the unique Pauline usage to which I drew attention. He points out that Paul himself does not offer an anthropological, theological, or cosmological explanation of this concept of Sin as a power alien to God and almost as potent, and does not himself attempt to identify precisely what Paul meant.

J. D. G. Dunn is much more perceptive in his magisterial *The Theology of Paul the Apostle*. He describes Sin as "a compulsion or constraint which humans generally experience within themselves or in their social context, a compulsion towards attitudes and actions not always of their own willing or approving" (p. 112), and concludes that "it [Sin] is the world as an organized system of social values which did not recognize God" (p. 113). Such commonsense confirmation of my definition of Sin as "the inexorable pressure of a false value-system that permeates society" (p. 97) is most welcome. Sin is not simply in the world; it is the world.

Both Sanders and Dunn correctly point out that Paul pays no attention to the origins of Sin. They in turn avoid the question. Sin simply entered the world (Rom 5:12). For Paul, however, in this very text, it did so "through one man." The allusion to the sin of Adam is inescapable, and from here it is but a short and logical step to the consequent exponential development of evil as described in Gen 4–11, to which I drew attention. Reflection on these passages concerning the origins of humanity remains the simplest theological explanation of the origins of Sin.

I would now also draw attention to another factor: Paul's personal experience. Just imagine a night in an inn as he tramped the roads in Turkey and Greece. Inns were notoriously insecure. Across the Roman province of Asia, they were spaced a day's journey apart—25 Roman or 22 English miles (35 km)—with a small establishment (*mutatio*) where dispatch riders could change horses roughly halfway between two inns. The rooms were grouped around three or four sides of a courtyard with public rooms on the ground floor and sleeping accommodation above. Those with money to spend could buy privacy, but those with slender purses had to share a room with strangers; how many depended on the number of beds the landlord could cram in or on his or her attitude to guests sleeping on the floor. Unless they wanted to cart their baggage with them, guests had to leave it unguarded while they visited the baths and/or a restaurant.

The ease of theft needs no emphasis. Roman legislation made innkeepers responsible for the acts of their employees, but not all guests were honest, and in a crowded room at night one had only to stretch out a hand to appropriate something from another's baggage.

Paul's conversion had made him a follower of Jesus who had given his life for the salvation of humanity. That totally other-directed mode of existence became Paul's ideal. His goal was to make it transparent in and through his own comportment, "always carrying in the body the dying of Jesus so that the life of Jesus may be manifested in our bodies" (2 Cor 4:10).

Yet every road he travelled forced him to worry about his personal safety (2 Cor 11:26). Every inn he visited obliged him to consider others as potential thieves, at least insofar as he had to take measures to protect the precious tools of the trade on which his livelihood depended. Circumstances conspired to push the self to the center of his consciousness, whereas he wanted to be totally focussed on the other. His life became a perpetual struggle against the insidious miasma of egocentricity. He was forced to be other than he wished to be. He experienced the alienation of the authentic self. "If I do what I do not want, it is no longer I that do it, but Sin which dwells within me" (Rom 7:20).

To a great degree Paul's concept of Sin is simply a generalization of his experience as a travelling missionary. It was this that gave life and force to his theological insight. People were not selfish because they chose to be. They were forced to be egocentric in order to survive. Their pattern of behaviour was dictated by irresistible societal pressures. They were controlled by a force greater than any individual, the value system that had developed within their society. The power of system became clear to Paul in the difficulty he experienced in being true to himself as the model of Jesus Christ (1 Cor. 11:1). Hence his anguished cry, "Who is not weak, and I am not weak? Who is made to fall, and I do not burn with anger?" (2 Cor 11:29).

VI. ALIEN BEING

Obedience to Law

The documentation that I provided for the idea that God was subject to his own Law on page 115 was greatly supplemented in my *Paul: A Critical Life*. If God appears as a student in *b. Avoda Zarah* 3b and the Jerusalem Targum on Deut 32:4, it is not surprising that he should take his place with other scholars:

> Now they were disputing in the Heavenly Academy ... the Holy
> One, blessed be He, ruled, "He is clean"; while the whole Heav-
> enly Academy maintained, "He is unclean." Who shall decide
> it? said they. Rabbah b. Nahmani; for he said, "I am pre-emi-
> nent in the laws of leprosy and tents." (*b. Baba Mezia* 86a; trans.
> Epstein)

Divine authority gives way before rabbinic expertise. Elsewhere
when questioned God can only say, "My son Abiathar says So-
and-so, and my son Jonathan says So-and-so. Said R. Abiathar,
'Can there be uncertainty in the mind of the Holy One?'" (*b. Gittin*
6b). On another occasion God throws his weight on the side of R.
Eliezer:

> A Heavenly Voice cried out: "Why do you dispute with R. Eliezer,
> seeing that in all matters the halakah agrees with him!" But R.
> Joshua arose and exclaimed, "*It is not in heaven* (Deut 30:12)."
> What did he mean by this? Said R. Jeremiah, "That the Torah
> had already been given on Mount Sinai. We pay no attention to
> a Heavenly Voice, because Thou has long since written in the
> Torah at Mount Sinai: *After the majority must one incline* (Exod
> 23:2)." R. Nathan met [the prophet] Elijah and asked him, "What
> did the Holy One, blessed be He, do in that hour?" He laughed
> with joy, Elijah replied, saying "My sons have defeated Me. My
> sons have defeated Me." (*b. Baba Mezia*; trans. Epstein)

As a good loser, God recognizes that he has been sidelined. He
had failed to realize that once he had given the Law to the Jewish
people, it was out of his hands. Now only the voice of the rabbis
counted. God himself is bound by their decisions!

Whatever their date, and even when given their most benign
interpretation as assertions of the freedom of human reason, these
quotations unambiguously illustrate what happens when intangible
grace is confronted with the concrete specificity of the Law.

Predominantly Jews debated points of the Law, not the mystery
of grace. Manipulation of the controllable took pride of place over
contemplation of the ineffable.

In his monumental *Paul and Palestinian Judaism*, E. P. Sanders offered a "new perspective" on Paul. He argued against the very common view that the Judaism criticised by Paul was a religion in which salvation was won by merit acquired by observance of the precepts of the Law. He had little difficulty in assembling texts that show that the fundamentals of Judaism are election and grace. Obedience to the Law, in consequence, did not win salvation. It was simply the means of staying in the life-giving covenant. To describe this type of religion, he coined the phrase "covenantal nomism," which has become common currency.

The fatal flaw in this vision is its entirely theoretical character. In reality subtlety always gives way to simplicity. The human mind instinctively takes the line of least resistance. If disobedience to the demands of the Law caused damnation, which Sanders admits, then to Jews who were not professional theologians it would seem natural to infer that obedience to such precepts won salvation. Moreover, the Law contained statements promising rewards for keeping the commandments, such as, "if, throughout your lives, you fear Yahweh your God, and keep all his laws and commandments, which I am laying down for you today, you will live long.... Listen then, Israel, keep and observe what will make you prosperous" (Deut 6:2–3). A religion of grace that expresses itself in covenant form quickly becomes a religion of meritorious achievement, at least in the popular mind, if not in the dissertations of theologians. Given what we know of human nature, it is practically impossible to have law without legalism. There is no metaphysical necessity. It just happens that way, as Paul knew from personal experience.

It should never be forgotten that Paul was a Pharisee. Had he been a member of the priestly caste, he might have seen Judaism differently. Then his duties would have been connected in one way or another with sacrifices and the uplifting of the mind to a merciful God. As it was, for the better part of fifteen years his days were devoted, not to silent contemplation of the Godhead or to the public chant of hymns extolling God's mysterious interventions in history, but to debates about the minutiae of the Law. This was what the Law demanded: "This book of the Law shall not depart out of your mouth. You shall meditate on it day and night, so that you may be careful to act in accordance with all that I written in it" (Josh 1:8); "He must read it every day of his life and learn to fear Yahweh his God by keeping all the words of this Law and observing these rules" (Deut 17:19; cf. Ps 1:2). According to the *Rule of the Community* from Qumran, "In the place where the ten are, let there not lack a man who studies the Law night and day, continually, concerning the duties of each towards the other" (1QS 6:6–7).

Paul's pride expressed in Gal 1:14 is intelligible only in terms of competitively controlled Torah-keeping. It would be interesting to inquire into the programs of modern rabbinic schools. With admirable commonsense Paul judged what was really important to his contemporaries by the time and energy they invested in it, not by the theoretical statements they made about it.

What Paul criticized was the *practice* of Judaism, just as Jews throughout history have criticized the *practice* of Christianity. I have no doubt that Paul's contemporaries paid lip service to election and grace, just as the majority of Christians pay lip service to the primacy of love. In theory Christianity is a religion of love, and no Jew should have ever suffered.

*****

On page 115 I quoted Rom 2:17–18. I still maintain what I said about it, but the point of Paul's criticism of Judaism is brought out much more forcibly if this text is put in parallel with Phil 1:9–10, where Paul offers the Christian perspective on precisely the same point in identical language.

Rom 2:17–18	**Phil 1:9–10**
(17) But if you are called a Jew and rely upon the Law and boast in God, (18) and know the will,	
	It is my prayer that your love may abound more and more with knowledge and all discernment

and **approve what is excellent** being instructed from the Law	so that you may **approve what is excellent**

In both texts the phrase in bold translates *ta diapheronta* as the object of the verb *dokimazein*. The verb means "to test, examine" or consequently "to prove, approve." In both contexts it clearly refers to the making of a moral judgment. The object of that judgment, *ta diapheronta*, is the polar opposite of *ta adiaphora*, which had become a technical term in popular Cynic-Stoic ethics for things that are morally neutral, neither good nor bad. As its antithesis, *ta diapheronta* means things whose moral character is completely unambiguous. They are either right or wrong. The translation I give is that of the RSV. Others differ slightly: "what is best" (NRSV); "tell right from wrong" (NJB); "able to make sound judgments on disputed points" and "to value the things that really matter" (NAB); "truly to appreciate moral values" and "to recognize the highest and the best" (Phillips).

How are right and wrong to be distinguished? This is where the two texts differ radically. The Jew knows "the will of God," and this is what is truly essential, because that knowledge derives from the Law. The Jew, in other words, is told what to do by the Law. The point is put well by Dunn, "The assumption criticized [by Paul] is not simply that of having a test ready to hand (= the Torah), but rather the assumption that the law has already decided such questions (cf. v 20c)" (*Romans*, 111). For the Jew, "the things that really matter" are the commandments. Obedience, not research, is the appropriate response.

For Paul, on the contrary, the place of the Law is taken by love (*agapē*). From it flow two types of knowledge. *Epignōsis* is the sort of knowledge that is operative in black and white situations, such as the judgment as to what must be done on discovering a boatload of refugees who have been adrift at sea for a week. Their needs are unambiguous. Clarity and justified certitude are the qualities of *epignōsis*.

Aisthēsis, on the other hand, "knows" in situations where no solution can be justified rationally. It is flair, discernment, an intuitive sense, an instinctive awareness, a sensitivity. The greater one's love, the more profoundly and accurately one understands not only the unspoken but perhaps also the unconscious needs of the other. For Paul, "the things that really matter" are the needs of one's neighbour.

Being a Christian was something that Paul's converts had to make up as they went along. They were continuously improvising, relying on an instinct for what was appropriate in interpersonal relations. Paul would have approved Augustine's *ama et fac quod vis* "love and do what you like," but with the qualification that the love in question must be modelled on the self-sacrificing love shown by Christ. Thus, if the Jew looked to the Law for guidance, the Christian must look to Christ for inspiration.

Other aspects of what has been said here are treated below in XI. THE MIND OF CHRIST under the subheading *No Binding Precepts*.

IX. LIBERATION

The Sinless Community

The texts that I quoted to demonstrate the Jewish belief in the sinlessness of the messianic people are sufficient to make my point. However, I omitted one text whose importance for understanding Paul is accentuated by the fact that it probably stemmed from the Pharisaic circles to which he had belonged for some fifteen years. The sanctity of the people is particularly emphasized in the mid-first century B.C. *Psalms of Solomon*:

> (23) Behold O Lord, and raise up unto them their king, the son of David.... (26) He shall thrust out sinners from the inheritance ... (27) and he shall reprove sinners for the thoughts of their heart. (28) And he shall gather together a holy people, whom he shall lead in righteousness ... (29) and he shall not suffer unrighteousness to lodge any more in their midst, nor shall there dwell with them any man that knows wickedness.... (36) And there shall be

no unrighteousness in his days in their midst, for all shall be holy
and their king the anointed of the Lord.... (41) And he himself
will be pure from sin so that he may rule a great people. He will
rebuke rulers and remove sinners by the might of his word....
(45) He will be shepherding the flock of the Lord faithfully and
righteously, and will suffer none among them to stumble in their
pasture. (17:23–45; trans. Gray)
He will direct everyone in the works of righteousness by fear of
God, and may establish them all before the Lord, a good generation living in the fear of God in the days of mercy. (18:9–10;
trans Gray)

My point in emphasizing the sanctity of the church as the
community of the Messiah Jesus Christ was to explain how Paul
understood Christians to be freed from Sin. If Sin is the false value-
system of society, one can be freed from its compulsion only by
belonging to a group in which those values are not operative. In
effect, one has to move to another environment. Paul puts this
idea thus, "He has delivered us from the dominion of darkness and
transferred (*metestēsen*) us to the kingdom of his beloved Son"
(Col 1:13).

It goes without saying that this is entirely speculative. It explains
how freedom works in principle. Paul, however, knew perfectly
well that practice does not always conform to theory. That is why
my treatment of the "how" of freedom (pp. 155ff.) deals with two
levels, first the theoretical and then the factual. Only when Paul's
theoretical perspective is firmly grasped can we understand how
he dealt with practical problems. He is able to identify the precise
point at issue by the gap between the real and the ideal.

It is all too often thought that just because we are baptized we
are free. For Paul, on the contrary, freedom from Sin is not a given
but an achievement, and a fragile one at that. "For freedom Christ
has set us free. Stand fast, therefore, and do not again submit to a
yoke of slavery" (Gal 5:1); "You were called to freedom, but do not
use your freedom as an opportunity for the flesh, but through love
be servants of one another" (Gal 5:13). Believers have to make

their freedom real by intensifying the quality of their community life. If their local church is only nominally a Christian community, then their freedom will be purely nominal, and their true state will be enslavement.

Only in freedom can the believer love, and thus exist both as a Christian and an authentic person. "Without love I do not exist" (1 Cor 13:2). Freedom, therefore, is fundamental (in the most literal sense) to Paul's understanding of the Christian life. Without freedom, nothing is possible.

Yet Sanders (*Paul and Palestinian Judaism*) does not mention freedom once, and Dunn (*Theology of Paul the Apostle*) refers to it only twice. In both instances he merely notes the fact as a feature of justification and as a blessing of the Spirit. No effort is made to determine "how it works." The answer to this question, however, is indispensable if we are to be able to guarantee or to protect our freedom.

A most instructive parallel is furnished by the teaching of the New Testament on the prayer of petition. To take the words of Jesus (Mt 7:7; Lk 11:9) at face value would seem to imply that such prayers would be answered directly by God. One of the acute problems of the early church, however, was the tension between the absolute promise of Jesus and the fact that worthy prayers, such as the request for food for a starving child, were not answered.

Two types of solutions developed. The more popular, drawing on Jewish precedent in the Old Testament (e.g., Isa 1:15; Ps 66:17–19; Prov 15:29), took the easy option and blamed the petitioner for various forms of inadequacy, notably lack of faith (e.g., Mk 11:24; Jn 9:31; Jas 1:5–8; 2:15–17). The promise of Jesus, however, lays down no conditions.

There were first-century theologians who saw that to blame the victim was completely alien to the spirit of Christianity (Rom 5:8; 8:32). Matthew, for example, added "whatever you wish that people should do to you, do so to them" (7:12) to the promise of Jesus. In context the meaning is clearly "If you wish others to meet your needs, then fulfil their needs." In the specific context of petitionary prayer it means, "If you wish others to answer your prayers, then answer their prayers." John, for his part, integrated "Love one another" into his statement of the infallibility of the prayer of petition (Jn 15:16–17).

Only in this perspective can we understand how Jesus could speak as he did. If anyone asked for what he or she truly needed in the community of love that Jesus was forming (Mt 5:43–48; Lk 6:27–35), then the response was guaranteed. No woman desperate for food for a starving child will be turned away empty-handed if her neighbours are dedicated to meeting the needs of others. Her degree of faith or her moral character is completely irrelevant. Her need and that of the child is paramount.

Prayers are answered only if believers accept the responsibility of being the hands and ears of God. If they do not listen, God does not hear. This is "how" the prayer of petition works. Were Christians to realise this, there would be no desperate silent prayers that produce no fruit and lead to despair. Similarly, it is only when we know "how" we are freed from Sin that we can take the measures to ensure the reality of that freedom.

Children and the Community

A thorough survey of Paul's usage reveals that "holiness" is essentially a dynamic concept. Those who in virtue of a divine call have been separated from the "world" are expected to exhibit a pattern of behaviour that is the antithesis of their former conduct. The "holiness" that is the fruit of love in action is what gives meaning to the qualification of the believers as "saints."

According to 1 Cor 7:14, the pagan partner in the mixed marriage is "holy" but at the same time "unbelieving." In the light of what we have seen of Paul's understanding of holiness, the most natural interpretation is that, although the pagan has not committed himself or herself to Christ in faith, he or she nonetheless exhibits a pattern of behaviour that is analogous to the conduct expected of the believing "saints."

Can this be verified? The context demands an affirmative answer. By consenting to live with the Christian, the pagan brings his or her behaviour into line both with the intention of the Creator concerning marriage ("The two shall become one flesh," Gen 2:24, which Paul quotes in 1 Cor 6:16) and with the dominical directive prohibiting divorce (1 Cor 7:10–11). In this precise respect, therefore, the behaviour of the pagan is identical with the conduct that Paul expects of Christians, and so the predication of "holiness" is justified.

It is most important to keep in mind that Paul predicates "holiness" only on the basis of behaviour. It is not an automatic concomitant of belief. This is clearly demonstrated by his attitude toward the Galatians. Even though they had responded to the call of God in Christ, he never once applies "to be holy" or any of its cognates to them. Their behaviour did not merit the qualification.

In Galatia, therefore, we have the reverse of the dichotomy in 1 Cor 7:14. The Galatians were "believers" but not "holy"; the married pagan at Corinth is "unbelieving" but nonetheless "holy." Just as Paul hopes that the "believers" will become "holy," so he hopes that the "holy pagan" will become a "believer." In each case the presence of one element of what should be an indissoluble pair founds the hope that the other will come into existence. In the second-next verse (1 Cor 7:15) Paul reminds the Corinthians of the real possibility of the conversion of a pagan who desires to stay married to a Christian.

It has been suggested that the perfect tense *hēgiastai* "he/she has been sanctified" militates against the emphasis that I laid on the comportment of the unbelieving partner, who *de facto* was behaving as a Christian. The perfect tense evokes a state, we are told, not an action. Undoubtedly, but as far as I am concerned, a consistent pattern of behaviour is a state. It is the way the person is.

It is also pointed out that the "holiness" of the unbelieving partner is something that is done to him or her, not something that he or she does, as I claimed. It is perfectly correct that "through his wife/her husband" must carry an instrumental connotation. In 1 Cor 1:2; 6:11 and Rom 15:16 the preposition indicates the means whereby sanctification is achieved. Here we can only say that it was through his or her marriage to a believer that Paul came to think of an unbeliever in terms of holiness. Without that instrumental/causal link, Paul would never have thought of categorizing the behaviour of an unbeliever in terms appropriate only to a believer ("saint"). This demands that the original past event evoked by the perfect tense (*hēgiastai*) be either the baptism of the converted partner, if they were already married, or the marriage of one who is already a Christian to an unbeliever.

In 1 Cor 7:14, however, Paul recognized that he had hitherto spoken of holiness to the Corinthians only in the context of commitment to Christ (e.g., 1 Cor 1:2). Here he was using the same concept, but only in an analogous sense. Hence, he had to provide a link that would permit them to understand him. To this end, therefore, he evokes their attitude toward their children: "Otherwise your children are unclean, but as it is they are holy."

I made a mistake in evoking the baptism of the Corinthian children. Nothing in the context suggests that Paul had this sacrament in mind. Once brought into the debate it gives rise to a series of questions to which no answers are possible and which are a distraction from the point at issue. Since the non-Christian partner is presented as unbelieving, then it is most probable that Paul thought of the children as unbelievers. This they were technically, because they had not made the act of faith required for salvation (Rom 10:9–10). Nonetheless, because they had been born into the freedom of a Christian community, their behaviour had never been influenced by Sin. Their comportment, in consequence, was "holy."

It is important to note that the major translations (RSV, NRSV, NJB, NAB) blur the fact that Paul says that the Corinthian children (like the unbelieving parent) are both "unclean" and "holy" *at the same time*. 1 Cor 7:14 really reads, "Otherwise your children are unclean, but now they are holy." Despite the "now," it is not as if in the past they had been "unclean" (the implication of the major translations) but now in the present are "holy." Clearly the children are viewed simultaneously from different perspectives. When looked at in one way (faith) the children are "unclean," but in another sense (behaviour) they are "holy." They were in fact unbelievers, but one could think of them as Christians, because of their exposure to the good example of the believing community which is the basis of Christian freedom.

Whose children are in question? I assumed that they were the children of believing Corinthians in general. It is possible, however, that the primary referent is the children of the mixed marriages under consideration, but an extension to all the children of the community should not be excluded.

X. THE LIVING CHRIST

Women in Christ

I would now completely change the interpretation of 1 Cor 11:10 that I gave on pages 195–96. The point of the section in which it appears (1 Cor 11:3–16) is that the difference of the sexes should be respected at Corinth. The first argument that Paul uses is drawn from Gen 2:18–23. The difference between the sexes is important because God did not create man and woman in the same way. Man was made from the dust of the earth, whereas woman was made from the side of man. Were the difference between male and female irrelevant, Paul argues implicitly, God would have created them in precisely the same way.

Paul's conclusion regarding the woman is enunciated in 11:10, in the translation of which the expression *exousian echein epi* followed by a genitive, in this case *tēs kephalēs*, must be given its normal meaning, namely, "Therefore the woman must exercise control over her head." In other words, she should dress her hair in the conventional way by wrapping the long plaits around the top of her head (11:15).

I would no longer translate *dia tous angelous* in 11:10 as "because of the angels." When *angelos* is understood as referring to otherworldly spiritual beings, the suggested meanings range from the barely possible (the one I proposed) to the patently absurd. *Angelos*, however, is well-attested elsewhere in the New Testament (Mt 11:10; Lk 7:24; 9:52; Jas 2:25) and in contemporary Greek (e.g., Josephus, *Life* 17 [87]) as meaning a human "messenger."

Paul never uses *angelos* in this sense, but he shows his awareness of it by introducing a qualification when the term alone would have been ambiguous, "If an angel *from heaven* should preach to you a gospel contrary to the one we preached" (Gal 1:8; cf. 4:14). The sense of human "messengers" is perfectly in place in 1 Cor 11:10 because it was no doubt Chloe's messengers from Ephesus (1 Cor 1:11) who reported to Paul the strange liturgical customs of the Corinthians. They had been scandalized by the way the woman leader in prayer and prophecy refused to dress her hair properly. Paul was always concerned about the impact the behaviour of the community made on outsiders who just wandered into an assembly (1 Cor 14:16, 23).

*****

My treatment of 1 Cor 14:34–35 and 1 Tim 2:11–14 on p. 197 was extremely sketchy, and I take this opportunity to elaborate it a little. A synoptic presentation immediately reveals the considerable extent to which these texts overlap not only in content but also in vocabulary.

1 Cor 14:34–35	1 Tim 2:11–14
The women should keep silence in the churches. For they are not	Let a woman learn in silence with all submissiveness.
permitted to speak but should be subordinate,	I permit no woman to teach or to have authority over men. She is to keep silent.
as even the Law says.	For Adam was formed first and then Eve,
If there is anything they desire to know, let them ask their husbands at home. For it is shameful for a woman to speak in church.	And Adam was not deceived, but the woman was deceived and became a transgressor.

Two reasons strongly indicate that 1 Cor 14:34–35 was not written by Paul. First, the silence it imposes on women stands in flat contradiction to their freedom to pray and prophesy in public, which is acknowledged by Paul in 1 Cor 11:5. It is most improbable that Paul would contradict himself within the space of four chapters. A choice between the two has to be made, and the criterion can only be closeness to the gospel. The freedom and full equality that women enjoy in 1 Cor 11:4–5 and 14:31 ("you can *all* prophesy") reflects the newness of the gospel, whereas the restrictions of 1 Cor 14:34–35 mirror the patriarchalism of the ambient world. Thus, Paul's thought is represented by 1 Cor 11:4–5.

Second, the phrase "women should be subordinate, as even the Law says" (14:34) is completely un-Pauline. Paul never appeals to the Law in this manner. Moreover, in 1 Cor 11:11–12 Paul shows that the use of Gen 2:18–23 to prove the subordination of women is illegitimate. The traditional argument was based on chronology: man was created first, then woman. This is overturned by the simple fact that in the divine plan every man now has a mother.

Despite the force of these arguments, there is still a large body of scholarship that believes that 1 Cor 14:34–35 can be reconciled with 1 Cor 11:5. It does so by postulating a difference in the intention of the two passages. One set of scholars claims that the two texts are addressed to different women. Others, on the contrary, insist that a different type of speech is envisaged.

Some maintain that 1 Cor 11:5 is addressed to single women, who are permitted to speak, while 1 Cor 14:34–45 has in view married women, who are obliged to remain silent. No such distinction, however, appears in either text, and it is excluded by the reference to the Law in 1 Cor 14:34, which clearly has women *as such* in mind. It cannot mean that only married women are subordinate. Moreover, in the patriarchal system that prevailed at the time of Paul, a daughter (and every single woman was somebody's daughter) was, if anything, more limited than a wife. No daughter could be accorded a freedom denied to her mother. In this sense, therefore, the distinction between single and married women is anachronistic.

Others start from the conviction that 1 Cor 14:34–35 cannot contradict 1 Cor 11:5. Thus, the prohibition of 1 Cor 14:34–35 cannot exclude speech as such, still less inspired speech. In consequence, it must be directed against a particular type of speech, namely, verbalization that is disruptive in one way or another. Some think of repeated questions that interrupt the flow of the liturgical assembly or prophecies that ramble on rather too long. Others are more concerned for the dignity of male members of the community and think in terms of criticism of the lifestyles of certain prophets or of wives sitting in judgment on the gifts of their husbands.

The obvious response to this elaborate hypothesis is the simple question: If this is what Paul meant, why did he not say so? He was perfectly capable of finding the appropriate words. Moreover, are we to assume that *all* women, and *only women*, were disruptive? Men can be just as much a threat to good order.

Supporters of the disruptive speech hypothesis consider the most severe form of disruption to be that of the conventional order of the male-female relationship. Women, therefore, are silenced in 1 Cor 14:34–45 in order to ensure that they could not pass judgment on prophecies (1 Cor 14:29) spoken by husbands or senior male relatives. Paul's concern, we are told, was to preserve the traditional order in which women were subordinate to men.

If this is in fact the meaning of 14:34–35, then it flatly contradicts Paul's explicit statement in 11:11–12 regarding the complete equality of men and women "in the Lord," that is, in the Christian community. There could hardly be more compelling confirmation of hypothesis that 1 Cor 14:34–35 is a post-Pauline interpolation.

A further absurdity follows from the disruptive speech hypothesis. The "established order" also put masters above slaves. The logic of the disruptive speech hypothesis demands that slaves should also be prohibited from evaluating the prophecies of their masters or mistresses. In other words, we are invited to rewrite 1 Cor 14:29, "Let two or three prophets speak, and let the others, *who must be of superior or equal social rank*, weigh what is said." This, however, is completely opposed to Paul's vision of the Christian community, where "there is neither slave nor free, nor male and female" (Gal 3:28).

1 Tim 2:11–14 makes the same point as 1 Cor 14:34–35 but much more strongly, and the chronological argument based on the Law is made explicit. The non-Pauline character of 1 Timothy is widely admitted, and the lack of authenticity of the passage under consideration is confirmed by what is said of Adam and Eve. It absolves Adam of all blame, whereas for Paul Adam was the transgressor par excellence (Rom 5:12–21; 1 Cor 15:21–22, 45–49). Eve is taken to represent all women, whereas for Paul she was the prototype of the entire Corinthian community and not merely of the feminine element (2 Cor 11:3).

The refusal to recognize the full equality of women in the Christian community that we find in 1 Cor 14:34–35 and 1 Tim 2:11–14 stems from the generation after Paul, when the churches he founded reverted to the patriarchalism of society. The male leadership felt itself threatened by gifted independent women and invented fictitious prohibitions by Paul to keep them from exercising any influence in the community.

XI. THE MIND OF CHRIST

No Binding Precepts

In this section I subscribed to the view of John Knox that Paul was radically antinomian. In his view there was no place in a Christian community, not only for the Law of Moses, which spelled out Israel's covenantal obligations, but for law as such. Paul came to this conclusion only at the end of a long evolution in the course of which his attitude toward the Law changed at least three times.

As a teenager Paul's attitude toward the Law must have been ambivalent. The mastery displayed in his use of rhetoric can only be the result of highly professional instruction followed by intensive practice over a considerable period. We know from Strabo (*Geography* 14.5.13) that Tarsus was well known for its schools of rhetoric. These are the obvious places for Paul to have studied, naturally in the company of pagans. In consequence, he would have spent part of his formative years in a Gentile environment permeated by the casual morality of young men. This would have been extremely stressful because of the Jewish stress on separateness. Age-old Jewish tradition (e.g., Lev 20:24–26; Ezra 10:11; Neh 13:3; *Pss. Sol.* 17:28; 3 Macc 3:4; *Jub.* 22:16) is perfectly summed up by the second or first century B.C. *Letter of Aristeas*:

> In his wisdom the Legislator ... surrounded us with unbroken palisades and iron walls to prevent our mixing with any of the other peoples in any matter.... So, to prevent us being perverted by contact with others or by mixing with bad influences, he hedged us in on all sides with strict observances connected with meat and drink and touch and hearing and sight, after the manner of the Law. (139–142)

On the one hand, the Law cut Paul off from full participation in the activities of his fellow students. He could not even share a drink of wine with pagan friends unless he brought the bottle. A certain resentment would be only human. On the other hand, the Law was a source of pride that grounded his identity. Exalted as the pinnacle of ethical insight, it was what held Jews together in an alien world.

Whatever ambivalence Paul might have harboured as a teenager vanished when he became a Pharisee in Jerusalem (Phil 3:5). Even though he is looking back on a lifestyle that he has now completely repudiated, the note of bursting pride in Gal 1:14 is inescapable. Paul had been totally committed to the Law and fully subscribed to the principle "an ignorant man cannot be holy" (*m. Aboth* 2:6).

Paul's third attitude toward the Law can be dated to the years immediately following his conversion. At the beginning of this Afterword (I. Paul and Jesus, *The Pharisaic Tradition*), I explained why Paul persecuted Christians. Their proclamation of Jesus as the Messiah said in effect that the Law was no longer relevant. The consequence of this either-or mentality was that, when Paul on the road to Damascus recognized Jesus as the Messiah, he abandoned the Law immediately. It was not a slow, drawn-out process as he struggled to break free from the conditioning of decades. He was already psychologically prepared for the choice. In a sense, the decision had already been made.

How, then, was Paul to treat Jews who had become Christians? He could stress his conviction that their distinctive customs (circumcision, dietary laws, sabbath rest) no longer had any salvific value. This would have carried obvious dangers for the delicate compromises on which the unity of a mixed community, such as that of Antioch-on-the-Orontes, depended. The charitable alternative was for Paul mentally to reclassify specifically Jewish practices as simple ethnic markers, no more worthy of criticism than the women of Tarsus who wore the full chador (Dio Chrysostom, *Discourses* 33.48). Thus, Paul's third attitude toward the Law was one of tolerance.

Such tolerance disintegrated in the furious row between Peter and Paul at Antioch (Gal 2:11–21), which brought Paul to his fourth and final stance, antinomianism. The effort of James to raise the level of Jewish identity in the community meant that Gentile converts would in effect have to become Jews, if the church was to survive as a unity. This brought Paul to the realization that the Law was a dangerous rival to Christ. The experience taught him that, if the Law was given even the smallest foothold in a Christian community, it would eventually assume a dominant role. Acceptance of one commandment would lead to observance of others to the point where the believer was following a rule book rather than imitating Christ.

A number of important scholars refuse to accept the full radicality of Paul's antinomianism. This is based not on any evidence, as we shall see, but in an emotional refusal to accept the consequences of his complete rejection of the Law. The Ten Commandments are part of the Law (Exod 20:1–21; Deut 5:6–21). If the Law as such is rejected, then so are they! But this cannot be correct. Hence, Paul's criticism of the Law must be so narrowly focused, we are told, that we can envisage him accepting the Ten Commandments and other moral directives of the Jewish Scriptures as valid for Christian believers.

According to Dunn, for example, what appalled Paul was the overweening pride of Jews in being the chosen people (*Romans*, lxiii–lxxii). Their distinctiveness was exalted into a sense of privilege, which took the place of genuine religious sentiment. What set Jews apart from others, however, were above all circumcision, food laws, and the sabbath rest. These then, according to Dunn, are what Paul repudiates, leaving the rest of the Law intact as the expression of the will of God. In other words, Paul rejects the Law only insofar as it was a source of ethnic pride for Jews.

There is no evidence in Paul's letters for this distinction between commandments that are ethnic identity markers and those that are not (see in particular S. Westerholm, *Israel's Law and the Church's Faith,* ch. 10 iii). Were Dunn correct, Christians would be partially under the Law. Paul, however, makes a radical distinction between Jews, who are *hypo nomon* "under the Law" (1 Cor 9:20), and Christians, who are *ou hypo nomon* "not under the Law" (Rom 6:14–15). The dichotomy is absolute.

If believers "have died to the Law" (Rom 7:4; Gal 2:19), they cannot be obligated by its commandments, just as a woman whose husband has died cannot commit adultery with an unmarried man (Rom 7:1–6). No restriction as to the type of commandment is asserted or implied. If Paul intended to say that Christians had "partially" died to the Law, and thus were "partially" freed from its demands, he certainly had the language to express himself precisely and would have been obligated to do so, were his churches not to have become completely confused.

The whole point of Gal 2:17–18 is that Paul cannot be said to transgress a Law to which he is no longer subject. Only Jews are bound to keep the Law (Gal 5:3).

It is true that Paul pays special attention to the ethnic markers that Dunn singles out as the sole object of his criticism. In Rom 14:14 Paul flatly refuses the Jewish distinction between clean and unclean food (Lev 11; Deut 14:3–21). In Rom 14:5 he makes the obligation of sabbath rest (Exod 20:8–11; Deut 5:12–15) entirely optional. Equally the calendar, which was fundamental to Jewish life (and the basis of the split between the Essenes and the Temple), is dismissed as part and parcel of a lifestyle that Christians have left behind (Gal 4:10–11). It is completely indifferent whether a Christian is circumcised or not (1 Cor 7:19).

What Dunn forgets, however, is that the Law did not permit anyone to pick and choose among its precepts. All parts of the Law were equally binding. To reject one precept was to reject all. "Be heedful of a light precept as of a weighty one, for you do not know the recompense of reward of each precept" (*m. Aboth* 2:1); "Run to fulfil the lightest duty even as the weightiest" (*m. Aboth* 4:2). These Pharisaic maxims make it certain that in rejecting certain precepts, which Dunn claims Paul was doing, Paul must have been fully aware that he was thereby repudiating the Law as such. If he never did anything to correct this impression, it must be because it in fact represented his entirely negative attitude toward the Law.

In is something of a paradox, in consequence, to find Dunn arguing that Paul desired believers to obey the *whole* Law:

> In both Gal 5.13–14 and Rom 13.8–10 Paul talks about "fulflling" the law as something which evidently meets the requirement of the law (Rom 8:4), and is still desirable and necessary for believers. In so doing he indicates clearly that he had in mind the whole law. Not just the moral commands within the ten commandments, but "any other command" too (Rom 13.9). His concern was not to abstract or separate the love commandment from the rest, but to emphasize the "whole law" as still obligatory for believers (Gal 5.14). To fulfil the law of Christ was to fulfil the law. (*Theology of Paul the Apostle*, 656)

This is to turn Paul's thought upside down. For Paul, one could not be a Christian without loving. "Without love I do not exist" (1 Cor 13:2). Love is so integral to the very idea of Christianity that Paul could say, "You have been taught by God to love one another" (1 Thess 4:9). One might think, therefore, that to love one's neighbour was the one precept that had to be obeyed. Dunn reflects the imprecise attitude of many by speaking of the "love commandment." In both Gal 5:14 and Rom 13:9, however, Paul deliberately refrains from calling "You shall love your neighbour as yourself" a precept. Instead, he calls it simply a "word" (*logos*), which contrasts vividly with the "commandments" (*entolē*) drawn from the Law (Rom 13:9). Subtly but unambiguously Paul indicates that

Christians belong to an entirely different world than Jews. He tells them to focus on loving and to set aside all other demands even if they originated in the Law of God.

In speaking of love as the "fulfilment" of the Law, Paul is not thinking primarily of the Law, as Dunn seems to think, but of what will in fact happen if believers truly love. Behaviour inspired by the self-sacrificing love of Christ will in fact conform to the original intention of the Law (Rom 7:10). It is only in this sense that they "fulfil" the Law. There is no question of conscious obedience to a list of precepts (the Law traditionally contained 613).

That this is what Paul has in mind is confirmed by his exhortation, "Bear one another's burdens and so fulfil the law of Christ" (Gal 6:2). This rendering is typical of the current translations (RSV, NRSV, NJB, NAB) but fails to do full justice to what Paul wanted to say. The last words might give the impression that Paul is thinking of the precepts of the Law taken over into a new superior law promulgated by Christ. This is not in fact the case. "Of Christ" is a genitive of content or apposition (BDF §167), and the phrase should be translated "the law *which is* Christ." Paul's letters contain other instances of the same phenomenon, such as the "law which is faith" (Rom 3:27) and the "law which is the Spirit" (Rom 8:2).

The use of the verb "to fulfil" links this text with Gal 5:13–14 and Rom 13:8–10, but there is a difference. Both of these have the simple form *plēroō*, whereas in Gal 6:2 Paul uses the complex form *ana-plēroō*. The prefix serves to introduce the notion of repetition (LSJ *ana* F3). To perform an act of love, for example, to bear another's burdens, is to repeat the action of Christ, "who loved me, that is who gave himself for me" (Gal 2:20), and thereby to do the will of God expressed in the comportment of Christ. Gal 6:2 should be translated "Bear one another's burdens and in this way repeat the self-sacrificing action of Christ, which made him the paradigm of Christian behaviour." This sums up all that Paul asked of his converts.

It should be unnecessary to stress that "the law which is Christ" would have been perfectly intelligible to Paul's contemporaries.

Philo, for example, wrote, "The lives of those who have earnestly followed virtue may be called unwritten laws" (*De virtutibus* 194).

I find it extraordinary that authors such as Sanders, Dunn, and Westerholm, who discuss Paul's attitude to the Law magisterially, do so in complete isolation from two sets of texts that have an obvious *prima facie* claim to be considered in any treatment of Paul's stance with respect to legal authority.

The first are the two commands of Christ, with which I dealt on pages 201–2 above. In 1 Cor 7:10–11 Paul cites the dominical prohibition of divorce, which as a negative precept applies to everyone in all circumstances. There are no exceptions. Immediately afterwards, however, Paul on his own authority permits a divorce (1 Cor 7:15). Similarly, in 1 Cor 9:14 Paul quotes a command of Christ to the effect that preachers should live from the support of their communities. Once again he does exactly the opposite by insisting that he preferred to earn his own living (1 Cor 9:15–18).

Paul's treatment of these two commands shows that he did not consider them binding precepts but directives whose utility could vary as circumstances altered. His respect for the authority of Jesus is evident in the fact that he twice quotes him. Yet Paul absolutely refuses to give Jesus' commands the force of law. This fact alone makes it extremely improbable that he according binding force to the precepts of the Law. Confirmation for this view is to be found in 1 Cor 9:15–18, where Paul adopts a course of action that flatly contradicts his own reading of Deut 25:5 as quoted in 1 Cor 9:9.

The second series of texts is Phlm 8, 14; 2 Cor 8:7–8; and 9:7, which I have discussed on pages 117–18 above. In both it is a question of the "compulsion, necessity" (*anagkē*) generated by a command. The goodness produced by obedience to a precept is forced, and in consequence has no moral value. Clearly, if one is "bound" to act in a particular way, one cannot do so freely. Yet it is only by actions freely chosen that the authentic personality comes into being.

The desire to maintain a rule book for believers is very deeply rooted in anyone connected with church leadership. In a way it is understandable. But it cannot be justified from Paul.

My final point is one that I made at much greater length in *Jesus and Paul: Parallel Lives* (pp. 63–68). In repudiating the Law Paul was only following in the footsteps of Jesus.

Two phases must be distinguished in the ministry of Jesus. At the beginning he operated as a disciple of John the Baptist (John 3:22–24), preaching the same prophetic message of repentance. To this phase we must attribute such texts as the praise of the eternal validity of the Law in Mt 5:17–20 and the action against the moneychangers in the Temple, which John correctly places early in the ministry of Jesus (2:13–17). Subsequently Jesus' attitude toward the Law changed.

Jesus prohibition of divorce contradicted the Law (Deut 24:1), which was understood to mean that Moses commanded the giving of a certificate of divorce (Mt 19:7). I have already noted in this section that the Law had to be accepted or refused as a whole. Selectivity in the acceptance of commandments was not permitted. To reject one was implicitly to reject all. In going against the Law in the matter of divorce, therefore, Jesus was in fact repudiating the authority of the Law as such.

This was not an isolated incident in the ministry of Jesus. When asked by a potential follower for leave to bury his father. Jesus said, "Follow me, and let the dead bury their dead" (Mt 8:22). Here Jesus consciously and deliberately issues an order to disobey the fifth commandment, "Honour your father and your mother as Yahweh your God has commanded you" (Deut 5:16; cf. Exod 20:12). As the formulation explicitly underlines, this was a binding divine precept, and respect for the body of a dead parent certainly came under the umbrella of filial piety. There is evidence that the obligation was considered as of the first importance at the time of Jesus. Certain texts of *m. Berakoth* read, "He whose dead lies unburied before him is exempt … from all the duties enjoined in the Law" (3:1; Danby); that is, burial takes precedence over all other obligations until it is completed. Once again Jesus is making a completely impermissible choice among the commandments of the Law.

Finally we come to the question of Sinners, those whose professions proclaimed contempt for the Law. If Jesus was judged to be a rebellious son worthy of death because of his association with Sinners (Mt 11:19), it can only be because he accepted them *as Sinners*. Had he pushed for their repentance, and the restitution of what they had stolen, he would have been applauded. In fact, however, his table-fellowship with Sinners was understood as proclaiming to the world that Sinners, *while remaining those whom the Law condemned*, would not suffer hell fire. In other words, Jesus' behaviour was an unambiguous statement that the Law was wrong in the way it judged such individuals.

In each of these three instances we have to do with an act that implies repudiation of the Law as such. In each case Jesus refuses to obey a specific commandment, thereby rejecting the Law as a whole. Given the knowledge of the words and deeds of Jesus that appear in Paul's letters, it would be extraordinary were he not aware of Jesus' antinomianism. This stance defined Jesus over against Judaism. As we have seen, Paul had his own reasons for repudiating the Law, but any residual irrational doubts would quickly have been laid to rest by recalling that Jesus had exhibited the same attitude toward the Law.

The Corinthian Error

On page 210 of this subsection I spoke rather generically of the pressure that the strong at Corinth, who had no trouble eating meat offered to idols, could bring to bear on the weak, who instinctively considered such food morally wrong. It might be helpful to provide a couple of concrete examples of the sort of thing that might have happened, which is in fact based on what the archaeologists have brought to light at Corinth.

Just inside the north wall of the city, where it got the fresh air from the Gulf of Corinth, is a beautiful colonnaded piazza some 20 meters square. The east side is taken up by three dining rooms whose doors give onto the piazza. Belonging to the temple of Asclepius, part of which is built above them, their design is identical. Around the walls are eleven couches for diners. In front are seven small serving tables. There is a hearth in the center. Plans of these structures are given on pages 187–88 of the third edition of my *St. Paul's Corinth.*

Let us suppose that John, one of the strong, rented one of these dining rooms to celebrate the birthday of his daughter. Meat that had been offered to Asclepius would certainly figure on the menu. All the family were gathered there when, after a couple of glasses of wine, John saw one of his employees, James, sauntering idly in the piazza.

James was there simply for the fresh air. Suddenly he hears the voice of his employer, "James, come and join us." He was shocked, because he was opposed in principle to idol meat. He knew that it was irrational to refuse to eat such food, but he felt very deeply about the matter and knew that his conscience would reproach him severely if he partook. Yet it was impossible to fabricate the excuse of another engagement. It was all too obvious that he was just killing time. He could not afford to offend his employer, who had issued the invitation out of sheer generosity. He had no choice but to go against his conscience and eat idol meat.

As an alternative scenario, one might imagine one of the weak receiving an invitation to the wedding of his favourite sister. Since she was still a pagan, it would be celebrated in one of the dining rooms of the temple of Asclepius. He could not decline on the grounds that his new faith did not permit it, because the strong were known to participate in such banquets. No matter how deeply rooted his conviction that he should not eat idol food, there was no way that he could make it either comprehensible or palatable to his family. To refuse to attend could only appear as a gratuitous insult to those whom he still loved. They would be deeply hurt. But if he gave in to the legitimate desires of his family, he would be suffer the pangs of conscience.

In both of these scenarios there would have been no moral dilemma for the weak without the attitude of the strong, which robbed the weak of their one reasonable excuse to refuse.

Suggested Readings

C. K. Barrett, *Freedom and Obligation: A Study of the Epistle to the Galatians*. London: SPCK, 1985.

J. D. G. Dunn, *Romans*. Word Biblical Commentary 38. Dallas: Word, 1988.

———. *The Theology of the Apostle Paul*. Grand Rapids: Eerdmans, 1998.

J. A. Fitzmyer, *The One Who Is to Come*. Grand Rapids: Eerdmans, 2007.

R. B. Hays, *Echoes of Scripture in the Letters of Paul*. New Haven: Yale University Press, 1989.

J. Louis Martyn, *Theological Issues in the Letters of Paul*. Studies of the New Testament and Its World. Edinburgh: Clark, 1997.

J. Murphy-O'Connor, *Jesus and Paul: Parallel Lives*. Collegeville: Liturgical Press, 2007.

———. *Keys to First Corinthians: Revisiting the Major Issues*. Oxford: Oxford University Press, 2009.

———. *St. Paul's Corinth: Texts and Archaeology*. Collegeville: Liturgical Press, 2002.

E. P. Sanders, *Paul and Palestinian Judaism: A Comparison of Patterns of Religion*. London: SCM, 1977.

———. *Paul, the Law and the Jewish People*. London: SCM, 1985.

S. Westerholm, *Israel's Law and the Church's Faith: Paul and His Recent Interpreters*. Grand Rapids: Eerdmans, 1988.

SUBJECT INDEX

Sacrifice, 103
Salvation-history, 42-43
Sanctification, 163-64, 203, 253-54
Sin (Personal)
    as alienation, 78-79, 93; culpability, 98-105; effect on community, 168
Sin (Societal)
    definition, 95, 98, 137, 159, 243; origin, 92-95, 244; individual responsibility, 98-105; religious observances, 111-12
Sinners, 267-68
Society, 125, 181
Son of God, 62-64, 224

Spirit, 156, 161, 166, 204
Testimonium Flavianum, 220
Tradition, 27-31, 181, 234
Ten Commandments, 262, 264

Vice lists, 132
Virtue lists, 185

Will of God, 201, 214
Wisdom, 65-67, 238-39
Witness, 145-49, 163, 188
Women, 129-31, 193-97, 256-60
World, 97-98, 111, 169, 228, 243-45

PAULINE TEXTS

ROMANS

1:3-4	62, 234, 239
1:3	29, 77
1:4	40, 46, 80
1:5	63
1:13	31
1:18-32	212-13
1:18	98
1:20	40, 97, 101
1:21	101
1:25	111
1:29-31	132
2:7	71
2:9-10	98, 101
2:12-15	98
2:16	65
2:17-21	116-17, 201
2:17-18	116, 215, 248
2:21	110
2:23	118
3:5	35
3:6	97
3:9	92
3:21-22	82
3:23	82
3:24	183
3:25	103
3:27	265
4:1	34
4:8	64
4:25	81, 103, 234
5:6-8	47
5:8	42, 252
5:9	103
5:12-20	260
5:12	92-93, 244
5:19	47, 95, 201
5:21	71, 92
6:3-7	156
6:5	178
6:6-7	169
6:6	70, 92, 160